Molders of the Jewish Mind

MOLDERS OF THE JEWISH MIND

A B'NAI B'RITH BOOK

B'nai B'rith Adult Jewish Education
Washington, D.C.

The B'nai B'rith Department of Adult Jewish Education, organized in 1954, has as its purpose to stimulate and promote the study of Judaism among adult Jews. Through annual Institutes of Judaism, year-round discussion groups, and authoritative and readable publications, it helps individuals and groups plan study programs on the religious and cultural heritage of the Jewish people.

B'nai B'rith Adult Jewish Education,
1640 Rhode Island Avenue, N.W., Washington, D.C. 20036.
Library of Congress Catalogue Card Number 66-27649
Manufactured in the United States of America

Contents

Foreword

There are no Napoleons in Jewish history. Though the Bible records the military triumphs of Deborah over the Philistines, it is as prophetess and judge of Israel "under the palm tree" that she is best remembered. Folk heroes like Judah Maccabee and Bar Kokhba are feted as warrior-defenders of their people, fighters for liberation against overwhelming enemy strength, rather than as empire-builders or conquistadores.

Moses led the people of Israel out of Egypt in a thrust for freedom and independence and nationhood. Over the centuries, it was battles of the mind rather than of force which concerned teacher-scholars like Akiba and Rashi and philosophers like Maimonides: these giants of the intellect sought through interpretations of Scripture and later Jewish "writings" to order the chaos of society and to clarify man's duties to man and to God.

Out of the *shtetlach* and ghettos of Eastern Europe rose righteous men *(zaddikim)* like the Baal Shem Tov, founder of *Hasidism*, to remind the people that religious faith was more than solemn obligation and joyless commandment: it could be a source of spiritual happiness and inspiration as well.

In modern times, new leaders emerged, like Moses of old, to help take the Jewish people once again out of bondage. Moses Mendelssohn in Germany saw as his task to lead the Jews out of their self-enclosed medieval ghettos and onto the larger arenas of Enlightenment and world civilization. Sholom Aleichem lovingly recorded the life of the *shtetl* and ghetto before it vanished, its joys and sadnesses.

The struggle for equality on the larger world stage brought in its wake a wave of Jewish nationalism built on the age-old deeply rooted longing for a Jewish homeland. Theodor Herzl gave this longing a political structure and a world address. Justice Brandeis, already eminent for his leadership in the field of American social legislation, led the Zionist movement in the United States. It was the poet Bialik who gave that movement its finest poetic voice.

This book brings together ten molders of the Jewish mind from different vantage points and in different ages. Selected from the first two volumes of the B'nai B'rith Great Books Series,* edited by Simon Noveck, the personalities included here are intended to be representative rather than all-inclusive. No attempt has been made to present a complete sampling or total cross-section.

Our thanks go to each of the authors represented who has kindly granted permission for the use of his chapter in this volume. Special gratitude must also be expressed to Professor Harry M. Orlinsky, Chairman of the Publications Committee, and Dean Harold Weisberg, Commission Chairman, for their guidance of this project and the selection of the actual chapters to be included.

LILY EDELMAN
Director, B'nai B'rith Adult Jewish Education

**Great Jewish Personalities in Ancient and Medieval Times*
Great Jewish Personalities in Modern Times

Molders of the Jewish Mind

1 . *Moses*

[c. 1300 B. C. E.]

HARRY M. ORLINSKY

AMONG the great personalities in the long span of Jewish history, extending over a period of some four thousand years, Moses must invariably stand at the head. Already in biblical times, he had become so revered and so much a legend that when classical prophecy made its mark in Israel, more than half a millennium after Moses' time, he emerged as *the prophet* par excellence: "And there has not arisen a prophet since in Israel like Moses, whom the Lord knew face to face" (Deuteronomy 34:10).

Israel Comes to Egypt

At the turn of the third millennium, about 2000 B.C.E., a Hebrew* named Abraham, accompanied by his wife Sarah and their wordly goods, started out on a journey that was to take them from one end of the Fertile Crescent to the other, from Ur in southern Mesopotamia to the southwestern border of Canaan, at Egypt. Abraham and Sarah had left family and friends in Ur, and in Paddan-aram too, in northern Syria, to make this trek; and although they and their offspring maintained their family and cultural ties with the place of their origin for some time,

* While the terms "Hebrew(s)" and "Israel(ites)" are used interchangeably in this essay, the first is older than the second. It was during the period of the Judges (12th-11th centuries) that the term "Israelites" (Hebrew *bene yisra'el*, "children of Israel") came to replace the term "Hebrews," just as "Israelites" was later replaced by "Judeans" and "Jews" after the Exile in Babylonia. For further explanation, see Orlinsky, *Ancient Israel*, pp. 51-2.

Canaan was to be their permanent home, and that of their descendants.

In the course of time, in the days of Ishmael and Isaac, of Esau and Jacob, and of their children and grandchildren—among whom the twelve sons of Jacob and his daughter Dinah are best known—many more Hebrews were to be found in the land, some of them as immigrants from the Syrian part of the Fertile Crescent and from the Arabian steppes. The first half of the second millennium was an exciting period, characterized by mass movements. People were being attracted in the thousands from their more primitive abodes in the grasslands and highlands to the more settled, sophisticated, wealthy, and comfortable towns and villages not far distant.

But drought and famine, also, were a common phenomenon in many parts of western Asia, and could change the historical direction of a people. It was one such period of desolation that brought Jacob and his family, and thousands of non-Hebrews as well, to Egypt, the country of full granaries. The periodic overflow of the Nile River, today no less than in the past, gave life to the land and helped regulate it as an agricultural society. Thus a thirteenth-century Egyptian document tells how the semi-nomadic inhabitants of Edom, south of Palestine, left their homes in time of drought to come to Egypt, "to keep themselves alive and to keep their cattle alive." And just as Abraham and Isaac in an earlier period had been compelled by famine to go south (Genesis 12 and 26), so too did Jacob in his time have to send his sons to Egypt to purchase grain.

Joseph, one of Jacob's sons, preceding his family to Egypt, had risen to high power, ranking next only to Pharaoh himself. When his father and brothers immigrated, they settled in the fertile Delta region of Goshen. This was the Eisodus, the "going into " Egypt.

The biblical tale concerns itself with the Hebrews alone. But in all probability the coming of the Hebrews to Egypt was part of a larger ethnic and military movement. During the first half of the second millennium Egypt had experienced an invasion and consequent degradation—reference to which was carefully, and, characteristically, avoided in its chronicles. A mixed group of Asiatics, apparently mostly Semites, and known generally as Hyksos (literally, "rulers of foreign countries"), appeared in the north, and in successive waves swarmed through Syria and Palestine. By about 1700 B.C.E. they had crossed the land bridge into Africa and conquered much of Egypt, a domination that was not to be completely broken until about 1550.

There appear to have been several points of contact between the Hyksos and the Hebrews during that century and a half. It is known, for example, that a certain Hyksos chieftain in Egypt bore the name Jacob-el (or perhaps: -har), which means "May El (or, Har—the mountain god) Give Protection." Another Hyksos leader was called Jacob-baal, "May Baal Protect." The verbal element Jacob, which means "protect," is identical with the name of the Hebrew patriarch who settled in Egypt.

Again, the historical kernel which resides in the dramatic story of Joseph's career in Egypt, of the coming to power of a Hebrew in the Egyptian royal court, could well have derived from the period of the Hyksos, when Semites, and in all likelihood Hebrews among them, were prominent among the new rulers of Egypt. It was not Egyptian habit to nourish the ambitions of strangers in their midst, and, furthermore, it would seem to be more than mere coincidence that in the Bible the Hebrews are said to have settled in the Delta, the very area which the Hyksos built up around their new capital, Avaris.

Israel in Bondage; Birth of Moses

"And Joseph died, and all his brothers and all that generation," the Bible relates (Exodus 1:6-7), "and the Israelites were fruitful and prolific; they multiplied and increased very greatly, so that the land was filled with them. But a new king arose over Egypt, who did not know Joseph . . ." On the grounds that the Israelites were becoming too numerous and strong for the native government to handle, the new regime introduced a system of state slavery: "They set taskmasters over them to oppress them with forced labor; and they built for Pharaoh store cities, Pithom and Rameses" (v.11).*

* Biblical quotations in the essay, where they do not derive from the 1962 *Torah*, the Jewish Publication Society's new Bible translation, or from the Revised Standard Version of the Old Testament (Nelson), are the author's own versions.

At this point the findings of archeology come to our aid, helping us to paint a broader picture than the biblical writers had deemed necessary. When the Egyptians finally succeeded in overthrowing their Hyksos oppressors, they drove many of them from the land and enslaved the rest. The erstwhile free rulers became captives of the state, subject to forced labor. It is now known that two centuries later, about 1300 B.C.E., Seti I of Egypt, who had done much to reorganize the empire in Palestine and southern Syria, began the rebuilding of Avaris, the old Hyksos capital. His son and successor, Rameses II, continued the building project on a much vaster scale, changing the name of Avaris to Rameses. This same Pharaoh also did much rebuilding at other sites, notably at Pithom. Slave battalions worked at all these places, and there is little reason to doubt that Hebrews were among them.

At this point, the biblical narrative introduces Moses. Pharaoh, the Bible relates, had given orders to drown in the Nile all Hebrew males at birth. But Moses' mother was able to hide her infant son for three months. At the end of that period, she placed the baby—who was of unusually striking appearance—in a waterproofed basket among the reeds by the bank of the Nile. A daughter of Pharaoh, coming down to the Nile to bathe, espied the basket. She sent a maid to fetch it, "and when she opened it, she saw that it was a child, a boy crying. She took pity on it, and said, 'This must be a Hebrew child' " (2:6).

Moses' sister, meanwhile, was stationed nearby watching for just such a development. She stepped forward and asked the Egyptian princess, "Shall I go and call you a Hebrew wet nurse to suckle the child for you?" And when the royal lady assented, she called her mother. When the child outgrew his mother's nursing and was brought back to the royal palace, the princess named him Moses (Hebrew *Moshe*): "because I drew him out (*meshitihu*) of the water" (v.10). So much for the biblical tradition.

All peoples in antiquity were given to embellishing the circumstances of the birth of their great heroes, and so too did ancient Israel. A story similar to that of Moses was told of Sargon I (about 2300 B.C.E.), founder of the world's first empire, at Accad in Mesopotamia. The legend reads in part:

My (?) mother conceived me, in secret she bore me.
She set me in a basket of rushes, with bitumen she sealed my lid.
She cast me into the river which rose not over me.
The river bore me up and carried me to Akki, the drawer of water.
Akki, the drawer of water, lifted me out as he dipped his ewer.
Akki, the drawer of water, took me as his son and reared me.
Akki, the drawer of water, appointed me as his gardener.
While I was a gardener, Ishtar granted me her love.
And for four and (?) years I exercised kingship.
The black-headed people I ruled, I governed . . .*

While the biblical tale credits the princess with knowledge of Hebrew, scholars have long recognized the Egyptian origin of the common name-element Moses, meaning "offspring, born of." The name "Moses" is no less authentically Egyptian than such other contemporaneous biblical names as Miriam, Hophni, Phinehas, Merari, and Puti-el. And these names, in turn, help to authenticate the Egyptian locale of the biblical account of the principal heroes and events involved in this phase of Israel's career.

Midian: The Call of Moses

All that we really know for certain, therefore, is that Moses was born in Egypt. How he spent his formative years no one knows. The Bible, having brought Moses into the royal family as the princess' adopted son, took him out of it in the very next verse (2:10-11), telling us nothing whatever about his youth.

Grown to manhood—in all probability in the same environment as that of his enslaved Hebrew brethren—Moses was aware and conscious of his Hebraic origin, and ready to avenge the affliction of his people. His first positive act, understandable under the circumstances even if committed impulsively, was to strike down "an Egyptian whom he saw strike down one of his Hebrew kinsmen" (v.11).

Moses had to flee the land, for he had been seen—by two Hebrew slaves—beating the Egyptian. He went to the land of Midian, generally located south of Edom, in Arabia. There he met the seven daughters of Jethro, a Midianite priest, and married one of them, Zipporah.

* "The Legend of Sargon," translated by E. A. Speiser, *Ancient Near Eastern Texts Relating to the Old Testament.*

This was the turning point of Moses' career, and that of biblical Israel. While tending the flocks of his father-in-law, Moses experienced his first contact with the God of his fathers. "When he came to Horeb, the mountain of God," the Bible reads (3:1 ff.), "an angel of the Lord appeared to him in a flaming fire out of a bush. He looked and, lo, the bush was aflame with fire, yet the bush was not consumed. And Moses said: 'I must turn aside and see this marvelous sight: why the bush does not burn up.' "

At this point the Lord revealed Himself to Moses: "I am the God of your father(s) . . . I have marked well the plight of My people in Egypt . . . I have come down to rescue them from the Egyptians, and to bring them out of that land to a good and spacious land, to a land flowing with milk and honey, to the region of the Canaanites . . . Come, therefore, I will send you to Pharaoh, and you shall free My people the Israelites from Egypt."

In this period, God's actions—and sometimes God Himself—were associated by the Hebrews with natural phenomena like fires, lightning, thunderstorms, mountains, and volcanoes. They believed that He manifested Himself and His will not merely by direct speech and in dreams, but also through these natural agents. Imbued as Moses was with the spirit of liberation and the desire to free his people at a time when the possibility of redemption was more favorable than before, it is understandable that he would see in natural phenomena, especially when they occurred unexpectedly or in unusual form, a theophany—that is, a visible appearance of God.

But Moses seems out of character in the dialogue that ensued. Rather than accept readily this mission from God to His people, he tried to find reasons why he should not become a spokesman for God (3:11-4:13). "Who am I?" Moses asked, "that I should go to Pharaoh and that I should bring forth the Israelites from Egypt? . . . What if they do not believe me or heed my voice, but say, 'The Lord did not appear to you?' . . . Please, O Lord, I have never been a man of words . . . for I am slow of speech and slow of tongue . . . Please, O Lord, send whomever else You will!" And Moses consented to go only after the Lord had assured him that his brother Aaron would be his spokesman.

In proper perspective, however, this biblically recorded conversation makes good sense. It was an ancient convention for one who felt himself chosen by God for a special mission to find reason for not responding at once and with eagerness to the call. Hesitancy, lack of confidence, fear of the consequences—these were conventionally attributed to God's chosen one when the call came. While Moses may have had a speech defect, and may also have felt some qualms about the enormity of the task, the biblical statement should not prevent us from recognizing in him a strong desire to lead his people out of slavery; for otherwise he would not have experienced the vision in the first place.

The Egyptian World in Moses' Time

What manner of civilization did Egypt constitute in this period so crucial to Israel? What were its material, artistic, and spiritual achievements?

The Near East, that quadrangle of land lying between the Mediterranean, Caspian and Red Seas, and the Persian Gulf, and connecting—at Israel and Sinai—Asia and Africa, is the birthplace of civilization. Egypt had long been one of the great powers in that part of the world. Indeed, during most of the third and second millennia B.C.E., Egypt was the principal power at the southwestern end of the Fertile Crescent, corresponding to the dominating regime at the northeastern end—Sumer, Babylonia, the Hittites, or Assyria.

The conquest at the hands of the Hyksos was Egypt's first full-scale and long-term experience as a subject people. Egyptian culture sank so low that this period has been described as "The Great Humiliation."

After the gradual expulsion of the Hyksos, the Egyptians began to devote their energies primarily to the reconquest of the neighboring regions, the rebuilding of the land, its army, shipping service, civil service, and temples. That accomplished, a decision had to be reached whether to venture into expanding imperialism or to remain essentially a localized economy. Queen Hatshepsut represented the latter view, her nephew Thutmose III the former. Ultimately, imperialism prevailed. And by the time that Thutmose had achieved his notable conquests (c. 1450 B.C.E.) Egypt was once more the greatest power in Western Asia. The revival that followed was on such a grand scale that the ensuing period of the New Kingdom, especially during the Eighteenth and Nineteenth Dynasties (down to shortly after 1200), has been called the Golden Age, and was the subject of a recent book suggestively titled *When Egypt Ruled the East* by G. Steindorff and K. C. Seele.

Ikhnaton and Atonism

During the reign of Amenhotep IV (c. 1380-1360), a fundamental split developed between the royal house and its supporters, on the one hand, and, on the other, the powerful priestly interests of the god Amon at Thebes. The latter group was apparently keenly interested in continued imperialist expansion and consolidation. The royal regime moved its headquarters from Thebes to a new site about three hundred miles to the north, and laid primary emphasis on another diety, Aton, the round disk of the sun. The king himself changed his name to Ikhnaton (Akh-en-Aton, "He Who is Serviceable to [or, "It Goes Well with] the Aton"), and named the new capital Akhet-Aton ("The Place of the Effective Glory of the Aton"), modern Tell el-Amarna. Art became more naturalistic than ever before. Women began to play a more prominent role in public life. Something of a democratization of social life was manifest in the public informality of the king, his wife, and their six daughters.

The virtually exclusive worship of Aton by the royal household has led a number of scholars to assert that Ikhnaton was a monotheist, the first in the world. Some scholars, going even further, placed Moses in Ikhnaton's period, and claimed that he obtained his knowledge of monotheism, directly or ultimately, from Ikhnaton. Sigmund Freud, in *Moses and Monotheism* (1939), made Moses an important Egyptian official in Ikhnaton's court who became a protector of the Hebrews, converted them to Ikhnaton's "monotheistic" religion, and led them out of Egypt. According to Freud, those passages in the Pentateuch that stood in contradiction to this theory were to be dismissed as invention and distortion; thus it was really Moses, not Abraham, who introduced the custom of circumcision among the Hebrews. This study of Moses by Freud is now regarded by many as a naive venture, constituting in reality a more important source of information for the analysis of Freud himself than of the prophet Moses.

According to more reliable treatments of the subject, however, it is clear today that Moses derived nothing from Ikhnaton's reign or outlook. Recent study has made it more than dubious that Ikhnaton was really a monotheist, or that his views circulated outside his royal court or subsequent to his death. What had been regarded by some as monotheism, the recognition and worship of Aton alone, has on closer study turned out to be a form of syncretism, a process by which several distinct gods came to be merged with a single deity so that all their functions were attributed to him. Ikhnaton, it is true, initiated a violent attack upon the god Amon, hacking the name out of inscriptions; at the same time, however, the many other less powerful and important gods were rarely disturbed. Indeed, the entire matter becomes clear when it is realized that Atonism was basically not a religious—let alone monotheistic—but an economic and political revolt against the powerful Amon interests.

Another important factor differentiated Moses' beliefs from those of Ikhnaton. Already in the preceding, patriarchal period, there had come into being among the Hebrews a concept of deity which, while not monotheistic in our sense of the term, was yet not polytheistic either. In a sense, the patriarchs may be said to have practiced monotheism, but without defining it. While they probably did not think of denying the existence of other gods, the patriarchs attached themselves to one God and worshipped Him alone. With Him, they entered voluntarily into a covenant which was binding forever, never to be broken under penalty of severe punishment and, theoretically at least, of complete rejection. In sponsoring monotheism, Moses was therefore not actually introducing a new concept to the Hebrews. He had a familiar, developable Hebraic idea of monotheism with which to work. Even the covenant of Sinai represented not so much a change in kind as a change in degree from the old way of binding oneself to the deity. Moses and the Hebrews, therefore, had little need of Egyptian assistance—which was not forthcoming anyway—in this direction.

The Age of Rameses II

Thanks largely to the findings of archeology during the past few decades, evidence has been accumulating from various sources to indicate that the career of Moses is probably to be sought not in the reign of Ikhnaton but about a century later, in the decades following 1300 B.C.E., during the long reign of Rameses II (c. 1290-1224). It is quite certain that Israel was in Canaan in some force around 1250; excavations at several sites point to the Israelites as conquering Canaanite settlements at about that time. Indeed, around 1230 B.C.E., King Merneptah of Egypt celebrated his victory over numerous foes in an alleged campaign in Western Asia. And the Pharaoh boasted:

> Israel is laid waste, its seed is not,
> Palestine is become a widow for Egypt.

If we add a few decades to 1250 to allow for the wilderness wandering under Moses, we arrive at a date well within the reign of Rameses II. It also seems clear that the store cities, Pithom and Rameses, said in the Bible to have been built by the Hebrews in bondage, were erected in the days of this same Rameses. All in all, one cannot be far wrong in dating Moses about 1300, and the Exodus during the thirteenth century.

Rameses II could well be the vainglorious Pharaoh whose heart softened and hardened by turn. Rameses was the king-god who walked into a Hittite trap at Kadesh on the Orontes River in Syria, and then turned his feat in escaping from the ambush into a great personal triumph. On his return to Egypt, he outdid all his predecessors—and, it turned out, all his successors too—in covering the wall space in the temples with carved representations of his remarkable "victory." Steindorff-Seele describes him bluntly as the "greatest of Egyptian boasters." The biblical Pharaoh of the bondage could scarcely be described better!

The Exodus

This was the Egypt to which Moses returned after his vision of God in Midian. His brother Aaron joined him, and the two together began the difficult and arduous task of persuading and organizing their fellow Israelites to leave their land of bondage. According to one version in the Bible, Aaron performed for them the signs that the Lord had commanded: he caused his staff to turn into a serpent and then into a staff again; he brought leprosy upon his hand and then cured it; and, finally, he poured on the dry ground some water from the Nile so that it became blood. "And the people believed," the Bible asserts (4:31), "when they heard that the Lord had taken note of the Israelites and that He had seen their plight; and they bowed in homage." But another version has it that when Moses told the Israelites what the Lord had told him, "they would not listen to Moses, their spirits crushed by cruel bondage" (6:9).

Pharaoh could hardly have been expected to consent to the release of so many thousands of unpaid workers. The biblical interpretation is different: God could readily have made Pharaoh free his captive Israelites; but He wanted to demonstrate for all time His power and glory. "The Lord said to Moses: Go to Pharaoh. For I have hardened his heart and the hearts of his courtiers, in order that I may display these My signs among them, and that you may recount in the hearing of your sons and your sons' sons how I made a mockery of the Egyptians and how I displayed My signs among them, that you may know that I am the Lord" (10:1-2).

And thus there began a series of ten events that have been retold by countless generations—the ten plagues. In the case of the first nine, neither blood nor frogs nor lice, neither insects nor pestilence nor boils, neither hail nor locusts nor darkness could stay Pharaoh from the swift completion of his appointed round. The tenth plague, however, brought matters to a head. "In the middle of the night the Lord struck down all the firstborn in the land of Egypt, from the firstborn of Pharaoh who sat on the throne to the firstborn of the captive who was in the dungeon, and all the firstborn of animals" (12:29). Pharaoh and his courtiers did not wait until morning. They arose in the night and summoned Moses and Aaron: "Depart from among my people, you and the Israelites with you! Go, worship the Lord as you said! Take also your flocks and your herds, as you said, and be gone! And may you," the divine Pharaoh pleaded with these two men, "bring a blessing upon me also."

For those who do not believe in miracles, the biblical account is understandable in natural terms. Scholars have long recognized that most of these plagues are natural phenomena that have afflicted Egypt throughout the ages. The Nile has long been known to acquire a reddish color. Frogs have on occasion plagued the country, their decomposition resulting in a vast multiplication of lice, insects, and pestilence. And what moderns explain as natural phenomena in aggravated form, the biblical writers accounted for in terms of God's direct and supernatural intervention in behalf of His people.

It seems clear that in the midst of some such upheaval, Moses and those slaves, non-Hebrew as well as Hebrew, who were courageous or desperate enough to follow him, made a dash for liberty. Their aim was to escape Egyptian territory to freedom. This they achieved. Thus Moses found himself at the head of an undisciplined collection of people—the Bible refers to the non-Hebrews as the "mixed multitude" and "rabble" (Exodus 12:38; Numbers 11:4)—numbering several thousand.*

Deliverance at the "Red" Sea

Moses' leadership was tested at once. Normally, he should have led the Hebrews directly to Canaan, the land that they believed God had promised the patriarchs to give to their descendants—and where, incidentally, some Hebrews had remained when the others went down to Egypt. But no. "God did not lead them by way of the land of the Philistines," we are told (Exodus 13:17), "although it was nearer; for God said, 'The people may have a change of heart when they see war, and return to Egypt.' " In other words, the Philistines were settled in Canaan when the biblical account of the Exodus was being written down, but not yet when the Exodus took place. Moses realized full well that he dare not make directly for Canaan lest his people run head on into several Egyptian fortresses and garrisons en route. This road, so important for economic and military reasons, was always closely guarded. Instead, Moses led the Israel-

* According to the census lists in Numbers 1 and 26, said to have been taken right after the Exodus and at the end of the forty years of wandering respectively, the number of male Israelites who left Egypt under Moses, not including the Levites (or the wives, children, and cattle), came to just over 600,000. This figure can scarcely be taken seriously, for sundry and sufficient reasons. It is not unlikely that these lists originally belonged to a later period, perhaps that of David. In any case, scholars generally tend to guess at the number of people involved in the Exodus and Wandering at about 5,000.

ites roundabout, south and east, by way of the wilderness at the Red Sea—more correctly, Reed (or, Marsh) Sea.*

After a short period of wandering, the Hebrews found themselves up against the Reed Sea. In the meantime, an Egyptian force had set out—the biblical narrator states that in order to recapture the fugitive slaves Pharaoh himself "hitched up his chariot and took his men with him: he took six hundred of his picked chariots, and the rest of the chariots of Egypt, with reserves in all of them . . ." (14:5-9)—and they overtook the Hebrews encamped by the Sea.

At this point, tradition recounts, when panic and the urge to surrender to the Egyptians overcame many of the Israelites, Moses stepped forth and said, "Have no fear! . . . The Lord will battle for you, and you hold your peace!" (14:13-14). The following morning the curtain came down on the final scene of Israel's first great act in the drama of man's attempt to achieve and maintain freedom. A strong east wind backed up the waters of the sea, "and the Israelites went into the sea on dry land, the waters forming a wall for them on their right and on their left. When the Egyptians came in pursuit after them into the sea . . . The waters turned back and covered the chariots and the horsemen of Pharaoh's entire host that had followed them into the sea; not one of them remained" (vv.22-26).

The Song of Triumph

Then Moses, assisted by his sister Miriam and the Israelites, sang this song to the Lord (15:1 ff.):

> I will sing to the Lord, for He has triumphed gloriously;
> Horse and driver He has hurled into the sea. . . .
> The deeps covered them;
> They went down into the depths like a stone.
> Thy right hand, O Lord glorious in power,
> Thy right hand, O Lord, shatters the foe! . . .
> The foe said,
> "I will pursue, I will overtake,

* The biblical term *yam suf* has been incorrectly translated "Red Sea." A clear discussion of this, as well as of the route of the Exodus, may be found in G. E. Wright–F. V. Filson, *Westminster Historical Atlas to the Bible* (revised edition, 1956), 38-9; or Wright, *Biblical Archaeology*, 60 ff.

I will divide the spoil;
My desire shall have its fill of them.
I will bare my sword;
My hand shall subdue them."
You did blow with Your wind, the sea covered them;
They sank like lead in the majestic waters.
Who is like You, O Lord, among the mighty,
Who is like You, majestic in holiness,
Awesome in splendor, working wonders! . . .
The Lord will reign for ever and ever!

Though Moses' song is ancient, it is scarcely his, for only one who had lived in Canaan and knew Canaanite poetic composition—from which ancient Hebrew poesy derived—could have written it. Exactly what transpired at the Reed Sea can no longer be determined. We do know that it was invaders from the east Mediterranean, known as Sea Peoples—among whom the Philistines are the best known—who were largely reponsible for the collapse of Egypt after about 1200. "The relentless surge of wave after wave of Sea Peoples," it has been noted by J. A. Wilson, "shows one great folk-wandering . . . The Sea Peoples alone did not deal the vital blow to Egypt's proud position in the southeastern Mediterranean world, but they were one strong factor among many in sapping Egyptian power and shrivelling Egyptian spirit." One may wonder whether the biblical song of Israel's triumph at the Sea of Reeds, composed after the Philistines had become neighbors of the Israelites in Canaan, does not reflect something of the later battles between the Sea Peoples and the Egyptians.

To biblical Israel the Exodus became the greatest event in her history. If only for his leadership in the Exodus, Moses would have become immortal in Jewish history. The Israelites interpreted this single act as demonstrating that God had chosen them as His own. Time and again in the Bible the Exodus is referred to as the physical proof of God's selection of Israel out of all the peoples of the world. Thus, when the Judeans were in the Babylonian Exile (first half of the sixth century B.C.E.), the Isaiah of the Exile could comfort and urge on his fellow exiles with the argument of God's first Exodus, and the new Exodus, soon to transpire (Isaiah 43:18 ff.). So it has been throughout the centuries, in the Diaspora, down to the several exoduses in our own time into the State of Israel from tyrannical countries in Europe, Asia, and Africa.

Passover, Matzot, and the Haggadah

Several later aspects of Israelite life in Canaan came to be associated with the Exodus. Such purely agricultural practices as sacrificing a lamb in the springtime, eating unleavened bread (probably in connection with the barley harvest), and dedicating everything firstborn—practices known in agricultural society from of old—came to be associated with Israel's coming forth from the Egyptian bondage. These nature festivals thus became historical feasts. And in time—especially when the Jewish people found itself exiled by Rome and again in need of an exodus—the Passover feast became the most popular occasion in Jewish religious life.

An essential part of the feast was the retelling (*Seder Haggadah*) of the Exodus and its by-products in accordance, of course, with the biblical account. The haste with which the Israelites had to leave was made responsible for the *matzot:* "And they baked unleavened cakes of the dough that they had taken out of Egypt, for it was not leavened, since they had been driven out of Egypt and could not tarry" (12:39); therefore, "seven days you shall eat unleavened bread (*maṣṣot*) . . . And you shall tell (*we-higgadta;* whence the term *Haggadah*) your son on that day, 'It is because of what the Lord wrought for me when I went free from Egypt' " (13:6-8).

Journey to Sinai

The career of Moses was really hammered out in the generation-long wandering in the wilderness of Sinai. The period of his mature life coincided with the older generation of Israelites that was to die, and with the younger one that was raised in the stimulating but harsh environment of Sinai's rugged terrain. Only the determined and hardy could withstand—and thus in a way thrive on—the many trials. This phase of Israel's history affords an excellent example of challenge and response in man's struggle with his environment.

After traveling three days in the wilderness of Shur, the Israelites were without any water; and when they came to Marah (Hebrew for "bitter"), they found its water bitter. But by casting a log into the water, the Bible asserts, Moses made it sweet. Not long afterwards the Israelites found themselves without food in the midst of the wilderness of Sin, between Elim and Sinai, and they cried out in anguish, "Would that we had died by the hand of the Lord in the land of Egypt, when we sat by the fleshpots, when we ate our fill of bread! For you have brought us out into this wilderness to starve this whole congregation to death" (16:3).

This was the occasion for God to provide the people with "manna": "In the morning there was a fall of dew about the camp; and when the fall of dew lifted, behold, something fine and flaky upon the face of the wilderness, fine as frost upon the ground. The Israelites saw it and said to one another, 'What is it?'—for they did not know what it was. And Moses said to them, 'It is the bread which the Lord has given you to eat' . . . The House of Israel named it manna; it was like coriander seed, white, and it tasted like wafers in honey" (16:14-31).

On another occasion, the "rabble" (Hebrew *asafsuf*) urged the Israelites on: "and they said, 'O that we had meat to eat! We remember the fish we ate in Egypt free; the cucumbers, melons, leeks, onions, and garlic. Now our strength is dried up, and we have nothing before us but manna!" (Numbers 11:4-6). In response, the Lord brought on enough quail to keep the people busy capturing them for two days and a night. But when the people began to gorge themselves with quail, the Lord became angry and struck many of them down for their lust (vv. 31-35).

At Kadesh, in the wilderness of Sin, the people were once again overcome by thirst: "This is no place for grain, or figs, or vines, or pomegranates; and there is no water to drink" (Numbers 20:5). Moses struck a rock—though the Lord had instructed him merely to speak to it—and it gave forth water for the people and their cattle.*

Here again, what the ancients considered to be God's intervention in their behalf—sometimes by a miraculous act and

* Scholars generally agree that the Books of Exodus and Numbers have probably preserved varying versions of the same event. Thus Exodus 16:13 and Numbers 11:31-35 deal with the quail; Exodus 17:1-7 and Numbers 20:1-13 deal with obtaining water from a rock by striking it.

sometimes by the miraculous timing of an act of nature—the modern scholar would explain more naturally. Quail fly over the vicinity of Sinai in large numbers every fall in their migration from Europe to Africa and Arabia. The limestone rock in Sinai has been known—and Moses may have known this from his previous sojourn in Midian—to give forth water when struck, the broken surface exposing the soft and porous rock underneath. And the manna was almost certainly the honey-like substance found on the tamarisk: ". . . manna production is a biological phenomenon of the dry deserts and steppes. The liquid honeydew excretion of a number of cicadas, plant lice, and scale insects speedily solidifies by rapid evaporation. From remote times the resulting sticky and often times granular masses have been collected and called manna." *

The Route of the Wilderness Wandering

To reach the Reed Sea, Moses led his people from Rameses to Succoth, "and they encamped at Etham, at the edge of the wilderness . . . Then the Lord said to Moses, 'Tell the Israelites to turn back and encamp before Pi-hahiroth, between Migdol and the sea, before Baal-zephon; you shall encamp facing it, by the sea' " (Exodus 13:20; 14:1-2).

This part of the Israelite itinerary can now be traced with fair certainty; previously, many thought it scarcely historical. Succoth has been identified with modern Tell el-Maskhutah (excavated since 1883, when numerous inscriptions were found), and Tell Defneh (Greek Daphne) is believed to be the modern site of ancient Baal-zephon.

The route taken to Mt. Sinai, however, is not as certain, and the identification of Mt. Sinai itself is disputed. Tradition has long placed the holy mountain at the southern end of the peninsula of Sinai. Others, however, locate it farther east, across the Gulf of Aqaba, in Midian. Still others place it in the north-central part of Sinai. Had the Israelis been permitted to remain longer in Sinai after their campaign in 1956, a team of scholars might have been able to determine the site of the famed mountain. As of now, there is insufficient reason to give up the traditional location, except that what is conventionally called "Mt.

* F. S. Bodenheimer in *Biblical Archeologist*, X (1947), pp. 1-6.

Sinai" may in reality be a range of mountains rather than a single peak.

Moses and Jethro

Even before the great event at Mt. Sinai, Moses was playing something of the role of arbiter and lawmaker. When differences of opinion arose, when disputes and recriminations resulted, even when simple inquiries had to be made, he acted as arbiter. Fortunately for Moses, Jethro, his Midianite father-in-law, came to the camp to see his daughter Zipporah and the grandchildren, and to congratulate Moses and Israel. "Blessed be the Lord," Jethro said, "who delivered you from the Egyptians and from Pharaoh . . . Now I know that the Lord is greater than all gods . . ." (18:10-11).

But when he saw how "Moses sat as magistrate among the people, while the people stood about Moses from morning until evening," Jethro advised his son-in-law as follows: "The thing you are doing is not good: you will surely wear yourself out, both you and this people with you, for the task is too heavy for you; you cannot do it alone. Now listen to me. I will give you counsel—and God be with you! . . . And Moses heeded his father-in-law," we are told, "and did all that he had said. Moses chose capable men out of all Israel, and appointed them heads over the people—chiefs of thousands, hundreds, fifties, and tens. And they exercised authority over the people at all times: the difficult matters they brought to Moses, and all the minor matters they decided themselves" (18:17-26).

There can be little doubt of the essential authenticity of this tradition. It is not likely that anyone would fabricate an Israelite dependence upon anything Midianite—the Midianites later became mortal enemies of Israel—especially one that involved Moses in relation to the administration of law. Then again, there is independent reason for recognizing an early and close relationship between some Midianites and the Israelites, e.g., by way of Hobab the Kenite, of the family of Moses' father-in-law (Numbers 10:29-32; Judges 4:11). Indeed, some scholars believe that the Lord, God of Israel, was originally the God of the Midianites (or Kenites), and that Moses adopted Him as God only after marrying into Jethro's family; this theory, however, is quite hypothetical.

Mt. Sinai: The Covenant

Israel was now ready for the corollary of the Exodus, the solemn establishment of the theocracy at Sinai on the basis of the "Book of the Covenant" (*sefer ha-brit*, Exodus 24:7), which consisted of the Ten Commandments and a code of laws (chaps. 20-23). The two events together—for Exodus and Sinai are really inseparable—formed the basis of the national covenant (*brit*) between God and Israel, a pact around which the entire Hebrew Bible was to revolve. It is impossible to comprehend the biblical view of Israel's career without recognizing the central role of the covenant; the entire rabbinic view of Judaism derives wholly and directly from it. Indeed, early Christianity found it necessary to alter this covenant between Israel and God by proclaiming a New Covenant (or, Testament) that was to replace the Old, one which Jesus was to mediate and which was to involve all the nations of the world (Matthew 28:18 ff.; Hebrews 8:6 ff.).

The great event at Sinai, befitting its status as The Revelation, is majestically and vividly described in the Bible. It is true that much of the biblical account is the product of a later period; thus many of the laws derive from the experiences of a settled community long occupied in agriculture. On the other hand, since they associated God with awesome aspects of nature, it was natural for Moses and Israel to choose a setting like Sinai, amidst desert thunder and lightning, for the consummation of the act of covenant. Whether the Ten Commandments were introduced by Moses to Israel for the first time at Sinai, or were simply formally confirmed on that occasion—the fact seems to be that Sinai was a real event at Israel's coming into nationhood.

For three days the Israelites purified themselves. On the third day, "Mount Sinai was all smoking, for the Lord had come down upon it in fire . . . and the whole mountain trembled violently. The blare of the horn grew louder and louder. As Moses spoke, God would answer him in thunder . . ." (Ex. 19:18 ff.).

In this setting, "God spoke all these words, saying: 'I the Lord am your God who brought you out of the land of Egypt, the house of bondage. You shall have no other gods beside Me . . .' " (20: 1 ff.) Then came the other nine commandments:

> You shall not make for yourself a sculptured image . . .
> You shall not swear falsely by the name of the Lord your God . . .
> Remember the Sabbath day and keep it holy . . .
> Honor your father and your mother . . .
> You shall not murder . . .
> You shall not commit adultery . . .
> You shall not steal . . .
> You shall not bear false witness . . .
> You shall not covet . . . anything that is your neighbor's.*

Accompanied by thunder and flashes, the blare of the horn and the smoking of the mountain, the people heard these words and agreed solemnly to the conditions of the covenant. The Israelites and their descendants voluntarily bound themselves exclusively to one God, who, in turn, obligated Himself forever to Israel. It was unthinkable that God, the incomparable, would fail to protect a law-abiding Israel and make it prosper; had He not already demonstrated by His acts His interest in Israel? But if Israel failed to heed God's commandments, then He could punish and even destroy her.

Yet over and above the letter of the law, another element was recognized in the covenant, namely, God's love for Israel and His devotion (*hesed*, traditionally rendered "lovingkindness") to her. It was believed that no matter how grievously Israel sinned and how undeserving she might be of God's protection, God would never cast her off completely. This concept is the core not only of the Written Law (the Bible), but also of the Oral Law (the Talmud, consisting of the Mishnah and the Gemarah) and of the liturgy.

The concept of covenant was not novel. Earlier, each patriarch had entered into a covenant with God. Abraham had entered into a mutually exclusive agreement with "the God of Abraham," whereby Abraham was to recognize and worship no

* This version of the Decalogue is that of Exodus. The Book of Deuteronomy (5:6 ff.) offers a somewhat different version; cf. S. R. Driver, *Introduction to the Literature of the Old Testament* (Meridian).

nly after Aaron persuaded Moses to appeal t
ehalf.

n the part of Aaron and Miriam to reduce th
authority of Moses failed. But other revolt
st Moses (Numbers 16-17). A Levite name
some two hundred and fifty chieftains, not al
"assembled against Moses and Aaron and said
ave assumed too much! For the entire commu-
of them, is holy, and the Lord is in their midst.
ou exalt yourselves above the congregation of
6:1 ff.). In defense, Moses bade them offer fire
he Lord at the sanctuary, "and the man whom
oose shall be the holy one." As a consequence,
th from the Lord and consumed the two hun-
en offering up the incense."

time, Dathan, Abiram, and On, all three of the
, led another segment of the people in rebellion
"Is it a small thing that you have brought us up
owing with milk and honey, to kill us in the
t you must also make yourself a ruler over
13-14). Unlike the ecclesiastical revolt of Korah
this was a rebellion of laymen against the civil
n Moses claimed. Their punishment and end were

of the revolt and its collapse came the next day.
raelite community murmured against Moses and
'You have killed the people of the Lord!'"
Lord then took matters into His own hands. He
to break out among the people, killing many of
according to v. 14). Had not Moses intervened
n atonement offering of incense, the biblical text
ople would have perished to the last man.

elements among the people at one time or another
s is certain; it is hardly likely that anyone gratui-
in a later period such hostile sentiment against
nding Founding Father. But what can never be
t extent the opposition to Moses was justified un-
mstances. Later writers naturally tended to put
ight, and use the divine acts as evidence against the

other deity but God, and God was to watch over the welfare of Abraham and his family. When Isaac renewed the pact, God became "the kinsman (*pahad*) of Isaac." For Jacob, God was "the champion (*'abir*) of Jacob."

This concept of covenant between two parties, it is now known, derived from earlier western Asia, where the covenant involved two equal rulers or a powerful ruler and a vassal. As in the case of the patriarchs, and later in the Mosaic period, the two parties of the covenant were bound by an oath, sometimes consisting specifically of blessings and curses; no legal means of enforcement was involved.

Significantly, however, only the patriarchs and their descendants are known to have entered into a covenant with a deity. They alone, it would seem, adopted a single god; but why they should have done so, in the midst of a polytheistic world, has not yet been determined.

In the wilderness, what had been a personal covenant involving God and an individual patriarch became for the first time a national covenant, one that brought together God and an entire people. As a result of the Exodus and Sinai, Israel came into being as a nation covenanted with God. The central figure and mediator in this epochal event was Moses.

The Law

As part of the covenant, Moses proceeded to set before the Israelites some of the laws by which they were to live. Law, from the very outset, has constituted a necessary and useful brake against oppression of the weak on the part of the strong. Indeed, law marks the beginning, and the basis, of the trend toward a democratic society.

Western Asia, and Mesopotamia in particular, was the birthplace of law on earth. Three lawbooks, two written in Sumerian and one in Babylonian, have recently been discovered; preceding by about two to three hundred years Hammurabi's famous Code of about 1700 B.C.E., these are the oldest known lawbooks, and they antedate the earliest known codification of Roman law by more than fifteen hundred years.

Law in the ancient Near East—Egypt produced no lawbooks because the god-king was himself the source of law and authority–reached its peak in the Bible. The constitution of ancient Israel was frequently called "the Torah of Moses" by the biblical writers. And while scholars today recognize several later strata, post-Mosaic layers of law, in the Torah, Moses came to be acknowledged as Israel's lawgiver, recipient of the Torah directly from God Himself.*

The collection of instructions (*torot*) that Moses is said to have set forth (Exodus 20:23-30; 38), regulating the social and religious life of the people, was called "The Book (or: Record, Document, Writ) of the Covenant." A better term could scarcely be found. Biblical law dealt with the individual's relationship to his neighbor—as an individual and as a member of society—and to God; all three parties, the individual, the state, and God, shared importance in the Mosaic code or covenant. Man's life, limbs, cattle, and fields (20:23 ff.) must be guarded and respected, according to the terms of the code, no less than the details of the Tabernacle (or, Tent of Meeting), the Ark, and the sacrifices (25:1 ff.). Social and religious responsibility were the two complementary aspects of the covenant, a view never lost sight of in biblical tradition. Thus the prophet Isaiah asserted (Isaiah 1:2-4, 10-23) that no matter how many sacrifices and prayers the Israelites offer to the Lord, He will reject them all if the worshipper has failed in the commandments pertaining to man and society.

The Tabernacle and the Ark

Closely connected with the event at Sinai are the Ark and the Tabernacle (Hebrew *mishkan*). In the former, the acacia chest, Moses is said to have placed the two tablets of stone on which the Ten Commandments were recorded; the latter was the movable shrine around which the political and religious life of the wandering Israelites revolved.

There can be little doubt that these institutions are the product of a nomadic or semi-nomadic society, even if later priestly writers embellished the original account considerably. Acacia wood—cedar, cyprus, or olive was later used in Canaan—ram-

* All lawbooks in western Asia were said by their compilers or royal patrons to have emanated from the gods and been given to the rulers as a trust to uphold.

skins, lambskins, cl
tations of nomadic
about many aspects
the religious—they
among some nomad
(sacred tents) were
The Tabernacle
Canaan, the "Tent o
replaced by the Ten
In the case of the Ar
in the Temple, and–
ing the reign of King
Chronicles 35:3)—w
Tent and the Ark w
significant role in th
conquered Canaan.

Desert Sojourn: Grumb

Having received the
ready to prepare then
problems still remained
the Amalekites, semi-n
Israel. Moses appointed
a picked group of men
which the Bible interpr
with the natural—Israel
aid of Moses, who kep
brother Aaron and Hur
thus ensuring the defeat
At Hazeroth (Numb
for having married an E
defense. "The man Mos
more than any other per
by this criticism. He sum
spoke only to the last tw
with all My house. Wit
Why then were you no
Moses!" Then the Lord st

she was cured o
the Lord in her b
This attempt
total power and
broke out again
Korah, heading
of them Levites
to them, 'You h
nity, every one
Why then do y
the Lord?' " (1
and incense to
the Lord will c
"a fire went fo
dred and fifty m
At the same
tribe of Reuben
against Moses:
from a land fl
wilderness, tha
us . . . ?" (vv
and his group,
authority whic
dreadful.
The climax
"The entire Is
Aaron, saying
(17:6 ff.) The
caused a plagu
them (14,700
hastily, with a
asserts, the pe
That many
opposed Mose
tously created
Israel's outsta
clear is to wh
der the circu
Moses in the

other deity but God, and God was to watch over the welfare of Abraham and his family. When Isaac renewed the pact, God became "the kinsman (*pahad*) of Isaac." For Jacob, God was "the champion (*'abir*) of Jacob."

This concept of covenant between two parties, it is now known, derived from earlier western Asia, where the covenant involved two equal rulers or a powerful ruler and a vassal. As in the case of the patriarchs, and later in the Mosaic period, the two parties of the covenant were bound by an oath, sometimes consisting specifically of blessings and curses; no legal means of enforcement was involved.

Significantly, however, only the patriarchs and their descendants are known to have entered into a covenant with a deity. They alone, it would seem, adopted a single god; but why they should have done so, in the midst of a polytheistic world, has not yet been determined.

In the wilderness, what had been a personal covenant involving God and an individual patriarch became for the first time a national covenant, one that brought together God and an entire people. As a result of the Exodus and Sinai, Israel came into being as a nation covenanted with God. The central figure and mediator in this epochal event was Moses.

The Law

As part of the covenant, Moses proceeded to set before the Israelites some of the laws by which they were to live. Law, from the very outset, has constituted a necessary and useful brake against oppression of the weak on the part of the strong. Indeed, law marks the beginning, and the basis, of the trend toward a democratic society.

Western Asia, and Mesopotamia in particular, was the birthplace of law on earth. Three lawbooks, two written in Sumerian and one in Babylonian, have recently been discovered; preceding by about two to three hundred years Hammurabi's famous Code of about 1700 B.C.E., these are the oldest known lawbooks, and they antedate the earliest known codification of Roman law by more than fifteen hundred years.

Law in the ancient Near East—Egypt produced no lawbooks because the god-king was himself the source of law and authority–reached its peak in the Bible. The constitution of ancient Israel was frequently called "the Torah of Moses" by the biblical writers. And while scholars today recognize several later strata, post-Mosaic layers of law, in the Torah, Moses came to be acknowledged as Israel's lawgiver, recipient of the Torah directly from God Himself.*

The collection of instructions (*torot*) that Moses is said to have set forth (Exodus 20:23-30; 38), regulating the social and religious life of the people, was called "The Book (or: Record, Document, Writ) of the Covenant." A better term could scarcely be found. Biblical law dealt with the individual's relationship to his neighbor—as an individual and as a member of society—and to God; all three parties, the individual, the state, and God, shared importance in the Mosaic code or covenant. Man's life, limbs, cattle, and fields (20:23 ff.) must be guarded and respected, according to the terms of the code, no less than the details of the Tabernacle (or, Tent of Meeting), the Ark, and the sacrifices (25:1 ff.). Social and religious responsibility were the two complementary aspects of the covenant, a view never lost sight of in biblical tradition. Thus the prophet Isaiah asserted (Isaiah 1:2-4, 10-23) that no matter how many sacrifices and prayers the Israelites offer to the Lord, He will reject them all if the worshipper has failed in the commandments pertaining to man and society.

The Tabernacle and the Ark

Closely connected with the event at Sinai are the Ark and the Tabernacle (Hebrew *mishkan*). In the former, the acacia chest, Moses is said to have placed the two tablets of stone on which the Ten Commandments were recorded; the latter was the movable shrine around which the political and religious life of the wandering Israelites revolved.

There can be little doubt that these institutions are the product of a nomadic or semi-nomadic society, even if later priestly writers embellished the original account considerably. Acacia wood—cedar, cyprus, or olive was later used in Canaan—ram-

* All lawbooks in western Asia were said by their compilers or royal patrons to have emanated from the gods and been given to the rulers as a trust to uphold.

skins, lambskins, cloth of goat's hair, and the like are all manifestations of nomadic existence. Again, while little is really known about many aspects of life among the nomads in antiquity, e.g., the religious—they left virtually no records—we do know that among some nomadic, pre-Mohammedan Arabs portable shrines (sacred tents) were employed.

The Tabernacle was to become later, after the conquest of Canaan, the "Tent of the Lord" at Shiloh, and it was ultimately replaced by the Temple that David planned and Solomon built. In the case of the Ark, Solomon placed it in the Holy of Holies in the Temple, and—except for a single unclear reference during the reign of King Josiah about two hundred years later (II Chronicles 35:3)—was heard of no more. It is clear that the Tent and the Ark were ancient institutions that played a more significant role in the wilderness wandering than they did in conquered Canaan.

Desert Sojourn: Grumblings and Uprisings

Having received the covenant at Sinai, the Israelites were now ready to prepare themselves to enter the Promised Land. But problems still remained. At Rephidim, on the way to Mt. Sinai, the Amalekites, semi-nomadic desert folk, came and fought with Israel. Moses appointed a promising young man, Joshua, to lead a picked group of men in battle. In keeping with the manner in which the Bible interpreted history—combining the miraculous with the natural—Israel was victorious because God came to the aid of Moses, who kept his hands erect—with the aid of his brother Aaron and Hur of the tribe of Judah—until the sun set, thus ensuring the defeat of hated Amalek (Exodus 17:8-15).

At Hazeroth (Numbers 12), Miriam criticized her brother for having married an Ethiopian woman. Moses said nothing in defense. "The man Moses," the text reads, "was very humble, more than any other person on earth." But the Lord was vexed by this criticism. He summoned Moses, Aaron, and Miriam, but spoke only to the last two: ". . . My servant Moses is entrusted with all My house. With him I speak mouth to mouth . . . Why then were you not afraid to speak against My servant Moses!" Then the Lord struck Miriam with leprosy, from which she was cured only after Aaron persuaded Moses to appeal to the Lord in her behalf.

This attempt on the part of Aaron and Miriam to reduce the total power and authority of Moses failed. But other revolts broke out against Moses (Numbers 16-17). A Levite named Korah, heading some two hundred and fifty chieftains, not all of them Levites, "assembled against Moses and Aaron and said to them, 'You have assumed too much! For the entire community, every one of them, is holy, and the Lord is in their midst. Why then do you exalt yourselves above the congregation of the Lord?' " (16:1 ff.). In defense, Moses bade them offer fire and incense to the Lord at the sanctuary, "and the man whom the Lord will choose shall be the holy one." As a consequence, "a fire went forth from the Lord and consumed the two hundred and fifty men offering up the incense."

At the same time, Dathan, Abiram, and On, all three of the tribe of Reuben, led another segment of the people in rebellion against Moses: "Is it a small thing that you have brought us up from a land flowing with milk and honey, to kill us in the wilderness, that you must also make yourself a ruler over us . . . ?" (vv. 13-14). Unlike the ecclesiastical revolt of Korah and his group, this was a rebellion of laymen against the civil authority which Moses claimed. Their punishment and end were dreadful.

The climax of the revolt and its collapse came the next day. "The entire Israelite community murmured against Moses and Aaron, saying, 'You have killed the people of the Lord!' " (17:6 ff.) The Lord then took matters into His own hands. He caused a plague to break out among the people, killing many of them (14,700 according to v. 14). Had not Moses intervened hastily, with an atonement offering of incense, the biblical text asserts, the people would have perished to the last man.

That many elements among the people at one time or another opposed Moses is certain; it is hardly likely that anyone gratuitously created in a later period such hostile sentiment against Israel's outstanding Founding Father. But what can never be clear is to what extent the opposition to Moses was justified under the circumstances. Later writers naturally tended to put Moses in the right, and use the divine acts as evidence against the guilty ones. If some of Moses' critics had actually been the victims of an epidemic, an earthquake, a fire, or a skin disease at about the time that they voiced their discontent, these occurrences were readily interpreted as indications and proof of God's view. It is more likely, however, that the biblical pattern of history-writing, in defending Moses, simply made use here of well-known natural phenomena.

Death in the Wilderness: Punishment for Disobedience and Lack of Confidence

In the second year of the Exodus, Moses took the first positive action in regard to the conquest of Canaan by sending spies from the wilderness of Paran to the Promised Land (Numbers 13-14). "See what kind of country it is," they were instructed by Moses, "whether the kind of people that dwells in it is strong or weak, few or numerous; whether the cities are open or fortified."

The report that the majority of the spies brought back was far from favorable. True, the land "flows with milk and honey," they said, "but the people that inhabits the land is powerful, and the cities are fortified mightily . . . It is a land that devours its inhabitants . . ." And a final touch: we saw such giants there that we appeared in their eyes like grasshoppers.

Caleb, son of Jephunneh, however, supported by Joshua, son of Nun, gave a dissenting report. "If the Lord delights in us," they exhorted the people, "He will bring us into this land . . . Only do not rebel against the Lord, and do not fear the people of the land . . . The Lord is with us, do not fear them!" Caleb and Joshua were about to be stoned by the people when the Lord intervened (14:6-10).

To what extent this story is true cannot be determined.* But it was made, or, as some scholars would say, created to serve as the reason that so few of the erstwhile slaves in Egypt lived long enough to enter Canaan. The assumption is that had the people rejected the pessimistic view of the majority of the spies in fa-

* It has long been recognized that the biblical text is made up of two versions of the story, and the older one did not include Joshua at all.

vor of the confident outlook of the minority, relying utterly upon the power and protection of God, they would shortly have marched into Canaan and conquered it. Instead, God decided, except for such as Caleb and Joshua, only the children would live to reach Canaan; all the older folk, those who had been twenty years and over when the first census was taken, were going to die in the wilderness. Hence the forty years of wandering.*

If the facts preserved in the Bible are essentially true, then one may posit simply that the forty years—which is sometimes only a round number used in the Bible to indicate a generation—of wandering were made necessary by the urgent need to train and discipline the horde of slaves for the conquest of Canaan. Disaster clearly stared them in the face were an all-out invasion of the land undertaken prematurely.

Moses, too, and Aaron did not enter the Promised Land. The Bible gives two reasons, both in keeping with its religious interpretation of history: they, too, like the people, were disobedient and lacked confidence in God. In the older version (Deuteronomy 1:37), Moses was excluded from Canaan along with the people because of their reaction to the pessimistic report of the spies (Numbers 13:20). According to the later version, when the people were overcome by thirst at Kadesh, in the thirty-seventh year of the Exodus, God had ordered Moses to take his staff, assemble the people, and "tell the rock before their eyes to yield its water" (Numbers 20:1-13). Instead, Moses used the staff to strike the rock. Whereupon the Lord told Moses and Aaron, "Because you did not believe in Me, by sanctifying Me in the eyes of the Israelites, therefore you shall not bring this congregation into the land that I give them." Why Moses is said to have struck the rock, instead of speaking to it as commanded, is for the folklorist to interpret; but if he had spoken to the rock, then the biblical writer would have had to look for another explanation.

Shortly afterwards Aaron died, on the top of Mt. Hor, on the border of Edom.

* A few scholars would reduce the total period of wandering to but a few years: cf., e.g., H. H. Rowley, *From Joseph to Joshua* (Oxford University Press, 1950); nowhere else will so full a bibliography on the subject be found.

On the Eve of the Conquest of Canaan: Moses' Death

The people were now approaching inhabited territory. They had reached the land of Edom. Moses sent messengers to Edom's king for permission to go through his land. "We will not pass through field or vineyard," they assured the Edomite government (20:14 ff.), "neither will we drink water from a well . . ." But the king refused permission, and the Israelites had, once again, to take a roundabout route.

Farther north, in Transjordan, the people approached the territory of Moab, then dominated by the Amorites under King Sihon, who also refused to grant transit permission. Instead, Sihon attacked Israel; for his pains he and his forces were defeated, and the territory was occupied by the victors (21:21-32). North of Moab, in the territory of Bashan, King Og, too, attacked Israel and was vanquished.

At long last the Israelites found themselves at the border of Canaan (22:1). And Moses had now reached the point of neither return nor advance. His mission was accomplished. He had played the central role in effecting the Exodus from Egypt, in achieving the crossing of the wildernesses in the peninsula of Sinai, and in preparing the Israelites, as a more-or-less united group bound by a national covenant to a single deity, for the conquest of Canaan. Even the vexing problem of successorship had been solved; no opposition seems to have arisen—among a people that was given so frequently to opposition—to Moses' selection of Joshua of the tribe of Ephraim as his successor.

After attributing to Moses a long review of his career just ended and a preview of his people's career about to begin (chapters 1-32), culminating in his famous blessing (33), the Book of Deuteronomy (34) tells us that "Moses went up from the steppes of Moab to Mount Nebo, the top of Pisgah, which is opposite Jericho," from which the Lord showed him Israel's land. After which "Moses the servant of the Lord died there in the land of Moab. And He buried him (or he was buried) in the valley of Moab opposite Beth-peor; but no man knows the site of his grave to this day. Moses was 120 years old when he died; his eyes were not dim, nor his natural force abated."

Jewish sources have embellished the story of Moses' death. Early legends differed as to whether Moses had experienced an unusual manner of dying or had simply not died at all. From the biblical text itself it is not clear whether God or someone else had buried Moses. The Septuagint (Old Greek) translation reads "they buried him." Philo, the Alexandrian Jewish philosopher of the first century, in his essay on "The Life of Moses," wrote: "He was entombed not by mortal hands, but by immortal powers . . ." And Josephus, the Jewish historian and Philo's younger contemporary in Judea, asserted: "While, after having taken leave of the people, he was going to embrace Eleazar and Joshua on Mount Nebo, a cloud suddenly stood over him, and he disappeared, though he wrote in Scripture that he died, which was done from fear that people might say that because of his extraordinary virtue he had been turned into a divinity."

The Man and His Legacy

For the modern Jew, who may or may not accept the legends that have sprung up around Moses,* the patriarch remains the prime mover in the actions and decisions that led to the founding of Israel as a nation. Even if it is not possible to delimit precisely his role, he alone was the leading personality and subjective factor among the objective conditions that made possible the Exodus from Egypt. In the wilderness of Sinai, not in Egypt, Israel was forged, hammered into the shape of nationhood amid appalling hardship. The weak and the weary perished, leaving the young and strong to drift yet another mile toward the Land of Promise, the ancestral home.

The struggle for power within the group that Moses led from Egypt was violent. Every faction in this group, religious and civil, including members of his own family, challenged the authority and wisdom of Moses. Only a man of iron will, patience, compassion for his people, and—above all—unlimited faith in his goal could have endured this endless bickering, scheming, and backsliding.

* No biblical character has been able to compete with Moses in sheer quantity of legend in post-biblical times. In Louis Ginzberg's monumental collection of *The Legends of the Jews,* the material on Moses fills more than one-third of the pages (611 out of 1728). Moses also played a prominent role in Christian and Muslim literature.

Moses comes through this struggle as a very human personality, revealing both positive and negative qualities. Several independent incidents would indicate that Moses had quite a temper. His act of beating an Egyptian to death for striking down a Hebrew is a case in point. When Dathan and Aviram accused Moses of authoritarianism, "Moses became incensed and he said to the Lord, 'Do not favor their offering! I have not taken a single ass from them, neither have I harmed a single one of them' " (Numbers 16:15). On several occasions he is also said to have betrayed indecision. At the "Red" Sea, with Pharaoh's superior forces approaching, the Israelites cried out to the Lord. "But the Lord said to Moses, 'Why do you cry out to Me? Tell the Israelites to go forward . . . !' " (Exodus 14:15 ff.). At Marah, too (15:22-25), and at Rephidim (17:1), when the people thirsted for water, Moses "cried out to the Lord."

It was indeed a difficult struggle, and about a generation—the traditional "forty years" of wandering—had to elapse before Moses could weld the heterogeneous, inexperienced, and uncultured mass together into something of a unified force and social group.

Besides founding the nation, Moses taught the concept of monotheism to his people. It used to be generally thought in scholarly circles, as has already been pointed out, that monotheism did not come to Israel until the period of the prophets (eighth century), and that Israel had little substantial origin or existence during the second millennium B.C.E. The patriarchs were frequently regarded as the figment of a much later writer's imagination. And those who credited them with something of an existence usually attributed to them the beliefs and practices of polytheism. Thanks to archeology, few scholars today would deny at least some historicity to the patriarchs; even fewer would refuse to grant some substance to the career of Israel in Egypt and to Moses.

There can now be little doubt that the patriarchs recognized the concept of covenant, each patriarch making his pact with God. It was under Moses that the covenant was made between a total nation and God.

This concept and act of covenant involving Israel and the deity was an integral part of a second concept, that of monotheism. It is impossible to postulate the covenant between the two without belief in the One. The biblical tradition is clear and consistent that Moses was the individual most responsible for emphasizing and cementing Israel's alliance with God. This is precisely what the very first of the Ten Commandments asserts: "I the Lord am your God who brought you out of the land of Egypt, the house of bondage. You shall have no other gods beside Me . . . !"

It has long been recognized that Moses is not the author of the Torah. This is a far cry, however, from denying to Moses all responsibility for helping lay the basis of Israel's legal system.

Judaism came to recognize the Talmud, the Oral Law, as no less authoritative than the Written Law, from which it derived. And just as Moses was credited with receiving the Written Law from God on Sinai, so did he become the ultimate authority also of the Unwritten Law.

Thus, Moses, the lawgiver, was the midwife of the Israelite nation. In the extraordinary career of Jews and Judaism, his figure and personality stands out as brilliantly today as it did more than thirty centuries ago.

2 . *Akiba*

[c. 40-137]

LOUIS FINKELSTEIN

RABBI Akiba ben Joseph dominates the whole scene of Jewish history for eighteen centuries—from the period of the prophets until the rise of the Spanish school of Jewish philosophers in the twelfth century. His originality of thought, his legislative insight, and his colorful personality combined to make him the most revered as well as the most beloved of Talmudic sages. Most of the great scholars of the following generation were Akiba's disciples, and an authority of the third century informs us that the Mishnah, the *Tosefta*, the *Sifra*, and the *Sifre*—those ancient compilations of rabbinic thought which have survived until our own time—all had their origin in his scholarly activity. The method he developed became basic to all later rabbinic reasoning, and everywhere in the massive tomes of the Talmud are traces of his remarkable influence on subsequent systems of Jewish law, ethics, and theology.

In a wider sense, the contour of western thought generally has also been affected by Akiba's philosophy. His ideas molded those of Maimonides, Gersonides,* and Hasdai Crescas.† The influence of these men was felt by a whole series of Latin writers from Thomas Aquinas to Spinoza, who in turn laid the foundations of modern thought. The amalgam of rationalism and mysticism which was basic to the advanced Jewish philosophy of the Middle Ages, the conception of a God who was real but not anthropomorphic, could hardly have taken the form it did with-

* Levi ben Gershom, 14th-century philosopher, mathematician, and astronomer.
† Spanish-Jewish philosopher (c. 1340-1412), author of *Milhamot Adonai* (The Wars of the Lord).

out the authoritative support of Akiba. Certainly the unequalled freedom and tolerance of later Jewish thought was, in large part, a result of Akiba's victorious assertion of his right to be original. Even the absorbing concern with ethics, which was characteristic of all Jewish thought, and has been perhaps its main contribution to the modern mind, gained in impressiveness from Akiba's teachings.

It is the reconstruction of the social conflicts of his time, however, which makes Akiba's life and thought particularly relevant to us. The issues which confronted him are with us yet, though in somewhat new form. The problems he posed of international peace, universal education, the status of women, the rights of laborers, the removal of superstition from religion, and the advancement of pure scholarship are still unsolved.

The rabbinic sages, always contemptuous of such accidental trivialities as physical characteristics, record only Akiba's exceptional stature and baldness. Surely the strange blend of humor and pathos, rigor and mercy, practical good sense and sentimental mysticism which characterized the man must have found some expression in the cheek, the forehead, and the eye. There must have been something singular and arresting in the contrast between the intellectual preoccupation of the statesman-scholar and the powerful physique of the one-time shepherd. But the Talmud records nothing of this. We are left to recreate Akiba in our imagination out of his pithy maxims, witty answers, ingenious arguments, penetrating decisions, mature theology, pedagogic method, and the memorable events of his life.

Akiba lived during an extraordinary period, intellectually and spiritually productive, marked by new thoughts, widening horizons, daring adventures, heroic martyrs, and memorable teachers. In little more than a century tiny Palestine produced the twin religions of rabbinic Judaism and Christianity.

These contributions to civilization were all the more remarkable in view of the political decline, social disintegration, and economic impoverishment of the times. Before Akiba was thirty years old, the ultranationalists of Judea, maddened by the oppression of the Roman procurators, had persuaded their brethren to undertake a hopeless rebellion which culminated in the capture of Jerusalem and the burning of the Temple (70 C.E.). Half a century later (115 C.E.) a second rebellion broke out because the Roman emperors violated their pledge to restore the Temple and Jerusalem; after another seventeen years came the final catastrophe of the Bar Kokhba Rebellion and its aftermath of unforgettable destruction. The Romans might well have thought that the destruction of Judea would end the spiritual life of its people. But the very opposite happened. Judea died, but she died in childbirth.

Akiba and Paul

In this miracle of destruction turned into creation and death into life, Rabbi Akiba and Paul the apostle exercised the greatest influence. Laboring in different fields and with different methods, the two teachers in middle life underwent conversions to causes which until then they had hated and persecuted. Both emerged as central figures in their respective faiths; both undertook reformulations of the traditions which they had accepted, and struggled unremittingly on behalf of their doctrines; both sought to universalize the teachings of their colleagues and to impose philosophic breadth and order on their religions; and, in the end, each crowned his career with a martyr's death.

True, Paul died before the year 70, and Akiba after the year 130; Paul taught the abrogation of the Law, Akiba its perpetuation; Paul gave himself to the Gentiles, Akiba to his own people; Paul became a Christian, Akiba remained a Jew. These wide divergences only emphasize their amazing similarities in life and circumstance.

It is not surprising that the transformation of rabbinic Judaism was less radical and occurred half a century later than that of Christianity. While Paul had to contend with traditions which were only twenty or thirty years old, those which Akiba undertook to recast had the authority of centuries. In the year 50, Christianity was still entirely fluid; even the founder's sayings had probably not yet been collected into fixed booklets.

The Oral Law, with which Akiba had to deal, had been handed down by a chain of teachers which reached back beyond the beginnings of Pharisaism (second century B.C.E.), and indeed antedated the origins of the Second Commonwealth. To effect even a moderate change in so ancient a system required extraordinary genius. Akiba met that requirement and was able to bring about the rebirth of Jewish law.

Humble Beginnings

Akiba was born in southwestern Palestine, probably in the vicinity of Ludd (modern Lydda), in the low-lying plain near the Mediterranean coast. His father Joseph was a poor, landless peasant, a laborer on the estate of a rich neighbor. He knew and cared nothing about the literature of his people or the learned traditions of the scribes. He could probably neither read nor write. His house had no hewn stone, marble, or wood of any kind; similar to huts still found among Arab peasants of the district, it had walls of sunburned brick, without openings for light or air. Straw mats were the only covering the inhabitants had over the bare earth. Their food was of the simplest—barley bread with cabbage, turnip, or garlic, cooked only if a jug of hot water could be obtained from a rich neighbor or from a central village supply.

Though Akiba knew hunger, toil, and exposure to the elements, he was outdoors most of the day, and could enjoy the bright sunlight and country air. Since he lived in the fertile coastal plain, he could look to the east and see the beauty of the Judean hills, and steal away to the sea which lay only a few miles off.

It was impossible for him, however, to acquire any book learning. Twenty years were to elapse before Joshua ben Gamala was to establish his first system of general rural education for Judea. In Akiba's day children could learn only from their parents, and Akiba could get from his father nothing more than the simple technique of sheep-tending. Condemned to the companionship of animals and inarticulate peasants, Akiba scorned the scholars. "When I was an *am ha-aretz*," he reported in later years, "I used to say, 'Would that I had a scholar in my hands and I should bite him like an ass.' " Those who knew Akiba in his older, mellow days, when he had attained profound learning, social charm, and gentle manners, could scarcely have credited him with such fierce words.

Marriage and a New Life

From this pit of ignorance, Akiba was fortunately saved by Rachel, who became his wife. Who she was and by what genius she was able to penetrate so graceless an exterior and see the immense potentialities within, we do not know. Whatever her background, she must be recognized as a most remarkable woman. Throughout his life Akiba insisted that he owed everything to her. "Whatever you have achieved, and whatever I have achieved," he said to his disciples when they gathered in hosts to greet him, "belong to her!" Rachel persuaded Akiba to leave his goats and sheep and become a pupil of the scholars whom he envied and loathed. After this decision was made, they were married and entered together on the struggle for his education.

Numerous stories are current about the discouragement which Akiba met and overcame in his first efforts to learn how to read and write. His wife's father, who had opposed the match from the beginning, refused to admit the poor, ignorant shepherd into his home; and Akiba had no house to which he and Rachel might go. His toil barely earned enough for food for the family. Added to these economic troubles were the disappointments over his attempts to learn. Apparently he found his studies so difficult that more than once he was ready to return to his sheep and his ignorance.

In truth, the system of education then in vogue was hardly adapted to the needs of an alert, mature mind. When the pupil had mastered the alphabet and was able to read Hebrew texts, he was introduced not to the fascinating narratives of Genesis, but to the difficult, technical laws of sacrifice in Leviticus. Akiba, unaccustomed to the discipline of book learning, and free to study only after the fatigue of a day's labor, must have found it difficult to keep awake as he struggled to remember which offering was sacrificed in the north and which at the door of the sanctuary; whether the sin-offering of the high priest was a bullock or a ram; whether the presence of yellow hair on a leprous person was a sign of impurity and disease or of purity and healing.

Meanwhile, Rachel had given birth to a child. Akiba may have wondered whether his child too was destined to remain an *am ha-aretz*. Brooding over his own unhappy lot, Akiba came one day, it is said, to a spring, where for the first time he noticed the deep groove which the falling waters had cut into the rock. The spring became for him what the almond tree had been for Jeremiah and the sight of the Temple for Isaiah—the catalytic agent of his conversion. Suddenly his thoughts crystallized, his mind became clear, his purpose assumed definite shape.

Akiba took his child, then a lad of four or five, to a teacher. "My master, instruct us," he said. The middle-aged father and the little boy began to learn the alphabet together. In the effort to help the boy, Akiba found his own learning less tedious and painful. He mastered Leviticus and then the other books which had legalistic significance: Exodus, Numbers, and Deuteronomy. Genesis, which contained only a few laws and was full of stories, was apparently not studied in the regular curriculum. In preparation for advanced rabbinic studies, Akiba also mastered the Prophets and the Hagiographa. He had now far outstripped his little boy, and was ready to apply for admission into the rabbinical academy.

As Akiba approached his fortieth year, in about the year 80, he had not yet entered on his career. But work was waiting for him. The momentous transformation in his private life had coincided with even more fundamental changes in the structure of the body politic. The double process of decay and growth characteristic of the period had already set in.

The Challenge of the Times

As it happened, while Akiba was still in his infancy, Agrippa's peaceful reign had come to an end, giving way to tumult and rebellion, denunciation and bitter strife. The ancient struggles between the Pharisees and the Sadducees, and among the various Pharisaic factions, had broken out anew, and with redoubled vigor.

This clash of social forces, which was to affect Akiba's public activity so intimately, becomes fully intelligible only in its historical perspective. The fundamental class division in Palestine was that between the semi-nomadic, landless shepherds and the landowning farmers. Neither the shepherds nor the small peasants of the hills could offer effective resistance to the great patrician landowners who dominated Palestinian culture and politics. The common people lacked organization, a program, and class consciousness; it was only in Jerusalem that they achieved partial victory. During the First Commonwealth the defense of the plebeians had been conducted largely by the prophets; in the Second Commonwealth, the prophet was replaced by the scholar, whose forum was his school room.

To emphasize the equality of the two groups within Pharisaism, however, a system of dual leadership was arranged, giving each equal representation. If the first sage (later called the *nasi* or president) was a patrician, the second or associate sage (later called *ab bet din*, or head of the court) had to be a plebeian, and vice versa. For many generations the two groups worked together, but during the insurrection in 66, which culminated in the destruction of the Second Temple, they became hostile to each other. Rabbi Johanan ben Zakkai was at this time the leader of the plebeians. Vespasian, having warned the Jews, reduced their cities one by one, and was ready, in the summer of 68, to lay siege to Jerusalem, virtually their sole remaining stronghold. This was a difficult moment for Johanan ben Zakkai, who had hitherto abstained from active participation in the rebellion, and had also refused to hold any communication with the Romans. But now a new situation confronted him. Even if the Romans should fail to make a breach in the city's walls, famine and thirst must ultimately compel surrender.

A plan was evolved requiring courage and unbelievable self-control. Johanan feigned illness, then death, and was taken out of the city by his disciples, as if for burial. He then sought out Vespasian in order to establish a new academy in one of the provincial cities already under Roman control. When Vespasian asked, "What shall I give thee?" he was doubtless amazed to hear that the aged scholar had risked his life for no greater boon than permission to establish an academy! The modest request was immediately granted.

Johanan was now ready for a more daring step. He declared the assemblage at Yavneh the true Sanhedrin of all Israel, the authorized successor of the body which had met for centuries in the "Chamber of Hewn Stones" in the Temple. Though the conclave was destined to meet there for only sixty years, while other centers of learning persisted for centuries, the Vineyard of Yavneh holds a permanent, unequaled place in Jewish tradition, for it was there that Judaism was saved in its direst crisis.

In the Vineyard of Yavneh

Shortly after its establishment, Akiba appeared at the Vineyard of Yavneh, seeking higher rabbinic instruction. Though Johanan had passed away and his place was still vacant, the academy had been so firmly established that there was no interruption in its activity, or diminution of its prestige.

It was easy to enter the Vineyard, where the scholars gathered for their deliberations. There were no guards at the gate; the sessions were held in public; the discussions were open. In the center of the whole magnificent group sat the two men who had helped Johanan ben Zakkai found the academy: Eliezer ben Hyrkanos and Joshua ben Hananya. Nothing could have illustrated more dramatically the composite nature of Pharisaism and the Sanhedrin than the juxtaposition of these two leaders, alike in their erudition and piety, but differing from one another in every other way. Eliezer, the foppish, rich landowner, reared as an *am ha-aretz*, had fled from his father's house in order to study Torah, and had finally attained such proficiency that Johanan had compared him to "a well-lined cistern which never loses a drop." Joshua ben Hananya, on the other hand, was ungainly in form and plain of face but possessed of remarkable wit and a melodious voice, a Temple singer who, after Jerusalem was destroyed, had become a needlemaker. In the midst of dire poverty, in a soot-covered hovel, he pursued his studies until he had mastered not only Jewish learning but also the secular sciences of mathematics and astronomy.

In this tumultous and dazzling assembly where so many types with differing gifts, temperaments, and social standing had gathered, Akiba turned first to Eliezer ben Hyrkanos, perhaps because he too had entered on his studies when he was a mature man. Eliezer, however, rejected Akiba, holding that just as God had given the Law to a generation which was fed with manna, so later teachers should accept as pupils only those who had no economic worries to distract them. But Akiba received a warm welcome from the poor Joshua ben Hananya; the latter sent him to Tarfon, Akiba's contemporary, who later became his closest friend. The tradition as he received it from Tarfon did not, however, satisfy Akiba because the former was really a member of the patrician wing of the Pharisees, while his own sympathies were with the plebeian group.

Finding himself in fundamental disagreement on the social issues of the day with Tarfon—in spite of the latter's love of the pupil—and unable to follow the slow-moving, good-humored, half-cynical, easily satisfied Joshua, Akiba turned to the brilliant but comparatively unknown Nahum of Gimzo. Nahum's value to Akiba lay in the new method of interpretation which he had developed, by which every word and indeed every letter in Scripture have significance.

Akiba's association with Nahum continued for twenty-two years. Long after he had become a famous scholar, he would travel back and forth between the village of Gimzo and the city of Yavneh, bringing the sick old man news of the conclave, and taking back to his colleagues ideas born out of those fleeting contacts.

Having mastered the plebeian doctrines of Joshua and Nahum, Akiba decided to return to Eliezer, who had originally rejected him. This time Eliezer did not refuse to admit him, but neither did he "recognize" him. We do not know how long Akiba remained associated with Eliezer in this way, but it is said that after he had spent thirteen years in study under his various masters, he decided to challenge openly the patrician traditions of the Shammaites, of whom his new master Eliezer was the foremost exponent.

The Great Debate: Akiba vs. Eliezer

One day, in the conclave of Yavneh, Eliezer offered an opinion to which Joshua raised an objection. There was nothing to indicate that the occasion would assume historical importance until Akiba, still comparatively unknown outside the limited circle of his teachers, stood up to oppose Eliezer, who, according to Johanan ben Zakkai, outweighed in learning the entire host of his contemporaries. What followed has become a saga of scholarship, and the arguments, even the invectives, used by the protagonists still echo wherever the Jewish tradition is studied.

Characteristically, the question which precipitated the combat was of purely academic interest at the moment. The law required certain sacrifices to be offered on Sabbaths and holidays, and it had always been agreed that the performance of the labor connected with these duties necessarily superseded the Sabbath and festival prohibitions. The priests further maintained that all ancillary activities, such as sharpening knives and preparing fuel, were also permitted. This the plebeians vigorously denied. The Temple had been in ruins for almost a quarter of a century when Eliezer mentioned the priestly tradition and defended it in the academy. He urged that since slaughtering an animal—a major activity— was permitted, sharpening a knife—a minor activity—must by implication also be permitted. Joshua made a feeble attempt to answer this argument but, in his usual fashion, was about to retire from the field when Akiba stood up to voice his opinion.

"Does not the Bible say," Eliezer shouted, " 'In its due season' (Numbers 28:2)? And does that not mean that sacrifices must be brought at their specified times whether on the Sabbath or on week days?"

"Indeed," Akiba replied, "but show me where it says that knives must be sharpened in the appointed seasons."

This first public argument presumably won Akiba his ordination and full membership in the conclave. The scholar could no longer be called a pupil; he was a master of the Law. By virtue of his new status, he was not only a recognized authority on all ceremonial questions; he could also sit as judge in matters of civil law, which were usually presented before three ordained teachers. He could also act as member of a court to exercise criminal jurisprudence in so far as the Romans permitted the Jewish community to enforce its law.

Both Akiba and Eliezer must have realized that this discussion was only an opening skirmish in a long-drawn-out battle. With unwearying persistence, Akiba returned to the struggle each day, lying in wait for any expression of Shammaitic opinion which he might need to refute.

During the eight or ten years which Akiba spent under the tutelage of Joshua ben Hananya and Nahum of Gimzo, he had become completely transformed: his interests now transcended his provincial origin; he had absorbed the whole plebeian outlook on life. Though his manners and speech were now those of a polished gentleman, his legislation protected plebeian interests. But it was expressed in terms of concrete legal rules and mature, sophisticated urban idealism.

So completely did Akiba win the hearts of both Eliezer and Joshua that when the latter traveled about the country to raise funds for the poor, they frequently invited him to join them. Only one member of the conclave regarded Akiba's rise with ill favor: the patrician scholar Elisha ben Abuyah. While Akiba could afford to ignore Elisha's envy, he could not dismiss as easily the tyranny of Gamaliel, whom the scholars had finally succeeded in making *nasi* or president.

At last, weary of the continual struggle against Gamaliel and the other patricians, Akiba left Yavneh and settled as a village teacher in the small town of Zifron in Galilee. He did not remain there long. The scholars who had taken him for granted while he sat with them in Yavneh suddenly realized all he had meant to them. "The Torah is outside," they declared, referring to his absence from their discussions. Yielding ultimately to their clamor, Gamaliel invited him to return to the conclave.

Though Akiba does not appear to have held any formal office in the academy, he was universally considered a dominant figure, the fourth member of the directing committee. Perhaps it was at this time that he was appointed overseer of the poor, a post for which he was admirably suited by character and which he filled for many years.

About fifteen years had passed since Akiba had come to the academy as a humble shepherd, with little hope. He had risen past colleagues and masters and stood, at last, on a high pinnacle, a dominant figure in Jewish life. At the age of fifty-five, still in the fullness of bodily vigor and mental alertness, he set out on his lifework—the reconstruction of the Law and the establishment of a permanent school.

Visit to Rome

The twenty years which followed a successful revolt against Gamaliel were probably the happiest in Akiba's life. Two sons and two daughters were growing up and showing high promise. His wife Rachel was sharing the fruits of their common sacrifices

—the friendship of their intimate co-workers and the approbation of the general public.

And yet the period began under a cloud. The Roman government, which for fifteen years had pursued a policy of friendship and conciliation, suddenly reversed itself and enacted a series of restrictive regulations against the Jews. In the autumn of the year 95, news reached Palestine of fresh threats against Jews in Rome. No time could be lost; a few days before the *Sukkot* festival, the four leading scholars, Gamaliel, Joshua, Eleazar ben Azariah, and Akiba set sail for the capital of the Empire.

The sages would probably have returned empty-handed had not Domitian died during their stay in Rome. He was succeeded in September, 96, by Nerva, the first of the "five good emperors," who, in his short rule of only sixteen months, managed to bring new hope to Jews, both in Rome and in distant Palestine.

The visit to Rome was a turning point in Akiba's life. Had he died before he undertook this diplomatic task, he would be remembered as the most brilliant member of the illustrious academy at Yavneh. But from that point on, his achievement as a leader competes with and eventually overshadows his reputation as a scholar.

Ordering of the Law

From the time of his return from Rome, in 97, Akiba was held in increasing reverence by both his colleagues and the masses. In the years that followed, while the Jewish community enjoyed unusual prosperity and peace, Akiba devoted himself to the formulation of his juristic principles, the clarification of his theological ideas, and the establishment of his school.

"To what may Akiba be compared?" asked one of his pupils, describing the activities in which the sage engaged at this time. "To a peddler who goes about from farm to farm. Here he obtained wheat, there barley, and in a third place, spelt. When he comes home he arranges them all in their respective bins. So Akiba went about from scholar to scholar, getting all the traditions he could; and then he proceeded to arrange them in an orderly granary." It is probable that the division of the Mishnah into six orders, and even the subdivisions into treatises, goes back to him.

Except for a few treatises describing the ancient Temple and its service, the earlier compilations of Jewish law were not arranged by subject matter at all. They were strings of legal norms put together according to the similarity of their literary formulation but without inner conviction. Akiba realized that while such a method was satisfactory for fragments of the Law, it was altogether inadequate for a complete code, which required logical division and subdivision.

Once he had decided on the method to follow in the arrangement of his material, Akiba even more boldly replaced ancient norms with others which represented his own opinions. Such was the authority he came to enjoy that within a generation the material he had rejected was almost unknown. The trenchant, epigrammatic style which he had developed for his apothegms and decisions proved invaluable to him in his new activity. The effective combination of brevity and precision was a boon to the student who had to memorize the text, and it set a good example for all future codifiers. His Mishnah became so popular in his own lifetime that even those parts which he rejected in his later years continued to be studied. Being oral texts, they could not be issued in new editions; once memorized they could not be withdrawn from circulation, as it were. The original statements were repeated in the academies, with the qualifying remark that Akiba had changed his mind about them, in part.

The later Talmudists rated these achievements so high that they declared Akiba had saved the Torah from oblivion. They ranked his work with the rediscovery of the Law in the days of Josiah. "Had not Shaphan arisen in his time, and Ezra in his time, and Akiba in his time," a homilist of the next century remarked, "would not the Law have been forgotten in Israel?"

For centuries the Mishnah of Akiba was recalled as an outstanding achievement of rabbinic learning. Not only Jewish scholars but Christian Church Fathers referred to it. One of the best-informed authorities of the third century tells us that it became the core of the Mishnah of Meir, which in turn was incorporated into the final redaction of Judah the Patriarch (or Prince)—which still remains the basic codification of rabbinic law.

"The truths which were not revealed to Moses," says a later teacher in his enthusiasm, "were uncovered to Akiba." When he left Palestine on his various journeys, "there remained not his equal in all the land," asserted his younger contemporaries. When he died, "the arms of the Law were broken, and the fountains of wisdom were stopped up."

Akiba's influence in the academy gradually became paramount. The principle, accepted by later Talmudists and codifiers, that Akiba's opinion must be given preference to that of any of his colleagues doubtless originated in the attitude taken toward him in his own lifetime.

Akiba the Teacher

In time Akiba, while still attending the sessions of the conclave, founded a private academy at the little village of Bene Berak, a short distance from Yavneh. The conclave at Yavneh had assembled in a vineyard and Eliezer had given his decisions from a rock; Akiba, however, preferred to lecture in the shade of a broad-leaved fig tree. Students from the most diversified groups flocked to him from all parts of the country.

In his relations with his students, Akiba displayed the same charm and courtesy which had won him the affection of his masters and colleagues. When any one of the young men fell ill, the master was sure to visit him. He did not consider it beneath his dignity on such a visit to arrange his pupil's room, sweep the floor, or perform any other service. "Whosoever neglects the duty of visiting the sick," he taught, "is guilty of shedding blood."

Akiba's power over his disciples arose not merely from his tenderness with them, but mainly from his pedagogic ability. In addition to the codification of the Law, he also arranged the laws and traditions as comments on the biblical verses from which they were derived. Two of his pupils, Judah and Simeon, preferred this method, which they developed even further, while two others, Meir and Jose, made Akiba's codes the foundation of their own compilations.

These works were not put into writing, for it was a cardinal principle of Pharisaism at the time that rabbinic traditions must be preserved orally. They were handed down from generation to generation by a special class of professional memorizers. Only in the fifth century, perhaps even later, when it became obvious that any further attempt to retain the old tradition would result in the disappearance of the whole law, was permission granted to entrust this material to writing. During the three centuries in which the books had remained an oral tradition, they had naturally changed considerably in form. Yet even now the stamp of the opposing schools is still clear, and permits us to reconstruct with reasonable accuracy the methods of teaching and inference current in the days of Akiba and Ishmael, seventeen centuries ago.

Akiba's mode of interpretation of Scripture is a development of that which he derived from his master Nahum of Gimzo. Superfluous letters, words, and verses were the meat whereon he thrived. By the use of them he was able to read his whole juristic program into Scriptures. But what he called superfluous words would hardly seem such to us. The juxtaposition of the various chapters had a meaning which must be discovered. He rejected the old Hillelite principle of inference by generalization from particulars, and replaced it with a curious and complicated rule of his own invention which he called "Inclusion and Limitation." Neither rhetoric nor grammar offered a bar to his imaginative argument. Indeed, were we to accept at face value the technical reasons he gave for his decisions, we should be forced to the conclusion that, far from being the greatest of the Talmudists, he was simply a brilliant example of extraordinary—but wasted—ingenuity. But the rules which he derived through his curious and intricate logic are so reasonable that when we examine them we are even more impressed with his judgment as a jurist than with his skill as debater. It is obvious that he considered the interpretation of the Written Law merely a form which had to be followed in the derivation of desirable rules from the biblical text.

Akiba was trying to change the complexion of the inherited law. To accomplish this he had to find an authority superior to that of his predecessors and accepted by everyone. Only one instrument could fulfill those requirements—Scripture itself.

The duty of teaching seemed to him paramount. "Though you have given instruction to some disciples in your youth, you must continue to teach in old age," he said. "This is the meaning of Ecclesiastes 11:6, which reads, 'In the morning sow thy seed, and in the evening withhold not thy hand; for thou knowest not which shall prosper, whether this or that, or whether they both shall be alike good.'" Akiba describes the value of a teacher to his pupils in three beautiful similes. "What I received from my teacher amounts to the fragrance given off by the citron, and the light taken from one candle to another, and the water drawn from a brook. The beneficiary enjoys the odor, increases the light, and is refreshed by the water; but the giver has lost nothing!"

Akiba's Juristic Philosophy

Akiba's various utterances regarding ethics, law, religion, theology, and politics form a complete, coherent, and unified system which we may rightly call a philosophy. His various decisions and maxims were applications of general principles which were clear in his own mind, although he did not organize them for posterity in the form of abstract propositions. This was due, first, to the nature of his judicial office, which required decisions in concrete cases rather than philosophic statements of general policy; and, secondly, to the Jewish tradition which, unlike the Hellenic, has never given up its preference for the concrete and individual.

Akiba's fundamental approach to juristic problems may be summarized as follows:

1. Whatever be the inequalities which we find in the world, we must not permit them to intrude on the worship of God. Hence, ceremonial law must be interpreted so as not to exclude the weaker social groups from participation, or to demand too heavy sacrifices from them. This implies that no opportunity may be given to the more fortunate to invent ceremonies or rituals which the poorer cannot imitate. Nor may expensive devices be utilized as evasions of burdensome laws.

In general, Akiba could not brook ostentation, especially in prayer. When he prayed in private, his disciple, Judah ben Ilai, tells us, "one would leave him in one corner and find him in another, to which he had wandered through the multitude of kneelings and prostrations." But when he prayed in public, he "would finish quickly, lest he keep others waiting for him."

2. So far as the civil law is fluid and open to interpretation, it can be used to rectify social inequalities. Hence the rules of law

should favor the oppressed groups: the plebeian, the artisan-merchant, the shepherd, the slave, the women and children.

3. It is especially important that the prerogatives of the priests be limited, and that the gross inequality between them and the Levites be minimized.

4. Akiba's attitude toward women and marriage was influenced by his own experience. When the usual question, "What is true wealth?" was raised among the sages, Tarfon, the great landowner, replied readily, "The possession of a hundred vineyards and a hundred slaves to work them."

Young Meir, Akiba's disciple, said more modestly, "Contentment and satisfaction with one's riches."

But Akiba said, "A wife who is comely in her deeds."

The possibility that the emancipation of women may lead to the disruption of family life should be met by the imposition of severe penalties for infidelity. Suitability in marriage meant not merely mutual compatibility and love; it also implied the absence of any legal or moral hindrance to the union. Hence, he was more severe than any of the other sages with regard to incestuous or forbidden unions, declaring them void, and maintaining that the children born of them were illegitimate.

On the other hand, his defense of the rights of women brought him into continual conflict with the patrician-provincial scholars, who objected to his violent reversal of the tradition of feminine inferiority. He conceded that a married working woman should turn over her wages to her husband, but he ruled that if she earned more than he spent on her maintenance the difference belonged to her.

5. In the attempt to ameliorate the conditions of slaves, care must be taken to protect the status and rights of free labor.

6. Pious merchants must be protected from the handicaps resulting from their observance of the Law.

7. There is no room for superstition in Judaism. In Akiba's opinion, anyone who believed in days of good or bad omen transgressed the biblical law against witchcraft; and those who used magical formulas to cure disease were unfit for immortal life. Tales of miracles which various sects told of their founders he considered pure fiction.

8. The ideals of peace and human equality are fundamental principles of religion. Akiba was determined to grant equality

to all free peoples. When the patricians proposed a rule varying the sum to be assessed for personal injuries according to the social status of the plaintiff, Akiba said, "The poorest man in Israel must be considered as a patrician who has lost his property; for they are all descendants of Abraham, Isaac, and Jacob."

Akiba made no claim that his decisions introduced anything new into Judaism. He regarded himself as the mouthpiece of the Torah, applying its principles to new cases as they arose. "Know before whom ye are standing," he said to the litigants at the opening of each trial. "Not before Akiba ben Joseph, but before the Holy One, blessed be He."

The Tragic Years: Rebellion of Bar Kokhba

The years 110-112 were epochal both in the life of Akiba and in the history of the Jewish people. In his seventieth year the great sage was still at the peak of his strength. His health was perfect, he had retained all the physical and mental vigor of his youth, and his native genius was now supplemented by the skill born of thirteen years of intellectual leadership. If the discovery and development of unsuspected faculties within one's self, the conquest of adverse circumstances, and the achievement of universal applause can give happiness to man, Akiba must certainly have been happy.

The situation of the community was equally happy. Never since the destruction of Jerusalem had Judea been economically more prosperous or politically more tranquil. The aftermath of the war had passed, and the ruined population had once more settled down to normal habits of work and trade; the city of Ludd in the lowland had partly replaced Jerusalem as the metropolis of Judea and had absorbed some of the destitute artisans and merchants. A new generation had grown up, accustomed to the Roman yoke and apparently willing to bear it. In distant Rome, the affairs of the Empire had for a dozen years been in the capable hands of Nerva and Trajan, the first and second of the "five good emperors."

To Akiba and many others it seemed that the Messianic era was at hand. Gradually, however, new oppressions were suffered, and about the year 125 the relations between Jews and Romans took a turn for the worse. It is not known whether the increasing rigor was due to the suspicion of nationalist activity on the part of some rabbinic scholars, especially Rabbi Simeon and Rabbi Ishmael. It is certain, however, that edicts were promulgated forbidding the practice of circumcision, the pretext being the Roman law against mutilation of the body, and it is probable that the recitation of the *Shema* at public services, the reading of the Book of Esther on *Purim*, and the sounding of the *shofar* (ram's horn) on New Year's Day were also prohibited as being ceremonies with specifically nationalist implications.

Some of the moderate nationalists were tempted to seek in exile both safety and the opportunity to observe the Law. But their consciences would not let them find so easy an escape. To dwell in Palestine was itself a commandment and, in the minds of many, one which outweighed all others.

While the scholars, like the people at large, were finding themselves involved in the various factions, the conclave assembled once more in Ludd to determine on a national policy. Standing between the extremists on both sides, Akiba insisted that the practical problem could not be solved until the scholars agreed on the basic theory of the place of observance in Judaism. The plebeians had always held that study was more important than observance; and it was entirely logical for them to maintain that should observance lead to the destruction of the Torah it would defeat its own purpose. The patricians had, however, always opposed this view.

It is highly probable that the severity of the recent enactment against Jews was related to the Emperor Hadrian's expected return to the East. To the Jews, however, the arrival of the emperor, in the year 130, seemed a most opportune occasion to present their petitions and their grievances in person. It must have been obvious to Hadrian that the Romans had committed an act of unjustified waste in razing Jerusalem to the ground. The interests of the Empire demanded the re-establishment of the great wealth-producing metropolis, which was the center of the country's commerce, industry, and religion. Hadrian decided to grant the request of the Jews and to rebuild their city.

The emperor also granted the Jews a temple. But—and in this he displayed the same blindness that had caused many tragedies in Roman history—the temple, like so many others he had founded, was to be dedicated to the worship of himself, as identified with the Capitoline Jupiter.

The effect of this pronouncement on Akiba, then in his ninetieth year, was crushing. The last hope for improved relations with Rome had disappeared; the teachings of his whole lifetime, that a pacific attitude toward the Empire would call forth reasonable treatment from it, were refuted by the event. For the first time in his life he began to be uncertain of his views. Endowed with extraordinary powers of introspection and self-examination, the old sage must have wondered whether his intellectual powers, which had so long resisted the years, had not failed him at last.

But the blow which had all but prostrated the old scholar stimulated the masses of the people to furious action. A decree of wholesale extermination could hardly have aroused them more than the news of the emperor's decision to establish his pagan sanctuary on Mount Moriah. The fanaticism which had been held in check for decades broke loose.

As the excitement grew, Ishmael and Simeon cast off the secrecy under which they had heretofore carried on their nationalist activities. The Romans arrested and condemned them to death, even before the revolution had broken out. Their faith endured to the last. While they were being led to the execution, they merely commiserated with each other on the fate which prevented them from sharing in the glory awaiting their people. Akiba, speaking over their graves, warned his hearers to expect no miracles. "Prepare yourselves for suffering," he cried to the weeping multitude. "If happiness were destined to come in our time, none deserved better to share in it than Rabbi Simeon and Rabbi Ishmael. But God, knowing what distress is in store for us, removed them from our midst, as it is written, 'The righteous is taken away from the evil to come' " (Isaiah 57:1).

The leadership of the rebellion passed from the intellectual sages, Ishmael and Simeon, to Simeon bar Kokhba, a soldier and strategist who at once set out to organize the straggling bands of patriotic peasants into a regular army. His first few victories aroused wild enthusiasm among the people, who saw in him not merely a second Maccabee but the Messiah. The private and public fortunes of a nation were staked on the personal prowess and military genius of the unproved leader.

Akiba himself did not long resist the contagion of Messianism. When he saw Roman legions yield to untrained Judean youths, new hope blossomed in his heart. "Yet once, it will be a little while," he quoted from Haggai (2:6), "and I will shake the heavens and the earth, and the sea, and the dry land." He went so far as to encourage the popular delusion concerning the miraculous role to be played by the new leader, and applied to him the verse (Numbers 24:17), "There shall step forth a star out of Jacob." On one occasion he even said outright, "This is the Messianic king."

The story of the denouement is well known: how in a little more than three years the Romans destroyed the last vestige of Jewish resistance, how in their fury they drenched the land with blood, slaughtering hundreds of thousands of people, how they sold tens of thousands into slavery, forbade the few remaining Jews to observe any of their ancestral customs, and took the children forcibly out of their religious schools and put them to manual labor. Hundreds of scholars fled to Babylonia, but many still felt that their duty was to remain in Palestine.

The fact that Akiba was not imprisoned shows that he had not implicated himself actively in the rebellion. Like other Jews, he could observe the Law only in secret; but he was permitted to move about and apparently even to give instruction. Clearly, the Roman generals who were trying to destroy Judaism root and branch did not at this time share the opinion of some modern historians that Akiba himself was the secret instigator of the whole rebellion and that his wide travels, ostensibly for the Sanhedrin and the Law, were really made to foment sedition.

Death of a Martyr

It was not long before the loyalty of Akiba and his colleagues to the principle of study was to be put to the ultimate test. The savagery of the repressions grew from month to month. It was probably in the year 134, just before the capitulation of Betar, that the Romans issued their drastic decree forbidding not only the practice but also the study of Torah. Akiba now knew that he had reached the end of compromise. He had counseled the people to accept the Roman gift of a temple when that had been offered; he had warned them not to be disappointed when the offer was withdrawn; he had asked them to sacrifice the right to observe the Law in order that its study might be perpetuated. But the last stronghold, the innermost shrine, was to be defended at all costs. If the study of Torah was abolished, there was no further purpose of living. And so, at the age of ninety-five, the compromising pacifist once more took up the weapons of non-resistant war. Calmly he gathered his students, gave his decisions, delivered his lectures. He disdained and feared gatherings in secret as unworthy of the dignity of Torah; they were certain to raise the suspicion of political activity. He had always taught in the open, in the shade of a tree; and he would continue to do so. He made only one compromise with necessity. He invited his disciples to dine with him; and they discussed the Law during their meal.

When his old antagonist, Pappias, warned that he was courting death by continuing to teach so publicly, Akiba replied with the parable of the fishes and the fox. The fox, coming to the river's bank, suggested to the fishes that they might find safety from the fishermen by coming on the dry land. But the fishes replied, "If in the water which is our element we are in danger, what will happen to us on the dry land, which is not our element?"

"So, too," continued Akiba, "if there is no safety for us in the Torah which is our home, how can we find safety elsewhere?"

Akiba could not have expected to continue teaching for long. Soon he was seized by the soldiers and carried off to prison. The Romans, still respecting his learning, his reputation, and his distinguished personality, and perhaps also remembering his pacifist and conciliatory teachings, hesitated to put him to death. They kept him in confinement for three years, treating him with consideration, even with courtesy. He was allowed the attendance of his disciple Joshua ha-Garai, who waited on him; and he was permitted to enjoy the visit of Simeon ben Yohai, who had returned from Zidon to be near the master in his affliction. "Continue to instruct me," Simeon begged of him. At first reluctant out of fear that he might endanger his pupil's freedom and even his life, Akiba finally yielded to his importunities. "My son," he said, "more than the calf wants to suck, the cow wants to suckle!"

Although he pursued these audacious activities secretly, Akiba must have known that the Romans would soon learn of them. When this happened, he was transferred to a prison in distant Caesarea, where no one but his servant-pupil Joshua ha-Garai was permitted to attend him.

And still Akiba carried on. The impoverished and leaderless community made unheard-of sacrifices to obtain decisions from Akiba during those days.

Finally Akiba was brought to trial; his judge was to be his former friend Rufus. There was no possible defense against the charges; Akiba had violated the Law by offering instruction to his disciples. He was found guilty and condemned to death. Still attended by his faithful Joshua, he retained his courage and strength of mind until the very end.

The popular story tells that the Romans killed Akiba by tearing his flesh from his living body. As he lay in unspeakable agony, he suddenly noticed the first streaks of dawn breaking over the eastern hills. It was the hour when the law requires each Jew to pronounce the *Shema*. Oblivious to his surroundings, Akiba intoned in a loud, steady voice the forbidden words of his faith, "Hear, O Israel, the Lord our God, the Lord is One. And thou shalt love the Lord thy God with all thy heart, and with all thy soul, and with all thy might."

Rufus, the Roman general, who superintended the execution, cried out: "Are you a wizard or are you utterly insensible to pain?"

"I am neither," replied the martyr, "but all my life I have been waiting for the moment when I might truly fulfill this commandment. I have always loved the Lord with all my might, and with all my heart; now I know that I love him with all my life." And repeating the verse again, he died as he reached the words, "The Lord is One."

3 . *Rashi*

[1040-1105]

SAMUEL M. BLUMENFIELD

RABBI Shlomo Yitzhaki, better known by his initials Rashi, though no longer read and studied as widely and assiduously as in previous generations, is still accepted as the authoritative commentator on the Bible and Talmud. The great impact which his teachings have had upon Jewry is due to the decisive role he played in maintaining the continuity and authenticity of Judaism at a critical juncture in the history of Jewish culture.

By the eleventh century, Babylonian and other Oriental Jewish communities had passed the zenith of their communal and literary creativity, while European Jewry was still in the throes of social and cultural adjustment to the new emerging patterns of western Christian culture. The world of the Bible had already receded to a seemingly hoary past, while that of the Talmud had become increasingly less intelligible since Aramaic was no longer the language of the majority of Jews, particularly in the West. There was, therefore, serious danger that the Bible would be relegated to the past, and, though revered, might no longer be considered relevant to the needs of a Jewry under totally new and different conditions. As to the rabbinic lore of the Talmud, it might have been lost altogether, owing to the sheer lack of knowledge of its language and the inability of most Jews to understand its involved legal dissertations and discussions.

Rashi's commentaries accomplished the remarkable feat of interpreting the Bible in terms and accents of eleventh-century Franco-German Jewry, and of providing the key to the sealed pages of the Talmud. Rashi's literary labors helped to link European Jewry to the chain of tradition of ancient Palestinian and Babylonian Jewries. Rashi's role in the history of Jewish culture can best be summed up in the words of the fourteenth-century Spanish rabbi, Menahem ben Zerah: "He (Rashi) wrote as if by divine inspiration. . . . Without him the Talmud would have been forgotten in Israel."

In spite of the widespread fame that Rashi attained during his lifetime and the many studies of his works by generations of writers after him, precious little is known about him as a person. Rashi, like other Jewish pietists of his day, did not consider it proper to reveal in his writings personal details about himself. The information that is available has been culled from scattered and indirect references in his own voluminous writings and the works of his disciples.

The Wandering Student

Rashi was born in the year 1040 in Troyes, the capital of Champagne in northern France. He came of a pious family which engaged in the prevailing economic, social, and religious pursuits of the Jewish community of Troyes. Rashi seldom refers to his father, but he does refer to his maternal uncle, Rabbi Shimon Hasaken, as "an expert scholar of the Talmud." Rashi married young and had three daughters, two of whom later married scholars of note and were the parents of renowned interpreters of the Bible and the Talmud, including the famous Rabbenu Jacob Tam. Descendants of Rashi, together with other illustrious disciples, became the founders of a school of commentators known as *Tosafists*. Their name is derived from the Hebrew root "to add," for they "added" to the commentaries and explanations of Rashi.

Until Rashi became famous, Troyes was not distinguished as a center of Jewish learning. Like other scholars of his day who were eager to pursue their education, Rashi traveled to Worms and Mayence, centers of Jewish learning in Germany. In these Talmudic schools Rashi received instruction from disciples of Rabbenu Gershom, known as the "Light of the Exile" because of his pioneering and creative rabbinic leadership in Central Europe in the tenth century. Rashi speaks of his own experience when he says that like "doves that wander from dovecote to dovecote in search of food, so they (students) go from the academy of one scholar to that of another in search of interpretations of Torah."

As such a wandering student, Rashi's life was full of hardships. "Lacking bread and decent clothes, with a millstone on my neck (burdened by marriage), I served before them (the masters)," he writes. After spending eight years of study in Germany, he returned to his native city of Troyes at the age of twenty-five where he began his lifelong career of teaching and writing. Rashi acquired his learning from the available literature on the Bible and the Talmud in Hebrew and Aramaic, but he also had access to writings in French, German, and possibly Latin. Soon after, he organized a Talmudic school of his own, and hundreds of students flocked to receive the benefits of his vast erudition and distinctive method of interpretation.

Influence of French Civilization

While our information about Rashi as a person is sparse, recent studies of Franco-German Jewry of the Middle Ages offer considerable information concerning the social and spiritual environment in which Rashi grew up and labored. Troyes was then a center of commerce, the seat of government, and the scene of important church conferences. Like most towns of Franco-Germany in those days, Troyes, whose total population at that period is estimated at about ten thousand, contained only about a hundred Jewish families closely knit by economic and religious ties—indeed, many of Rashi's disciples were his relatives. (To this day Troyes has retained an alley named "Rue de la Synagogue.") Like the other residents of this rural community, the Jews of Troyes were farmers and wine-makers. Grape-growing was a major occupation in which Rashi himself engaged for his livelihood. Some Jews also carried on commerce with neighboring communities as well as with those beyond the borders of Franco-Germany.

Contrary to conventional notions about the ghetto character of the Jewish communities in the Middle Ages, French Jews in the eleventh century maintained close relations with their non-Jewish neighbors. They used the French language in their daily speech, bore French names (one of Rashi's daughters, according to some scholars, was named Belle Assez), and shared with non-Jews in social and economic pursuits. Jewish scholars had such names as Leontin and Bon Fils, while pious poets composed prayers in French. Recent studies indicate the existence of both isolated *piyyutim* (religious poems) in the vernacular and entire prayer books in French. There are also indications that Jews used Gentile tunes for the lullabies they sang their children, and on occasions taught synagogue melodies to Christian priests. Jews often presented gifts to their Christian friends on *Purim*, while non-Jews would offer their Jewish neighbors on the eighth day of Passover leavened cakes, eggs, and the like. Rashi himself was the recipient of many such amenities. Indeed, according to L. Rabinowitz, "from the detailed account of the social, economic and religious life of the Jews of Northern France during the twelfth to fourteenth centuries in all its important aspects, there emerges one fact with unmistakable clarity, viz., that apart from the purely religious life, the Jews lived in a state of complete social assimilation with their non-Jewish neighbors."

In such friendly circumstances, it was natural that much of Rashi's life and experience should have been influenced by the French society and civilization in which he was born and lived practically all of his life. He refers to French as *bilshonenu* ("in our language"), and in his interpretation of events in the Bible and Talmud he avails himself of terms used in his time to describe political and technical subjects. Some scholars have even suggested that the clarity of Rashi's writings may be attributed in part to the influence of the French language, which because of its preciseness has long been the language of international discourse and diplomacy.

Relations with Non-Jews

Though close social and economic contacts existed between the Jews and their non-Jewish environment, there was little common ground in the area of religious and cultural ideas and practices. The Jewish community of the eleventh century was heir to a cultural tradition of about two thousand years and an institution of education at least a thousand years old, whereas the Christian community of this period was witnessing only the beginnings of what later led to the growth of scholarship and the founding of universities. Education did not become compulsory or universal until the end of the nineteenth century, and in eleventh-century Europe was almost exclusively limited to the training of religious teachers and ministers in monastic centers of scholarship, ecclesiastical authorities, and certain royal courts.

While Christian scholars like Anselm, the Archbishop of Canterbury and a contemporary of Rashi, made a dichotomy between knowledge and faith, Rashi and other Jewish scholars and teachers saw faith leading to the search for knowledge, and knowledge or Torah as the foundation of faith. Had not the rabbis of the Talmud taught long before that "an empty-headed man cannot be a sin-fearing man nor can an ignorant person be pious" (*Abot* 2:6)?

The difference in educational practice between the Jewish and non-Jewish community was fully noted by Christian spokesmen in Rashi's days. A pupil of Peter Abelard made the following comparison: "If the Christians educate their sons, they do so not for God, but for gain in order that the one brother, if he be a clerk, may help his father and mother and his other brothers. . . . A Jew, however poor, if he had ten sons would put them all to letters, not for gain, as the Christians do, but the understanding of God's law, and not only his sons, but his daughters."

This appreciation of the Jewish devotion to learning on the part of some Christians did not, however, lead to an understanding of Jews or to continuous friendly relations with them. Owing to strong spiritual and communal disciplines from within and the rivalries between the political interests of the church and state from without, Jews of Troyes and neighboring communities until the end of the eleventh century enjoyed rights and privileges accorded to ecclesiastics, noblemen, and the ruling count's vassals. They were free to choose their residences, and rulers could not legally seize the property of Jews who had decided to move to other localities. But in 1096, with the advent of the Crusades and the ensuing era of lawlessness and persecutions, these rights and privileges were curtailed and even abrogated. The Crusades must have brought about so many forced conversions that Rashi deemed it necessary to make allowances for unwilling Jewish converts. He called upon his people to show sympathy and forbearance to those who returned to the fold, saying: "Their defection was made under the menace of the sword, and out of their free will they hastened to return to the God of our fathers in penitence."

The Crusades also renewed disputes with Jews in regard to the merits of Judaism and Christianity, especially on the subject of Jesus. Commenting on the verse, "Lord, in Thy strength the king rejoiceth" (Psalms 21:2), which Christian theologians claimed was a reference to Jesus, Rashi argued that "it is more correct to speak of King David." Alluding to the bitterness of the disputations with Christian theologians, Rashi commented: "They hate me . . . because I do not pursue after their falsehood to follow their errors."

Rashi's rebuttal of Christian ideas is to be found in his reference to claims made by the Christian clergy to property rights over the Holy Land. In his first commentary on the Bible (Genesis 1:1), Rashi argues that the Holy Land does not belong either to Christians or Muslims, quoting from rabbinic writings: "The land belongs to the Lord, He created and gave it to whom He pleased. When He willed, He gave it to them and when He willed, He took it from them and gave it to us." In another connection Rashi expressed his views on the same subject even more forcefully: "The Holy Land does not belong either to the Christians or to the Muslims, but remains the perennial property of the Jewish people down to eternity."

Traditionalist and Realist

Far from being a cloistered scholar, confined to the proverbial "four ells of *Halakhah*" associated with the ghetto tradition of later centuries, Rashi displayed broad interests and warm sympathies in worldly affairs. There is hardly an area of human experience of his day that seemed alien to him. His commentaries and writings reveal familiarity not only with the wine industry in which he engaged but also with such subjects as carving, engraving, falconry, fishing and bee husbandry, glasswork, botany, ship repairs, and military affairs. For example, commenting on "the Lord trieth the righteous" (Psalms 11:5), Rashi says:

"The nature of the Holy One, blessed be He, is to chastise and to try the righteous more than the wicked. Just like the flax-man who knows that the better the quality of his flax, the more he beats it; when the quality is poor he does not beat it, as it would dribble away."

Other illustrations of Rashi's interest in everyday affairs and his use of homely similes follow:

> Interest is like the bite of a snake. At first it is a small wound on one's foot, and suddenly it swells up as the head (Exodus 22:24).

> One does not wait on his master while dressed in the garments he used in the kitchen (Leviticus 6:4).

> Merchants show the bad wares first and afterwards show the better ones (Numbers 13:17).

This wide range of interest undoubtedly contributed to what might be described as Rashi's pragmatic and wholesome views on a number of questions of Jewish law and practice. On the question of wine handled by Gentiles (*Yayin Nesekh*), for example, Rashi took a liberal position. According to the Talmud, a Jew was forbidden to use or to benefit from wine touched by non-Jews. Since wine was frequently used among Gentiles for idolatrous purposes, the rabbis of Talmudic times had felt justified in keeping Jews from any possible contact with Gentiles that would lead to a breach of law against idol-worship.

In France, however, many Jews, including Rashi himself, derived their livelihood from the making of wine in a predominantly non-Jewish community. Because of the many restrictions limiting the economic pursuits of Jews in medieval Europe, they were confronted with the choice of either withdrawing from the wine industry and being reduced to poverty, or disregarding the law and breaking with Jewish tradition. Rashi, like other courageous rabbinic personalities, shunned both these alternatives. By facing realistically the new circumstance of Jewish life in Europe he sought and found a formula which made it possible for the Jews of his time to adhere to another important tradition, "Ye shall therefore keep My statutes and Mine ordinances which if a man do, *he shall live by them.*" He maintained that the prohibition against wine handled by Gentiles does not apply to Christians on the principle that they are not idolaters. Therefore Jews should be permitted to employ Gentiles in the production and distribution of wine.

Rashi is also quoted by his grandson, the Rashbam,* as interpreting the prohibition against doing business with Gentiles on their holiday to be limited only to certain specific festivals, and as ruling that even on such occasions one need not be overly strict. Among the reasons given for this leniency is that "we are in exile and cannot afford to refrain from dealing with people among whom we live . . . and from whom we derive our sustenance." There is also the implied reason that since Jews disregard these prohibitions and restrictions, there is no sense making matters worse by branding those who violate the laws as transgressors. This is based on the rabbinic principle: "It is better that they (the Jews) err unknowingly than deliberately."

Like his contemporaries, Rashi sought to conform to tradition, but this formal loyalty to rabbinic teachings did not preclude his suggesting changes in the Law in order to meet a new and urgent need for survival in a Christian community. Indeed, the *pilpul* method of interpreting the Talmud with its ingenious dialectic perfected by Rashi's disciples was another device for squaring innovations in beliefs and traditions with older views and practices. Rashi's views on the wine problem and his decisions on similar questions reveal his courage and ingenuity in meeting new realities while preserving the spirit of old laws and traditions.

Rashi's Major Contribution

The secret of Rashi's influence is to be sought chiefly in his methods and skills as a commentator and teacher. The Jewish and secular lore contained in his writings influenced Jews in all walks of life, from lowly laborers to men of wealth, from young students to accomplished scholars. Indeed, most printed texts of the Pentateuch and the Talmud were subsequently accompanied as a matter of course by Rashi's commentary, which enriched the imagination and warmed the hearts of generations

* Rabbi Samuel ben Meir, also a distinguished French biblical commentator (1085-1160).

of school children and mature students. In fact, Rashi's commentary was among the first to be printed in 1475, seven years before the printing of the Bible itself.

Because of the type of script used in Rashi's commentaries by the first printer (which was then current among the Jews of Spain) and by many printers in succeeding generations, this script became associated with the name of Rashi, and is known to this day as Rashi script.

To understand the extraordinary interest shown in Rashi, one must appreciate the method he used in teaching the Jewish heritage. The question of how to hand down Jewish ideals and practices was a matter of controversy between the Sadducees and Pharisees several centuries earlier, one of their major points of dissension being whether the Scripture should be understood and transmitted literally or freely according to its spirit. This same controversy later led to disputes between the Karaites and Rabbinites.

Clearly, Rashi's problem was a difficult one. To interpret Jewish lore literally or to explain it only rationally would render the Torah a dogmatic, spiritless code. On the other hand, the method of free interpretation had its dangers, for in departing from the literal and rational approach, one incurred the risk of lapsing into farfetched allegory and mysticism. That Rashi was conscious of these dangers appears from the following comments: "Let the interpreter keep on interpreting, but we are interested in the simple, natural meaning of the text" (Exodus 6:9), or from his denunciation of those "who pervert the sense of the Torah by wrong and misleading exegesis (*Berakhot*, 126).

Rashi's contribution consists in his blending of both *peshat*, literal exegesis, combined with *derash*, free interpretation and homiletic comment. In his *peshat*, Rashi explains the text and conveys its meaning in terms of logic, grammar, common sense, and experience. This rational and logical treatment helped clarify many obscure passages and ideas, and to this day Rashi remains the most widely used commentator by students of Bible and Talmud.

Not being too far removed from the Talmudic age, Rashi was able to project himself into the world of the Talmud and share in it as though he were a contemporary. He succeeded also in steeping himself in the world of the Bible. Having shared vicariously in the life of biblical and post-biblical Jewry, Rashi was able to interpret the civilization of ancient Israel to his contemporaries in a lucid and vivid style which still remains a model of clear, precise Hebrew writing.

When Rashi was in doubt as to whether his contemporaries would understand a certain Hebrew or Aramaic term, he did not hesitate to translate it into French. Rashi's use of the vernacular is another indication of his eagerness to bring the teachings of Judaism to as many people as possible. He used some three thousand *Loazim* or French words, which have been studied by scholars of Romance languages as an important source of information about the French language of the eleventh century. When he was not certain that words alone would suffice to convey the full meaning of a passage, Rashi used drawings (I Kings 6:31) or cited graphic illustrations from daily life and the experiences of artisans and men of affairs.

When Rashi was not certain of the meaning of a text, he would quote an authority, adding that he was not convinced; or he would confess: "I do not know." At times he pointed out his own errors. Even in old age, when men's minds ordinarily tend to become less flexible, Rashi confided to his grandson that if he had the time, he would rewrite his biblical commentary in the light of more recent findings. Such freedom from dogmatism is all the more significant when considered against the authoritarian spirit of the age.

Rashi as Educator

Rashi's method is noteworthy for its sense of fitness and balance. He neither leaves passages unexplained, nor does he explain more than is necessary. As a skillful teacher he veers carefully between "not enough" and "too much," aiming to "help the student to help himself," to use William Kilpatrick's description of the ideal teacher. Drawing upon the distinction made by the rabbis between the *hakham* who relies upon authority, and the *nabon*, who from his knowledge of one situation understands another, Rashi advises the learner: "Do your own investigations in order to be able to infer one case from another." In his commentaries, instead of doing the work for the student, Rashi stimulates the learner and thus achieves one of the major goals of education.

While Rashi employed the rational approach, he was fully cognizant of the place of emotions and imagination in education. Though it is unlikely that Rashi was influenced by Plato's theory of character-building through the arts, as a true pedagogue he sensed the power of myth and poetry in elevating the spirit and enriching the imagination of the learner. This explains how a man with as clear and realistic a mind as that of Rashi could so often be at one with the world of imagery and poetic fantasy—the Midrash—the rich treasure of rabbinic lore from which he took so many references. Rashi, however, chooses his selections with discriminating taste and with a sense of harmony. "There are many Midrashim (interpretations)," he remarks a number of times, "but I have chosen the *Aggadah* which interprets Scripture according to its proper meaning in its appropriate place" (Genesis 3:9).

In many instances, Rashi, in order to convey more graphically a rabbinic thought or image, departs from the original text and freely uses his own intimate style. That his versions have proved to be more appealing than the originals can be judged from the fact that the one hundred rabbinic dicta which are most current in the Yiddish language are those quoted from Rashi and in his style.

An example of Rashi's effectiveness in selecting rabbinic material rich in emotional content and human appeal is his often-quoted commentary dealing with Jacob's request to be buried in Canaan and his allusion to the burial of his wife Rachel (Genesis 48:7):

> And although I trouble you to take me into the land of Canaan for burial, and I did not do this for your mother, though I might easily have done so since she died quite close to Bethlehem. . . . I know that in your heart you feel some resentment against me. Know, however, that I buried her there by the command of God, that she might help her children when Nebuzaradan will take them into captivity. When they pass along the road, Rachel will come forth from her grave and stand by her tomb weeping and seeking mercy for them as it is said, "A voice is heard in Ramah . . . . the sound of weeping. . . . Rachel weeping for her children." And

the Holy-One-blessed-be-He replies to her, "Thy children will return to their own border."

The tender voice and the moving appeal of Rachel pleading for her perpetually wandering children as expressed by Rashi in these lines have found their echo in the hearts of millions of Jews who studied the Pentateuch with Rashi's commentary, and had much to do with preserving the hope that Zion would one day be rebuilt.

Pedagogic Insights

An important pedagogic principle which has its origin in Talmudic literature and is particularly stressed by Rashi is the idea that the learning process can best be achieved if it starts on the level of the learner and with his interest. Rashi missed no opportunity to urge the teacher to consider the student—his tastes, interests, and capacities. He emphasizes that learning can best be achieved through love and joy rather than through fear and pain: "He who does not care for the words of Torah, even reasonable explanations do not appeal to him; but he who desires them, even those parts which he learns with effort and bitterness become sweet to him." He also stresses the thought that "there is no comparison between one who does things out of love and one who does them out of fear. He who does things for his teacher out of fear leaves him the moment they become burdensome."

Rashi further advises the teacher ". . . . teach only the tractate that (the pupil) requests; for if the teacher will use another tractate, the pupil would not know it, for his heart is bent upon the things he likes." Commenting on the expression, "early rain which falls gently," Rashi plays on the similarity between the words *moreh* (teacher) and *yoreh* (rain), and suggests that it refers to a "person who teaches his students with gentleness." Rashi also maintains that "when a person explains his words well to a student and makes his words sweet, he (the pupil) will increase in learning, and if the teacher approaches the learner in a pleasant way, the pupil will succeed in his studies; otherwise, he will not." He exhorts the student: "Learn out of joy and with good cheer in accordance with your heart's dictation and understanding." These exhortations in behalf of the child as the subject (and not object) of education, which are in complete harmony with modern educational theory, are eloquent testimony to Rashi's pedagogic insight.

Rashi is aware of the value of firmness, reproof, and occasional chastisement. He has, however, a fine sense of discernment among types of students and the effect of punishment on individuals of differing intelligence. He stresses the thought of Scriptures that "the humiliation of rebuke will impress a man of understanding more effectively than a hundred blows dealt a fool" (Proverbs 17:10). He also suggests that it is better to inform the student in advance that he will be punished rather than administer sudden punishment. Rashi goes out of his way to warn against unreasonable and harsh treatment: "You are not to punish him more than is necessary to remove him from your presence, but he should sit there together with others and thus he will become attentive." Rashi also suggests that once punishment has been meted out, an effort should be made at immediate conciliation to end unpleasantness as soon as possible.

This liberal attitude to the pupil was quite unusual in his time, which was largely under the influence of St. Augustine, who taught that "a birch, a strap, a cane" are indispensable to "overcome ignorance." Even in the days of colonial New England, schools viewed children as "limbs of Satan" and therefore sought to inhibit their natural appetites and interests as inclinations toward evil.

Like his contemporaries, Rashi stressed the value of drill and systematic study, but at the same time he placed an unusual emphasis upon explanation, understanding, and reasoning. According to Rashi, it was not enough for the teacher to say, "this is the tradition that I received," but he must explain and give reasons for everything possible. Commenting on Exodus 21:1, Rashi interprets "thou shalt set before thee" to mean that one must "set the material (before the student) and give reasons which will satisfy the learner." Rashi expresses the same thought in a letter to his son-in-law Meir ben Samuel. The rabbis of old arrived at decisions, he says, "not because of tradition or proofs from the Talmud but because of the understanding of their heart."

Rashi himself, in spite of his reverence for his teachers, did not hesitate to express himself vigorously against them when he found their views unacceptable. The person who gathers information without understanding Rashi describes as "a basket full of books," carrying a load without appreciating its contents. Rashi used all possible devices to simplify his subject matter and make it understandable to different types of students. That is why his commentaries on the same subject may differ in form, depending upon the kind of student for whom they were intended.

Rashi, aware of the importance of a well-balanced personality, states that "he who kills himself over the words of Torah is not worthy that his views be received and quoted." He thus disregarded the Talmudic statement (*Berakhot*, 63b) that "the words of Torah endure only with him who kills himself over them." Rashi is fully conscious too of the great educational value of habit formation and says, "The education of an infant is essentially to enable him to follow his habits when he grows up" (Proverbs 22:6).

Rashi in his utterances is not lacking in a sense of humor. He supports the advice of some rabbis of the Talmud not to dwell in a city which is led by scholars "because they are intent on their studies rather than on the affairs of the town" (*Pesahim*, 111a). Critical of the negligent appearance of many a scholar, Rashi stresses the need for cleanliness. Likewise, he realizes the difficulties of being a servant of scholars for they usually display ill temper (*Sabbath*, 11a), in spite of all the encomium that tradition showered upon them.

Legacy as Rabbi and Teacher

Rashi is in the main stream of Jewish tradition, in which the rabbi and teacher, rather than the ruler and priest, guide the development of the people. Moses is known as Moshe Rabbenu, "our teacher," and the reconstruction of Jewish religious life after the Babylonian Exile is associated with Ezra, the leading teacher of his day. Following the destruction of the Second Temple, the continuity of Jewish development was ensured by the activity of a third great teacher, Rabbi Johanan ben Zakkai. Rashi too made his contribution as a rabbi and teacher.

In his own day, Rashi brought the rabbinic world into the

very life of his people. As a result, Jewry for many centuries did not know of the distinction that existed in Christendom between the clergy and the laity. Because of his lucid, warm style and his intimate manner of interpretation, Rashi helped bring an ancient heritage to life, not for the scholar alone, but for the Jewish people as a whole. While education was until modern times restricted to the few, and in the days of Rashi to the clergy, Jewish learning, because of Rashi, was so widespread that the average Jew could quote Scripture and adorn his quotations with Rashi's commentaries.

In Rashi's writings, one finds sublime expressions of the value of study and teaching. There is hardly an utterance on education recorded by generations of scholars and pietists who preceded him which is not quoted directly or indirectly by him. Torah was to Rashi more than a means of imparting knowledge, training in skills, or even character-building. It was an integral part of religion itself, an essential element of faith and observance.

Like many a great Jewish personality, Rashi shows a deep appreciation of the historic mission of the teacher in the centuries-old struggle for survival of the Jewish people. Teaching to him was not a chore to be relegated to someone else, as among the ancient Greeks and Romans, where the slave performed the function of teacher. To Rashi, teaching was a divine function and the teacher a kind of spiritual father. By bringing out the potentialities of the learner, the teacher helped recreate the human personality and thus partook of the function of God. God Himself is often referred to in Jewish tradition as scholar and teacher. In the words of Rashi, "Even the master still needs instruction, and the Holy One teaches him" (*Temurah*, 16a).

Rashi's impact on Jewish learning can be judged by the fact that more than two hundred super-commentaries have been written upon his commentaries on the Bible and Talmud. His writings stimulated generations of scholars and opened for them new areas of studies and investigation. Recent studies have shown that the contribution of Rashi and his disciples, known as the *Tosafists*, was more than a successful attempt at explaining or interpreting Bible and Talmud. Just as the rabbis of the Talmud, while apparently seeking only to explain the Bible, in reality initiated a new era in the history of Jewish culture, so Rashi and his followers, through their interpretations of the works of their predecessors, ushered in an even newer era in the growth and development of Judaism, namely, the institution and tradition of the rabbinate. Solomon Zeitlin maintains that Rashi was "the founder of the rabbinate in western and central Europe" and "responsible for the institution of the rabbinate."

What is particularly significant about the literary labors of Rashi and his disciples is that they also influenced to a considerable degree Christian theologians and commentators in spite of the latter's ingrained bias against the Talmud and rabbinic teachings. It is well known, for example, that Rashi's commentaries were generously used by Nicholas de Lyra, a Christian scholar who in turn exercised a great influence on Luther. Recent studies indicate that Rashi's influence is also to be perceived in earlier Christian scholars as well.

Beryl Smalley, a Christian student of medieval Bible commentaries, speaks of Philo, Rashi, and Maimonides as major influences on Christian scholars. "We hear of controversy between Christian and Jewish scholars, in the form of polemics and disputation," he goes on to say, "yet a Christian wishing to learn Hebrew which he revered not only as the language of the Scriptures but also as 'the mother of tongues,' and which he expected would be the current speech in heaven, was obliged to take a Jew as his teacher. . . . We also hear of the Jew as a 'carrier' bringing Arabic science to Western Europe. But the exegesis of the North French school of Rashi was no imported article: it was a native product, of Jewish manufacture. So collaboration between biblical scholars may have involved a real contact, in which a specifically Jewish method influenced the Christians."

The esteem in which Rashi was held by Jewish posterity is evidenced by the many legends about him—the tribute of inarticulate masses to their favored master. Some legends relate to his forebears, tracing his descent to a venerable Talmudic sage; others deal with Troyes, his birthplace; the honor of being his first home is also claimed by Worms and Lunel. Still another tale tells how his mother, when pregnant, was caught in a narrow street in the midst of a collision of two carriages; to avoid being crushed she pressed against a wall which miraculously opened to receive her. There is also the legend about a chapel Rashi built in Worms and the bench used by him, which are exhibited to tourists.

Rashi has remained a potent influence into our own period, judging by the eloquent testimonies of recent writers. A. S. Yahudah records his memories of the time when he studied Rashi: "Great joy seized me when I used to study something difficult that I finally succeeded in grasping. . . . At times I would jump from my seat, startled by the power of Rashi to clarify the most difficult passage by adding one or two words, and at times just one letter." Another writer, I. Avinery, states: "Since my childhood, Rabbi Shlomo Yitzhaki fascinated me by his spirituality, kindliness and humility; by his simplicity and wholesomeness; and by the sweetness of his gentle and lucid words that speak to and penetrate the heart."

In his own time and to this day, Rashi succeeded in opening the vast treasures of Jewish lore to the masses of Jewry, thereby setting a unique example of democracy in education.

4 . *Moses Maimonides*

[1135-1204]

SALO W. BARON

IN Moses ben Maimon (fondly known as Rambam) medieval Jewry produced its greatest jurist, philosopher, and scientist. Already in his lifetime he enjoyed wide recognition throughout the Jewish world extending from Yemen to France, and when he died a grateful posterity coupled his name with the first Moses: "From Moses to Moses, there was none like Moses." Although opposing voices were not altogether lacking and a short time after his death some Jewish zealots persuaded the Christian Inquisition to burn his philosophic work in a public bonfire, his achievement has remained memorable among both Orthodox and progressive forces in Judaism. His code of laws is still among the most authoritative guides for Jewish ritualistic observance, while his attempt at reconciling the Jewish faith with the postulates of science has illumined the road for many of his "perplexed" contemporaries and successors. His personality and thought have also left an imprint on the larger Christian and Muslim worlds.

Early Years in Cordova

The son of a distinguished Spanish family which included several outstanding judges among his immediate forebears, Moses ben Maimon was born in Cordova on March 30, 1135 (*Nisan* 14, 4895), a crucial period for his people and the world at large. This was the era of the great Crusades, during which the young though still backward Christian nations had assumed the offensive against the richer, more civilized, but decaying world of Islam.

In this divided world, Jews maintained a precarious existence as a sort of "neutralist" group. While in actual warfare they were supposed to side with their respective rulers, they neither were expected nor did they wish to participate in the ideological struggle between the two dominant civilizations. Devoid of military power and dependent on the good will and "toleration" of their Christian and Muslim masters, Jews often suffered severely from their position between the two hostile worlds. At the same time they unwittingly served as the bridge between them. In science, philosophy, and economics, they were able to perform an important mediating role between the awakening West and Islam. Spain, in particular, at the border between expanding Christendom and retreating Islam felt with particular poignancy the great challenge of these world conflicts. Individual Spanish Jewish thinkers and poets had already offered many an answer to that great challenge in Judaism's "Golden Age" of the preceding two centuries. In the twelfth century, as the situation came to a climax, the works of Moses Maimonides provided the most authoritative Jewish response.

The city of Cordova, in which young Moses spent his childhood and adolescence, was a shadow of its former self. Once a great capital, it had in its glory embraced a population of several hundred thousands and prided itself on its famed academies of learning and a royal library of some four hundred thousand manuscripts. In the subsequent period of anarchy and internecine strife among the "petty princes," the city had suffered severely. Most noticeable was the decline in mutual understanding among the various racial and religious groups. Voices of intolerance, certain of which demanded that Muslims not consult a Jewish or Christian physician or lend scientific books to "unbelievers," now developed into a powerful chorus under the impact of the "crusading" spirit on both sides. The Almoravid regime of Spain had already injected a large measure of persecution of non-Muslims. Now, in a direct counter-reaction to the Christian Crusaders, the new Muslim Almohade sect, which believed in the absolute unity and incorporeality of God, felt obliged to suppress both Christianity with its trinitarian dogmas, and Judaism. Sweeping rapidly through North Africa and Muslim Spain, the Almohades completely outlawed all non-Muslim faiths, a policy theretofore unprecedented in the history of Islam.

Maimonides was thirteen when the Almohades conquered Cordova, closing all its churches and synagogues, and demanding the conversion of Christians and Jews to Islam. Since there was no effective inquisitorial body to investigate the private lives of individual citizens and to institute trials against those suspected of secretly adhering to their ancestral faiths, the Almohade authorities had to be satisfied with lip service on the part of their new converts. Maimon and his children may well have successfully dodged any such formal declaration and merely exercised great caution in performing certain indispensable Jewish rituals at home. Outwardly, nevertheless, every subject of the Almohade Empire was considered a professing Muslim, and for this reason Maimonides had to face in later years the accusation of being a relapsed convert, a mortal offense in Islamic law.

Emigration to Morocco

As time went on and Almohade intransigence hardened, the number of secret adherents to the older faiths must have greatly diminished. Continuous clashes between the Muslim and Christian kingdoms ultimately led to the reconquest of nearly the entire Iberian Peninsula by the Christian Crusaders. In the meantime, however, the situation of the "secret" Jews became ever more precarious, many suffering outright martyrdom. In 1158 and 1159 Maimon and his family decided to emigrate to more hospitable regions. Curiously, the Maimonidean family did not seek shelter in Christian Spain or the Provence. Although the people in those regions had made great strides in their economic and cultural pursuits, they must still have appeared backward to citizens of Muslim Andalusia. Jewish refugees found it easier to adjust to conditions in North Africa where, because of the lack of an immediate Christian menace, the surveillance of recent "converts" was less thorough.

Some "secret" Jews, nonetheless, were disturbed by the concessions they had to make to their outward profession of Islam, even in Morocco. To pacify their consciences, the elder Maimon circulated in 1159 an *Epistle of Consolation*, in which he tried to strengthen the heart of his perplexed coreligionists—an epistle which undoubtedly served as a model for the somewhat similar *Epistle of Conversion* later published by his famous son. Both authors urged their fellow sufferers to stand firm on their faith, and to look forward to an opportunity to emigrate to a more tolerant country.

Undoubtedly themselves planning to depart before long, Maimon and his children spent several years in Morocco, from about 1159 to 1165. In the city of Fez they found an intellectually vigorous and alert community which in the preceding two centuries had produced an array of distinguished Jewish thinkers, philologists, and jurists, including Isaac Alfasi, whom Maimonides acknowledged as the greatest of his teachers. Here young Maimonides received further training in both Jewish and general subjects, and in medicine. He also continued with his literary activities, on which he may have embarked as early as the age of sixteen. While still in Spain he had composed a brief manual on logic, analyzing some seventy basic philosophic terms and classifying the sciences, as well as a tract on "Intercalation," which reviewed the main principles of Jewish calendar computation. At the age of twenty-three he began his *Commentary on the Mishnah*, which, when completed ten years later, became a classic in its field. These works were written originally in Arabic, although they became far more influential in their later Hebrew translations.

We are not told what particular event persuaded the Maimonides family, in 1165, to turn their backs on the Almohade Empire. Possibly a new outburst of intolerance in Morocco resulting in the execution of one of Maimonides' teachers forced their departure. In any event, after a stormy voyage, the surviving of which Maimonides thereafter commemorated annually in two family fast days, they reached the Holy Land. They remained there a year or less, probably because most of the country was then part of the Latin Kingdom of Jerusalem, which, at least in its early years, was even more fanatical than the Almohades. Maimon and his family turned to Egypt which, even under the then declining Fatimid domination, was still one of the great economic and cultural centers of the Near East.

Egypt: Physician and Communal Leader

Moses and his family adjusted themselves in a remarkably quick manner to the new Egyptian environment. His younger brother David became a successful merchant, engaging in risky but lucrative trade with India. On one journey to the rich subcontinent, however, David was shipwrecked and lost at sea, along with most of the family's fortune (1174). In a letter dated 1182 Maimonides wrote: "When the bad news arrived, I became ill and depressed for a whole year; I thought I was lost. Eight years have passed; I am still mourning and cannot find consolation. I brought him up; he was my brother and my pupil." Under the impact of that loss and the ensuing financial responsibilities which he had to assume toward his brother's family, Moses began to practice medicine. Quite early he achieved a considerable reputation among his fellow physicians at Fustat, Cairo, who, when requested by a Christian prince of the Latin Kingdom to send him an expert physician, selected Maimonides; he, however, declined the invitation. He soon entered the services of the vizier and counselor of Saladin, Egypt's new and colorful ruler. Maimonides' success was so great that his medical services were sought by many princes and dignitaries of state and mosque. In an often-quoted letter to his French Hebrew translator, Samuel ibn Tibbon, Maimonides described his busy career:

> I live in Fustat while the king resides in Cairo at a distance of two permissible journeys on Sabbath (about three miles). My duties at the royal court are very exacting; I must see the king every day. But if he feels unwell, or if one of his children or concubines falls ill, I must spend most of the day at the royal palace in Cairo. Similarly, if one or another official is sick, I must attend to his medication . . . In any case, I do not return home before noon, quite hungry (and exhausted). But I find my waiting rooms filled with people, Jews and Gentiles, distinguished and common, judges and surveyors, friends and enemies, a mixed multitude awaiting my return.

In spite of his professional responsibilities, Maimonides found time to concern himself with the problems of the community in which he lived. Almost immediately after he arrived in Egypt he assumed a position of leadership in the Jewish community. The general respect for learning and personal integrity overcame whatever resentments may have been nurtured among local Jews by the interference of this "foreigner" in their domestic affairs, which had been quite unsatisfactory for some time. All of Egyptian Jewry was controlled by a single official bearing the distinguished title of *nagid* (prince), and some of the *negidim* used their authority and court connections for personal gain and aggrandizement. The regime of the *nagid* Zuta, shortly before and after Maimonides' settlement in Egypt, proved particularly obnoxious and had embroiled the community in endless controversies.

Maimonides evidently entered the ranks with reluctance. Deeply involved as he was in his studies, he resented any loss of time occasioned by communal strife. He also believed that "all the house of Israel are in duty bound to be united in one indivisible whole, and there should be among them no conflict whatsoever." At the same time, he held to the principle of the obligation of each individual to prevent wrongdoing whenever possible. "He who can protest and does not do so is himself guilty of the transgression for which he had failed to reprimand the transgressor." The growing authority of the great jurist doubtless helped depose the abusive Zuta, but he apparently refused to become *nagid* himself.

Nevertheless, Maimonides was soon recognized by all Egyptian Jewry as its outstanding leader. As early as 1176 he and nine associates issued a sharp ordinance aimed at reducing the Karaite influence on Rabbinite Jews. Although past its intellectual heyday, the Karaite sect generally enjoyed a high social and intellectual standing in Egypt, and their members sometimes intermarried with prominent Rabbinites. A series of other ordinances likewise bears Maimonides' signature and the imprint of his personality.

Maimonides' influence was also soon felt beyond the confines of Egypt. Ancient Yemenite Jewry, in particular, had long maintained intimate relations with the major Jewish centers of learning in both Babylonia and Egypt-Palestine. These relationships had been strengthened by the political and religious influence exercised upon Yemen by Egypt's Fatimid ruler. Maimonides' reputation spread from Egypt to this South-Arabian community, and in 1172, or some seven years after his arrival in the East, he was asked by Yemenite leaders to resolve certain theological difficulties connected with Jewish Messianic beliefs and practices. These difficulties assumed new significance with the appearance in Yemen of a Messianic pretender who found a wide following among his oppressed coreligionists. In his *Epistle to Yemen,* Maimonides delved deeply into both the doctrinal and historical aspects of the problem. Apart from citing numerous Messianic movements up to this time (some unrecorded elsewhere), he presented the traditional Messianic teachings which he sharply differentiated from the related Christian and Muslim doctrines.

The apologetic parts of the *Epistle* enjoyed wide popularity both in their Arabic original and in three independent Hebrew translations. So grateful were the Yemenite communities that they inserted Maimonides' name, while he was still alive, alongside that of the reigning Exilarch in their daily recitations of the *Kaddish.* The historical section of the *Epistle,* however, as well as its outspoken polemics against Christianity, was considered either uninteresting or too dangerous for Jews to be disseminated in the Hebrew version. The Arabic manuscript lay dormant until its publication in recent years.

Jurist and Legal Philosopher

Maimonides was both a jurist and a legal philosopher. His ordinances and responses enabled him, like the other Jewish *Halakhists,* to extend the Law, civil as well as ritualistic, by applying it to ever new cases. Reinterpretation of older laws by way of commentaries and recodification had also been a time-honored device to adjust the Law to novel conditions in each particular environment. But beyond his concerns with legal practices, Maimonides always searched also for the deeper reasons behind them and, in his systematic mind, formulated categories into which their disparate elements might logically fit.

Not that Maimonides felt the need to defend Jewish "legalism" as a matter of principle. Living in a Muslim environment, which was as little antinomian (opposed to law) as Judaism, he did not have to argue for the necessity of legal orderliness in societal and individual behavior. It sufficed for him to consider mainly the spiritual versus the physical elements in Jewish law and its impact on both body and soul. As he wrote in his *Guide:*

> The general object of the Law is twofold: the well-being of the soul, and the well-being of the body. The well-being of the soul is promoted by correct opinions communicated to the people according to their capacity. Some of these opinions are therefore imparted in a plain form, others allegorically; because certain opinions are in their plain form too strong for the capacity of the common people. The well-being of the body is established by a proper management of the relations in which we live one to another. This we can attain in two ways: first by removing all violence from our midst; that is to say, that we do not do every one as he pleases, desires, and is able to do; but every one of us does that which contributes towards the common welfare. Secondly, by teaching every one of us such good morals as must produce a good social state. Of these two objects, the one, the well-being of the soul, or the communication of correct opinions, comes undoubtedly first in rank, but the other, the well-being of the body, the government of the state, and the establishment of the best possible relations among men, is anterior in nature and in time.

Maimonides profoundly believed in the rationality of all laws. If his great predecessor Saadia Gaon had tried to draw a line of demarcation between rational laws which the human mind can explain, and irrational laws which must be followed merely because of the divine command, Maimonides rejected this distinction as almost bordering on blasphemy. To him the idea that God might have enacted laws without any good and valid reasons appeared abhorrent, although he admitted that human reason may not always be capable of comprehending their import. But whether one knew the reason or not, Maimonides agreed with all other Jewish jurists that one had to adhere to the commands of tradition undeviatingly. He even recognized unreasoned obedience as a highly meritorious act before the Lord.

Commentary on the Mishnah

A few years after he arrived in Egypt Maimonides completed his *Commentary on the Mishnah,* which he had begun at the age of twenty-three. Seeing in the Mishnah—as well as in the other *Tannaitic* sources—the chief repository of Oral Law, Maimonides early concentrated on deducing from it the principal Jewish legal teachings and spreading their knowledge among the masses. Overtly, his *Commentary* pursued only pedagogic aims. "What induced me to compose this work," he wrote, "was the recognition that the Talmud explains the Mishnah in a way no one could guess through mere reasoning." To understand it, moreover, it was not enough to study the Talmudic comments on a particular Mishnah, but one also had to remember many other rabbinic discussions scattered through the vast "sea of the Talmud." To help students understand, he embodied in his *Commentary* a summary of those far-flung debates in the ancient academies, and pointed out what he considered to be prevailing law. He also wrote commentaries on several tractates of the Babylonian Talmud, and, as one of few medieval rabbis, also studied intensively the Palestinian Talmud. The former are unfortunately lost, while his summary of the Palestinian compendium entitled the *Hilkhot Yerushalmi* appeared a few years ago.

Maimonides stressed the underlying principles alongside the specific provisions contained in the Mishnah. Unlike Roman law and its continental offshoots, but more similar to Anglo-Saxon, Muslim, and other legal systems, biblical-Talmudical jurisprudence was largely "case law." Inductive processes were necessary to reach an understanding of general principles, which Maimonides' logical mind tried to emphasize. At times he felt impelled to expatiate on them in lengthy introductions to individual Mishnaic tractates or even chapters. For example, the introduction to the *Sayings of the Fathers* was divided into eight sections. It soon began to circulate as an independent treatise called *Eight Chapters,* and became an outstanding classic of Jewish ethical literature.

Maimonides' ethics, too, has an intellectual slant. He believed that man's "only design in eating, drinking, cohabiting, sleeping, waking, moving about and resting should be the preservation of bodily health, while, in turn, the reason for the latter is that the soul and its agencies may be in sound and perfect condition, so that he may readily acquire wisdom and gain moral and intellectual virtues, all to the end that he may reach the highest goal of his endeavors." His introduction to the last chapter of "Sanhedrin," in which Mishnah and Talmud dealt at great length with the problems of resurrection and the Messianic era, enabled Maimonides to elucidate the fundamental doctrines of Judaism as a whole. Here he formulated his famous thirteen principles, which stated the beliefs in (1) God's existence, (2) unity, (3) incorporeality, (4) eternity, (5) exclusive claim to worship, (6) prophecy, (7) Moses' uniqueness among the prophets, (8) the Law of Moses as in its entirety given by God, (9) its eternal immutability, (10) God's omniscience, (11) reward and punishment, (12) coming of the Messiah, and (13) resurrection of the dead. Preceded in each case by the declaration "I believe (*Ani Maamin*)," these principles were embodied in the daily ritual of Ashkenazic Jewry. A broader reformulation has been recited monthly in Sephardic congregations for many generations.

The Book of Commandments

Despite his comprehensive treatment, Maimonides must have recognized the inadequacy of his *Commentary* for the practical guidance of judges and students. Gone was the time when the entire Jewish intelligentsia concentrated exclusively on the study of rabbinic letters. While concern with the Law remained the major preoccupation of a substantial segment of Jewry, the wider horizons of the renaissance of Islam had attracted many to the study of philosophy, philology, poetry, and the sciences. At the same time the new articulateness of Jewish literature and its diffusion from Persia to the Atlantic Ocean taxed the erudition of even the most learned *Halakhists*. Recodification of Jewish law in well-organized and clearly written handbooks had, therefore, become imperative.

Following established precedent, Maimonides in his Arabic *Book of Commandments* summarized the entire body of Jewish law under the headings of the traditional 613 commandments. From ancient times it has been assumed that the Torah had presented the Jewish people with a set of 248 commandments, similar in number to the limbs of a human body, and with 365 prohibitions resembling the days of the solar year. But nowhere did the Talmud offer any detailed enumeration; it was left to the medieval rabbis to fill in that gap on the basis of their individual traditions and reasonings. Deviating from all his predecessors, Maimonides attempted a new classification beginning with such general principles as the belief in the existence and unity of God and finally descending to individual laws and rituals. Each positive commandment as well as prohibition embraced many specific provisions. Together they covered the broad areas of Jewish law, both ritual and civil. Although some scholars disagreed with one or another individual decision, immediately after publication of the *Book of Commandments*, Maimonides soon claimed with great satisfaction that "many copies of that book have reached Babylonia, the extreme west and the cites of Edom (Christendom)." He only regretted that he had written it in Arabic and hoped that some day he would have the opportunity of translating it into Hebrew.

Here, as elsewhere in his juridical works, Maimonides insisted that all commandments were equal in rank. He refused to follow the gradation of commandments made by Abraham ibn Daud into those relating to faith, morals, social life, and those pertaining to ceremonies. He believed that the very assumption of such a differentiation in biblical laws had been King Manesseh's main transgression because it had led him to take certain commandments more lightly than others. The sage of Fustat would certainly have viewed with dismay those persons of our time who rather arbitrarily consider certain laws as more or less obsolete, while they rigidly adhere to others.

The Mishneh Torah

Still dissatisfied, Maimonides decided to reformulate all of Jewish law in a new systematic code. In intensive labor extending over more than a decade (1166-1176) and with many revisions thereafter, Maimonides restated the entire law of the Talmud. Using the Mishnah as a model, but going beyond it, he omitted all discussion pro and con or the citation of controversial points of view, but merely stated in his own lucid way the general principles as well as the specific laws. He gave considerable thought even to the succession of chapters and subchapters; for he so strongly believed that such orderliness had already guided Judah the Patriarch in his redaction of the Mishnah that he sometimes deduced points of law from Mishnaic sequences. Legitimately, therefore, Maimonides' commentators and other students of *Halakhah* paid special attention to the implications of the sequences in the Maimonidean code as well. He was proud of the simplicity of his Hebrew style and staunchly resisted appeals by friends to translate it into Arabic. Disregarding the traditional division of the material into six orders and sixty-three tractates, he reorganized it into fourteen logically integrated sections. Concerned with presenting the totality of Jewish law, the codifier drew no distinction between regulations still valid in his time and others which had become totally obsolete. He treated the laws governing the ancient Temple and its sacrificial ritual with the same care and detail as he did, for instance, those affecting marital relations, holiday observance, or the consumption of ritual food. Most remarkably, he devoted the first section of his work to a discussion of the "fundamentals of the Torah," that is, to the credal and ethical elements of Judaism, which had hitherto been left to homilists and preachers rather than to jurists.

This unprecedented method aroused misgivings among those students of the Law accustomed to the traditional arrangement, and even greater objection was raised to Maimonides' failure to supply his sources. Although any keen *Halakhist* could detect behind each formulation the author's familiarity with Talmudic sources and his careful weighing of the often contradictory evidence, Maimonides' authoritative declarations sounded presumptuous and arbitrary. At times, indeed, in spite of its clarity, many a Maimonidean statement lent itself to misinterpretation and misapplication by less informed judges and communal leaders. Only the citation of the older sources themselves, many leading jurists believed, would enable such legal practitioners to comprehend the arguments underlying each decision and to arrive at a more reliable judgment. Maimonides himself, constantly engaged in revisions of his *Code*, was aware of that shortcoming and at one time contemplated supplying brief references to the sources. He never accomplished this task, however, and it was left for the later host of commentators to do.*

Most shocking to traditionalists, however, was Maimonides' self-assurance and his opening declaration that he was trying to summarize the entire body of Oral Law so that "none will be required to study any further book concerning the laws of Israel . . . The present treatise," he promised, "will assemble the whole Oral Law, together with the ordinances, customs, and enactments which had been issued from the days of Moses to the completion of the Talmud, as they have been interpreted by the authorities in all writing composed after the Talmud. For this reason I have called this treatise *Mishneh Torah* (the Second Torah), for one need but read the written Torah first, and then study this book, to learn the entire Oral Law without being required to peruse any intervening tract."

This declaration evoked in the minds of many readers the specter of total neglect of Talmudic studies. For example, the distinguished and self-assertive *Halakhist*, Abraham ben David, of Posquières, reacted immediately with a series of sharp strictures to the *Code* (which he seems to have received in installments). Abraham's *Hassagot* (Objections) have since accompanied most editions of the *Code* itself. By thus stimulating the independent thinking of readers, they helped prevent blind reliance on the *Code* and the ensuing "petrification" of Jewish law, fear of which had long served as an argument against any attempt at codification. In fact, as Maimonides himself boasted to the scholars of Lunel, the distribution of copies of his *Code* in Yemen and vicinity had, from the outset, restored interest in Talmudic learning in communities as far east as India. Ultimately, a fifteenth-century North-African scholar could claim that without the *Code* "we would be unable to fully comprehend the Talmud."

Religious Philosopher

Maimonides became the greatest Jewish religious philosopher not so much out of an inner drive to speculate on the riddles of existence as in response to an urgent social need. Not that he

* No less than 220 commentaries were enumerated in a bibliography compiled some seventy years ago by the famous Viennese preacher Adolph Jellinek; many more have appeared since.

lacked intellectual curiosity; in fact, all his life he was deeply concerned with theoretical problems and voraciously read Arabic literature in most fields of learning. His personal contact with Muslim scholars, the influence of a philosophically-minded Jewish intelligentsia in Spain, Morocco, and Egypt, and the teachings of rabbinic scholars like his own father Maimon all combined to arouse his profound interest in philosophical speculation. Had not an outstanding leader of *Halakhic* Judaism, Saadia Gaon, and some of his successors pointed the way toward the reconciliation of *Halakhah* with philosophic studies?

None of these men indulged in speculations in a vacuum. As intellectual spokesmen of their people they were confronted with the powerful challenges of the majority culture, and often had to react to direct attacks on Judaism by Muslim thinkers. Even more important loomed the need to justify the traditional teachings before the growing Jewish intelligentsia itself. True, the outright agnostic trends noticeable in eastern Islam in the ninth and tenth centuries had given way to a more fundamentalist reaction, and in the western Muslim countries the impact of the Almohade reaction had almost obliterated all radical tendencies. Nevertheless, there were still many Jews of Maimonides' generation who were uncertain and perplexed about the seemingly irrational character of many Jewish teachings. To some of them, numerous statements in the Bible appeared controverted by scientifically demonstrable facts and sound speculation. Without abandoning their faith, they searched for guidance in reconciling the verities of their own religion with the philosophical and scientific teachings of the Greek schools now available in Arabic translations, and their further elaborations in Arabic commentaries and independent tracts.

Guide for the Perplexed

It was to such "perplexed" Jews rather than to outright agnostics or atheists (whose number in the medieval Jewish community must always have been small) that Maimonides addressed his *Guide for the Perplexed*. This philosophic masterpiece grew out of a series of essays in Arabic in which he answered some incisive questions put to him by a former pupil, Joseph ibn Aknin. In this work he sought "to enlighten a religious man who has been trained to believe in the truth of our holy Law, who conscientiously fulfills his moral and religious duties, and at the same time had been successful in his philosophical studies." He was addressing himself to persons attracted by reason who found it "difficult to accept as correct the teaching based on the literal interpretation of the Law."

Speaking to that intellectual minority, Maimonides had to be very circumspect so as not to offend the sensitivities of extreme traditionalists. The major question was how to reconcile the apparently naive and often legendary statements in the traditional sources with the dictates of reason, in whose supremacy Maimonides staunchly believed. Without entering into discussions of the complex philosophical problems concerning the reliability of human reason such as had been heatedly debated in Saadia's generation, Maimonides insisted that whenever reason was absolutely certain of its findings, the contradictory statements in the Bible must be explained in an allegorical way, that is, by searching out their hidden rather than literal meaning.

For this purpose Maimonides devoted most of the first section of his *Guide* to a lengthy semantic discussion. He tried to show that the Bible often used homonyms, or words which had one meaning when applied to man and another when used in connection with God. Even the simple formulation that "God is One" did not have the same connotation as that of "oneness" employed in human affairs. Whereas the latter really means that something consists of one rather than of two or three entities, all of which are equally possible, in the case of God double or triple existence is logically unthinkable; hence, God's oneness really means that He is one of a unique kind. This was the core of Maimonides' famous doctrine of "negative attributes," which held that anything attributed to God was intrinsically different from a similar attribute to man, and that we really know what God is not rather than what He is. Whether one asserts that God exists, has power, or knowledge (the three attributes originally used by the Syriac Christians to rationalize the trinitarian dogma), or whether one adds any number of other attributes, they all have a meaning peculiar to God's unique essence.

None of these doctrines was deeply controversial. The overwhelming majority of Christians, Muslims, as well as Jews agreed on the oneness of God and His differentiation from human beings. Nevertheless, like most medieval philosophers, Maimonides went through the motions of proving again the existence of God in Aristotelian terms. He mainly used the argument that a world in motion, caused by previous motions, logically leads back to a prime unmoved Mover, just as the usual chain of causality must somewhere end in a postulated First Cause.

Only one aspect of Godhead led to sharp controversies. The unsophisticated reader of the Bible saw in God a personality of a superhuman kind but one endowed with many corporeal features. God's actions and sentiments were expressed by the biblical writers in purely human terms (God seeing or saying something, His being angry, and the like). The rabbis, too, often stated that the "Bible speaks in the language of man," by which they meant that many of its statements need not be taken literally. Nonetheless, these biblical anthropomorphisms and the even more elaborate descriptions of human qualities in God found in the rabbinic *Aggadah* and mystical literatures became ready targets for Christian and Muslim critics. Some Muslims actually accused Jews on this score of lacking a purely monotheistic belief. They also claimed that the ancient rabbis must have altered statements in the Bible which could not have been given by God to Moses in that materialistic form.

Like other Jewish philosophers, Maimonides strained his ingenuity in explaining these passages; he declared most of them were homonyms having an entirely different meaning when applied to God. In any case, he felt that since human reason repudiated ascribing human qualities to God, Jewish readers were perfectly free to interpret away the most clear-cut biblical anthropomorphisms. He even counted rejection of the corporeality of God among his thirteen articles of faith. "Therefore bear in mind," he wrote, "that by the belief in corporeality or anything connected with corporeality, you would provoke God to jealousy and wrath, kindle His fire and anger, become His foe, His enemy and adversary in a higher degree than by the worship of idols." Such a rejection angered many of the traditionalists of the time, especially in Europe where the Bible still was largely read with its unsophisticated *Aggadic* elaborations. Thus Abraham ben David of Posquières noted that "greater and better men than he have followed that trend of thought."

The sage of Fustat was not prepared to accept, however, the somewhat related philosophic teachings concerning the eternity of the world which ran counter to the accepted religious doctrine that it had been created by God out of nothing. He felt that in this respect the Aristotelian demonstrations could be countered by equally valid counter-arguments and that, hence, there was no "sufficient reason for rejecting the literal meaning of a biblical text and explaining it figuratively." More generally he accepted almost all Aristotelian teachings concerning the physical aspects of the earth and its inhabitants, but he declined to follow the Stagirite thinker in matters affecting the superlunary world.

In discussing the relation between God and the universe, or man, Maimonides saw no need of arguing for the prevailing geocentric view of the world. Having accepted the creation of the world in time, he also had little difficulty in persuading himself that the same creator had inspired the biblical writers to compile this authentic record of the divine revelation to man. True philosophically-minded readers required an explanation of the nature of prophecy and miracles, and particularly of the manner in which the incorporeal God had communicated His will to man. Maimonides argued that the same omnipotent creator who had fixed the laws of nature could also alter them at will. Such a breach in the course of nature was not really their reversal but a temporary adaptation to new needs set in advance by an omniscient providence. God also willed it that certain individuals be endowed with special prophetic gifts enabling them to perceive His wishes and to communicate to their fellow men truths unattainable to human reason unaided by revelation.

In Maimonides' analysis of prophecy, which had given him the original impetus to compose the *Guide*, because it was the main line of demarcation between believer and non-believer and even between members of different denominations, his rationalism conceded the existence of an imaginative quality in certain extraordinarily gifted individuals which was infinitely superior to human reason. In his methodical fashion Maimonides graded the prophecies recorded in Scripture in eleven degrees.

Above all prophets towered the unmatched personality of Moses, who, in Maimonides' opinion, was as superior to the other prophets as the latter were to ordinary men. Only the poverty of human language accounted for the inability to give the great lawgiver a different and unique designation. Next to psychic endowment, piety, and virtue were qualities indispensable for a genuine prophet, distinguishing him from a false prophet.

Clearly, such doctrines easily lent themselves to an emphasis upon the uniqueness and exclusive truth of the Jewish religion. Mohammed's prophetic endowment was sharply rejected as was Jesus' Messianic mission. True revelation was limited to the Law of Moses, given to him on Sinai in the presence of a whole people. Later Israelitic prophets amplified the Pentateuchal teachings by special messages, but, unlike the founders of Christianity or Islam, did not alter them in any fundamental way. The fact that the Jewish people was the sole recipient of that revelation made it the "chosen people," which it has remained in spite of all suffering and persecutions, and which it would unalterably remain until the advent of the genuine Davidic Messiah.

It is because of the Jew's membership in the "chosen people" that he is obliged to observe the 613 commandments in all their ramifications. Next to the first two commandments of knowing that there is a God and believing that He is one, Maimonides placed as the third and fourth commandments the duties of loving and fearing Him. To explain love of God, he wrote: "It means that we ought carefully observe and meditate on His commandments, words, and works, until we grasp Him and enjoy such recognition with the profoundest of pleasure . . . This commandment also includes our obligation to urge all men to the service of God, and the belief in Him."

Although not averse to propagandizing the Jewish faith among Gentiles, Maimonides knew that under both Islam and Christianity such conversion was a capital offense. In Muslim lands even the conversion of Christians to Judaism was sternly outlawed. But in answering the appeal by a particular convert, Maimonides went out of his way to stress the law that after conversion a proselyte enjoyed essentially the same rights as a full-fledged Jew. Maimonides' primary concern in enjoining man's duty to love God was to make each and every Jew not only observe all commandments for himself and his family, but also to induce him to share in the responsibility for his fellow Jews and the community at large.

In general, man's ethical behavior must transcend the requirements of formal law. The moral aspects of Judaism deeply permeated all Maimonidean philosophy and colored his psychology. In his *Eight Chapters* particularly, Maimonides tried to combine the teachings of the fathers with those of Aristotle's *Nicomachean Ethics*. Like most Jewish teachers, but more explicitly, the Fustat sage stressed the doctrine of the "golden mean" as the major rule of human behavior. In his famous "Code of Benevolence" he placed assistance toward self-support of impoverished persons high above outright charity. Maimonides allowed himself occasional outbursts against existing communal practices which he abhorred. Following the old Talmudic preference for the study of Torah without expectation of reward, he sharply censured the widespread commercialization of learning and the professionalization of teaching and the judiciary. "Every Jew," he taught, "is in duty bound to study the Torah, be he poor or rich, healthy or ill, young or old and decrepit; even a pauper living on charity or begging from door to door and obliged to provide for a wife and children is bound to set aside time during the day and night for the study of Torah." Maimonides also condemned sharply the mania for titles which, in emulation of an Arab fashion, had spread in the Jewish community since the tenth century. He saw in them a violation of the old rabbinic ideal of humility which, together with inward piety, law observance, and intellectual aspiration, formed the backbone of Jewish ethics.

Medical Writings

The last dozen years of Maimonides' life were largely devoted to his intensive medical practice. Yet he found enough time to write a number of important responsa and epistles on legal and theological subjects. Some of these letters tried to explain to questioners moot points in his earlier works which he kept on revising to the end of his life. To this period also belong various important tracts which established his reputation as one of the outstanding Jewish medical authors during the Middle Ages.

As a student of sciences Maimonides was primarily concerned with those scientific data which had a direct bearing on his legal and ethical teachings. An assiduous reader of contemporary mathematical and astronomic literature, he effectively utilized the findings in the elaboration of certain rabbinic teachings. He was most interested in expanding his views on medical subjects. Most of his monographs—on hemorrhoids, sexual intercourse, asthma, poisons, fits (of melancholia), and even his semi-medical and semi-ethical tractate on the *Regulation of Health*—were written at the request of various dignitaries, which explains their frequently casual tone and numerous repetitions. Only two major medical tracts seem to have been written on his own initiative.

One of these was a large compendium on drugs, discovered about two decades ago in a unique Istanbul manuscript transcribed by one of the leading medieval Arab pharmacologists a generation after Maimonides. Apparently one of Maimonides' earliest medical works, it may have been written for his own benefit to help identify drugs used in his new Egyptian environment with similar preparations made in Morocco and Spain, which frequently bore different Arabic designations. Moreover, even the study of Hippocrates and Galen require a more precise knowledge of the medical compounds, for many of their prescriptions could not be filled in Egypt because of the absence of certain plants or their extremely high price. In the ensuing quest for substitutes a clearer understanding of drugs of similar qualities, or their linguistic "synonyms," became an urgent necessity.

Maimonides spent many years in formulating aphorisms of a medical-ethical nature, which came to be known under the name of *Pirke Moshe* (*Chapters of Moses*). While frequently quoting Hippocrates and Galen, he also dared to deviate from and at times even opposed the teachings of those ancient masters. In this and other works he tried to instill in his readers the conviction that a physically and mentally healthy way of life was the best means of preventing and curing disease. He was an ardent believer in "mental therapy" and often devoted considerable space in his medical treatises to advising patients to apply psychological cure. In his *Regulation of Health*, written at the request of a sultan who complained of mental depression and forebodings of death, Maimonides describes his approach: "The soul may become accustomed to resist passion by considering the ethical books, the literature and the rules of the religious law, and the sermons and the wise sayings of the sages, until the soul is strengthened and sees the right as right, and the idle as idle. In this way the passions diminish, the bad thoughts disappear, the unsociableness is removed, and the soul is gladdened in spite of all the conditions which may happen to man." Equanimity and calm acceptance of adversity were the keynotes of Maimonides' ethical-medical teachings.

After Maimonides' death, a Muslim student of medicine, with the typical exaggeration of the panegyrists of that age, wrote a poem extolling the mental therapy used by the Fustat sage above Galen's exclusive concern with bodily ills.

> Contrast Maimmi's with famed Galen's art:
> Health to the body Galen can impart,
> But the wise Hebrew, with a two-fold skill
> Relieves both mind and body from all ills;
> Shows how base ignorance can hurt the soul,
> While wisdom, counteracting, makes it whole.
> Even the moon, obedient to his cure,
> From periodic taint would be secure;
> No spots the brightness of her disc would stain,
> Nor would rebirth entail her death again.

Though some Muslim physicians denounced him as a relapsed convert to Islam, the majority placed him among the ranking medical authors of his age.

Following the prevailing fashion, Maimonides relied on book learning rather than experimentation. Though in his medical practice even more than in his mathematical and astronomic calculations the scientist had to make use of his personal observation and experience, Maimonides leaned heavily on earlier authorities. Primarily a student rather than a practitioner, he was annoyed at having to attend to the minor or imaginary ailments of his highly placed patients, which left him little time for the study of medical literature. "For you know," he declared, "how exacting and difficult is this profession for any person of conscience and precision, who refuses to make a statement without knowing how to prove it, or else how to indicate its source, or the kind of analogy leading up to it."

Scientific Works

In his astronomic studies Maimonides was even more dependent on literary sources; calculations of the movements of the moon and the ensuing calendar regulations had long been established in the Jewish tradition, and any deviation therefrom was a sign of heterodoxy. Like most of his Jewish confrères, moreover, Maimonides had little access to the few extant astronomic observatories, which had been erected for Muslims by royal patrons. Hence he could not possibly have reached novel conclusions on the basis of direct astronomic observation. Nevertheless, by using sound deductive methods he was sometimes able to improve upon the findings of certain distinguished Arab predecessors.

On the whole, Maimonides' world outlook was confined to the current views of Ptolemaic astronomy. Although some ancient thinkers and even such near contemporaries as the author of the *Zohar* had suggested an earth rotating around its axis or even around the sun, the overwhelming opinion held the earth to be a stationary globe around which the moon, the seven planets, and the sun all rotated. Erroneous as many of Maimonides' underlying hypotheses undoubtedly were, his practical conclusions were on the whole quite sound. In the field of calendar regulation especially, they still form the basis of the Jewish calendar today.

At times, however, when scientific findings ran counter to traditional teachings, a serious dilemma was created for Maimonides. In such instances, he consistently taught that rational certainty must take precedence over the literal meaning of the traditional sources, and that the latter must be reinterpreted in the light of scientific facts. In his *Commentary on the Mishnah* he had stated bluntly: "Thus have taught all the gaonim whose opinions we know, yet I have come to the conclusion that the opposite is true." Later in summarizing the laws governing the calendar, he declared: "Since all these teachings are demonstrated by clear and incontrovertible proofs one does not doubt them because of their authors, be they Israelitic prophets or Gentile scholars." On the other hand, his own medical learning had undoubtedly taught him that predictions of life expectancy always carried with them an element of doubt. That is why he refused to deviate from the Talmudic classification of *terefot* (maimed animals unable to survive), even where it was controverted by veterinary evidence. He apparently felt that even an animal, whose expected life span appeared very short, might nevertheless live much longer.

Fortunately for Maimonides and other orthodox students of science, scientific findings rarely came into conflict with *Halakhic* regulations. The latter were largely concerned with subject matter from the domain of *Aggadah* which, from the outset, had developed in so uncontrolled a fashion that it carried with it inherent contradictions and was subject to an endless variety of interpretations. Its unauthoritative nature had long been conceded by prominent *Halakhists*, and enabled Maimonides and other scholars to follow established scientific facts more freely and to rely on their own reasoning powers.

Death of the Sage

The incessant travail which characterized Maimonides' life —his medical practice, communal activities, and constant writing and revisions of his books—gradually undermined his health. In a letter to Ibn Tibbon he wrote:

> Patients go in and out until nightfall or sometimes, I assure you, until two hours in the night. I talk to them lying on my back because of weakness. When the night falls I feel so weak, I cannot speak any more.
>
> Thus no Israelite can have a private discussion with me except on the Sabbath. Then they all come to me after the services and I advise them what to do during the week; afterwards they study a little till noon and depart. Some of them come back and study again until the evening prayers.

In spite of his strict regime, to which he devoted a special monograph and according to which he seems to have lived himself, Maimonides did not complete his seventieth year. He died on December 13, 1204 (*Tevet* 20, 4965), and all Egyptian Jewry observed a three-day period of mourning. According to his wish, Maimonides was buried in Tiberias, where his tomb has ever since attracted pious pilgrims. He left behind one son of his old age, Abraham Maimonides, who, as the official *maggid* (preacher) of Egyptian Jewry as well as a jurist and philosopher in his own right, became an important leader of Near Eastern Jewry in the first half of the thirteenth century.

Impact of His Works

The controversy which Maimonides' works had aroused during his lifetime continued after his death. He had purposely written his *Guide* in a more involved style than he had employed in his juridical works and had repeatedly warned his readers to study his words very carefully lest they understand them "to mean the exact opposite of what I intended to say." It is not surprising that his views were condemned not only by ignorant persons, but also by thoughtful and informed traditionalists. Maimonides' insistence that belief in God's corporeality stamped one as a heretic may have been a necessity in the Muslim world, but those residing in the Christian West felt little of that pressure. After all, Christianity itself had gone much further in its doctrine of Incarnation of God, born, living, and dying as a human being. Some other teachings of Maimonides sounded even more extreme and dangerous to western traditionalists.

The assumption of the supremacy of reason and the need to harmonize the revealed word of God with Aristotelian philosophy aroused sharp opposition. In the Provence, particularly, that area of confluence of Islamic and Christian cultures, the anti-Maimonidean controversy reached its climax. Ultimately, the obscurantist faction invoked the aid of the Christian Inquisition. In 1233 it succeeded in persuading the Inquisitors of Montpellier that the Maimonidean *Guide* contained many heretical teachings, dangerous not only to the Jewish community but also to the orthodoxy of Christians. Before very long, however, an enlightened Pope himself promoted a Latin translation of the *Guide* so that he might study it at its source, and then the leading Christian scholastics, Albertus Magnus and Thomas Aquinas, frequently cited "Moses the Egyptian" with approval and respect. Little did the Jewish anti-Maimonidean informers realize that by inviting the Inquisition to interfere with Jewish literature, they were paving the way for the prolonged trial and burning of the Talmud.

At the same time, Maimonides' work inspired more moderate Jewish scholars the world over to concern themselves with philosophic and scientific studies. An ardent admirer like Yedaiah ha-Penini of Beziers exclaimed with the typical exuberance of youth: "We cannot give up science; it is as the breath of our nostrils. Even if Joshua were to appear and forbid it, we should not obey him. For we have a warranty which outweighs them all, namely, Moses ben Maimon who recommended it, and impressed it upon us. We are ready to set our goods, our children, and our lives at stake for it." With less vocal enthusiasm but equal devotion, many students, including some Muslims and Christians, studied the *Guide* with great care. A thirteenth-century Muslim even wrote a commentary on some of its sections. Several distinguished Jews, including Don Isaac Abravanel, wrote extensive commentaries on the whole work, while all later Jewish philosophers constantly took a position for or against some of its individual teachings. With Spinoza, whose philosophy was greatly indebted to that of Maimonides, the teachings of the Fustat sage entered the arena of modern philosophy and have ever since fructified human thought on basic religious problems.

Even more influential within Jewish life and thought was his great *Code* and other legal writings. Many distinguished *Halakhists*, including Joseph Karo, author of the similarly authoritative compilation, the *Shulhan Arukh*, wrote lengthy commentaries on it. Some poets, even if not endowed with grace divine, reproduced the regulations of the *Code* in verse form. Still today, students of Talmudic lore often exert their ingenuity in first detecting supposed contradictions in the *Code* and then harmonizing them by the use of advanced Talmudic dialectics. The very *Kabbalists* whose mystic teachings were so completely alien to Maimonides' rationalistic mind tried to claim the master as their own. Shem Tov ben Abraham ibn Gaon, one of Maimonides' outstanding commentators, actually reported to have read in an ancient scroll the following autograph entry: "I, Moses ben Maimon, descended into the chambers of *Merkabah* (the divine chariot of Ezekiel's vision)." Modern *Hasidic* rabbis likewise derived many significant teachings from the sage of Fustat. Hence, Saadiah ibn Danan (fifteenth century) was not guilty of an overstatement when he wrote that "under Ben Maimon's guidance all Israel walked from sunrise to sunset."

The Man and His Legacy

As for the Jewish masses, they took a cue from the poet Yehudah al-Harizi, who had sung:

> Thou art an angel divine,
> Created in God's image,
> Though formed in our shape,
> For thy sake did God say,
> "Let us make man in our image, after our likeness."

A rich web of tales and legends were spun around the personality of the master. He became one of the great heroes of Jewish folklore in both East and West. After the appearance of an alleged portrait of the sage, in an Italian work by a Christian scholar, Ugolinus (1744), reproductions were spread throughout the Jewish communities. In the nineteenth century there were, indeed, few Jewish homes which were not adorned with this alleged likeness of the jurist-philosopher.

What does Maimonides mean to our generation? Answers to this question will depend on the personal *Weltanschauung* of each individual. Certainly much of the sage's world outlook, his picture of the astronomic and geographic world, his acceptance of the four basic physical elements (earth, water, fire, and air), and even many remedies suggested in his medical works have become decidedly obsolete. His metaphysical discussions and his intense preoccupation with the problems of creation versus eternity of the universe, his proofs for the existence and oneness of God, or his doctrine of the negative attributes—all bear the imprint of the scholastic philosophy of his day and carry little immediate conviction to men searching after ultimate religious verities today.

Nevertheless, Maimonides' ingenious attempt to solve major religious problems through the instrumentality of reason, and his penetrating effort to build bridges between the traditional sources and the new facts presented by philosophy and science, have set an inspiring example for the following generations. The fact that religious philosophies advanced by such diverse thinkers as Avicenna, Maimonides, and Thomas Aquinas had so much in common and were accepted with relatively little opposition in that religiously enthusiastic age, when denominationalism was the most divisive force in mankind, has served as a testimony to the basic unity of the human mind.

Maimonides' legal and ethical teachings have suffered far less from the obsolescence of the ages. Perhaps because human progress in law and ethics has been much slower, or non-existent, the teachings of ancient and medieval thinkers, as reformulated in his writings, still have a direct bearing upon human behavior today. Certainly, Orthodox Jews living in accordance with the 613 commandments of Judaism still try to live up to the postulates of the thinker of Fustat, even though they know that *Halakhah* has long since overruled many of his individual decisions.

The extraordinary lucidity and persuasiveness of Maimonides' formulations, his penetrating methods of dealing with complex legal concepts, and his monumental effort to derive from the vast, often contradictory, traditional sources a uniform and self-consistent legal system may still serve as a model for all new juridical compilations. In the field of ethics practically nothing taught by Maimonides has become wholly obsolete. Perhaps our generation prefers to place different emphases on and ascribe different values to certain segments of the Maimonidean doctrine. But just as Maimonides himself attempted few innovations in the realm of ethical behavior, so have his successors until the present day departed relatively little in this area from the memorable structure erected by the masterbuilder. Moreover, like other classics, Maimonides' works have provided different values for different generations. If we, too, restudy them in the same creative way as Maimonides did in reinterpreting the older authorities, we shall indeed find that he may serve as a guide for the perplexed of our generation as well.

5 . "*The Baal Shem Tov*"

[1700-1760]

LOUIS I. NEWMAN

ISRAEL ben Eliezer, better known as the Baal Shem Tov or Besht ("Master of the Good Name"), is, without doubt, one of the world's greatest spiritual leaders. A warm, sympathetic, and colorful personality, he made a great impact on his own and subsequent generations. The movement he founded, which came to be known as *Hasidism,* effected a veritable spiritual revolution in the life of the Jewish people in Eastern Europe of the eighteenth century. In recent years, not only the personality but also the message of the Besht have won increasing recognition.

Israel ben Eliezer was born about 1700 in Okup, near Kamenatz-Podosk on the old Polish-Turkish boundary, in a region known as Podolia. Early in his childhood, Israel lost both parents; his father's last words, urging him to fear nothing since God would be with him, made an indelible impression on the boy. Okup's community leaders took him under their protection, but in the *heder* he proved to be a free-roaming, imaginative lad, constantly breaking school regulations to go his own way into the woods. No amount of ordinary discipline served to control the boy, and finally the authorities permitted him to express his own remarkable nature and temperament as he saw fit. Israel became assistant to the schoolmaster at the age of twelve, escorting the pupils to and from school and singing joyfully all the way. Later he became a *shamash* or synagogue attendant, who seemed to sleep during the day, but in the stillness of the night devoted himself to his studies, chiefly the *Kabbalah.* At eighteen he was married, but his young wife died immediately after the ceremony. Young Israel left Okup; he served as a helper and assistant teacher in various communities of Galicia, and then settled in Tlust near Brody as a teacher in the *heder*.

In Tlust his magnetic personality and keen human insight won him many friends, and intricate human problems were constantly laid before him for judgment. Ephraim, an affluent and learned resident of Kuty, impressed with Israel's wisdom, promised him his daughter in marriage. But Ephraim died before the betrothal, and his son, the proud aristocratic Rabbi Abraham Gershom, sought to prevent his sister's marriage to Israel. The latter was pretending to be a shabby, ignorant peasant, a disguise which he assumed, in part, as a protest against the ostentation of some rabbinic leaders. Hannah insisted on the marriage, however, not only in fulfillment of her late father's wish, but because she had fallen in love with Israel. Indignant at his sister's act, Rabbi Gershom compelled the couple to leave Brody, their only possessions a horse and wagon he had given them. The exiled pair settled in a Carpathian village between Kuty and Kassov, earning their livelihood, chiefly through Hannah's industry, by the sale of a weekly wagonload of lime from nearby quarries. Israel continued to be a *luftmensch* (Yiddish for "rootless person"), spending most of his time in a forest hut, communing with animals, flowers, and trees in the Carpathian mountains.

Teacher and Healer

Later Israel accepted a post as *shohet* in Koshilowitz, near Jaslowitz. Rabbi Gershom, the brother-in-law, repenting for his harshness toward his sister and her husband, purchased a tavern for the pair, which Hannah competently managed while her extraordinary husband continued his hermit's life in the forest. Through his friendship with the peasants, non-Jews as well as Jews, Israel acquired the secrets of herbs, plants, and roots for medicinal purposes. By reason of his congenial and magnetic nature, he soon became a beloved counselor, and was sought out by the wealthy and learned as well as the lowly. After seven years, he established himself in Tlust as a teacher and healer, where he "revealed" himself, winning the title "Baal

Shem Tov" or "Good (Kind) Master of the Name" (The Ineffable Name of God).* From his Tlust headquarters he visited neighboring communities in Galicia, Podolia, Volynia, and the region adjoining Kiev; once he journeyed as far as Slutsk in Lithuania on a "healing" mission.

In 1740 he established himself in Medziboz, a strategic center on the frontiers of a number of important areas of Poland, the Ukraine, and Lithuania. Without doubt his migration from Tlust to Medziboz was motivated in part by the Besht's desire to shed his reputation as a miracle-worker, and to extend his renown as an ethical and religious mentor. But it must be admitted he wrote amulets and gave advice to his followers for monetary payment (very much like a contemporary psychiatrist) to such an extent that his livelihood was assured. The Besht was always generous in his charities, his resources being so abundant in his later years that even if the house was without food and money, fresh supplies always seemed to arrive in time.

At Medziboz, where the Besht was active the rest of his days, he attracted from all walks of life disciples who, as his fame increased, were able to free him from the financial anxieties which had so long plagued him. So manifold were the requests made to the Besht from all parts of the Ukraine that in his later years he was compelled to engage the services of a second secretary to answer letters and transmit advice. Multitudes of disciples were drawn to the Besht because of the charm and animal vitality of his nature. He persuaded many doubters, among them Rabbi Yehiel, later the "Maggid of Zlotchov." Whenever a disciple was in doubt he traveled to the Master; one such was Pinhas of Koretz, who found the Besht expounding the verse (Exodus 17:11) which tells that the hands of Moses were "held up in the hour of the struggle with Amalek." "The influence of a leader," said the Besht, "is likened in the Talmud (*Abot* 2:15) to a burning coal. Do not hold yourself aloof from the Master; you will remain cold. Do not approach him too closely; you may be burned. This applies also to your re-

* The "Name" thus used was believed to possess supernatural powers both in Christian and Jewish life, both in the domain of thought and of practical healing. The addition of the adjective *Tov* or "Good" set Israel ben Eliezer apart from the professional and less gifted aspirants to the title.

lationship with your friends." We can "cleave unto the wise," the Besht explained, "by searching out those gracious traits which are common" to a vulgarian and a sage. In order to win the tempestuous Rabbi Jacob Joseph of Polonnoye as an adherent, the Besht told the story of the rabbi who impatiently struck a water-carrier, and who later repented his anger. "If he should come to me," said the Besht, "I could indicate to him a path of repentance." The Polonnoye rabbi, of course, became one of the Besht's most ardent disciples.

The Besht instituted a "fellowship" at Medziboz, which included great throngs of disciples and adherents. Out of the multitude arose certain eminent personalities; among them, in addition to Rabbi Jacob Joseph, were Rabbi Dov Baer of Mezeritz, known as "The Great Maggid"; Rabbi Pinhas of Koretz; Rabbi Yehiel Mikhal of Zlotchov, and numerous others, who, in turn, raised up disciples, followed by later generations of *Zaddikim.** The Besht ordained a number of pupils who became preachers, rabbis, *shohetim,* cantors, and leaders of prayer in numerous smaller communities; in this way the influence and message of their master and patron were disseminated. Hosts of unnamed lay visitors served as advocates of the Besht's teachings. Thus the *Hasidic* movement gained ever-increasing popularity among the East European masses, and served as an effective antidote to the arid rationalism and *pilpulism* which had impeded the flow of creative religious thought and action.

The Besht as a healer and an alleged wonder-worker provoked hostility among the more rationalistic Jews of his time, but among his devout followers, many of them non-Jewish peasants and Polish nobles, he was greatly revered. He became adept in prescribing homeopathic folk remedies based on knowledge gained from peasants and from his own extensive study of the curative powers of herbs, roots, and plants, many of which serve as the basis for drugs used by physicians today.

* The title *Zaddik* was applied not only to the "righteous man" in general, but also to the particular leader who gained the loyalty and adherence of the *Hasidim* or "Pious Disciples" who gathered about him. With the *Zaddik* as their leader, they formed a community or society in the spirit of the Master, the Besht, and in accordance with the special teaching or emphasis of the religious leader they had chosen to follow. Many of these *Zaddikim* were known by the names of the towns where they taught, thus, the Berditschever, the Lubliner, the Ladier.

Often he cured his devotees by fervent prayer, profound ecstasies, gesticulations, and other seemingly magical means; it is said that he also revealed secrets and foretold the future. But he was no ordinary Baal Shem who employed conjuring, incantations, and amulets. "To his credit, be it said that he was far from practicing the quackery of his fellows in the craft. In treating, for instance, those who suffered from melancholy, or the insane, he sought to influence their minds." So states Louis Ginzberg.

His Psychological Insight

The Besht was clearly a penetrating student of individual and group psychology; he understood the people with whom he dealt, and wished ardently to communicate with them in a language and by methods which, in the light of the current culture, they could understand. The "miracles" attributed to him can be explained in psychological terms. That some of the ailments apparently "cured" by the Besht were of a psychosomatic character is illustrated by a number of tales. For example, Rabbi Nahum of Tchernobil, a hypochondriac, felt the pain leave his limbs when the Besht himself read aloud from the Scriptures the passage of reproof on "The Sabbath of Blessings." Once the Besht refused to pray for a *Zaddik*'s recovery, but the latter's pain left him a few days later when a band of brigands was captured by the police. The Besht explained that the *Zaddik*'s pains had served to delay the brigands until they could be discovered. "The sufferings of a *Zaddik* act as a shield," he said. If a man believes he can dispel his tribulations by moving to another place, he is like an invalid who imagines his illness will similarly depart if he moves. The real cure, said the Besht, is obtained by repentance, by prayer from the heart, and by petitions for God's mercies.

The psychological effect of the Besht's influence can be seen in the story of the rabbi whose grandfather had been a disciple of the Besht. In pursuance of the dictum that "a story must be told in such a way that it constitutes help in itself," he narrated: "My grandfather was lame. Once they asked him to tell a story about his Master, the Besht. And he related how the holy Baal Shem used to hop and dance while he prayed. My grandfather rose as he spoke, and he was so swept away by his story that he himself began to hop and dance, to show how the Master had done. From that hour on, he was cured of his lameness. That's the way to tell a story." Such an example of auto-suggestion would have gladdened the heart of Émile Coué, the faith-healer of Nancy, France, in the 1920's.

Did the Besht himself believe in the healing powers attributed to him? If neurasthenic or psychotic persons seemed "possessed by spirits," the Besht, following the folk-beliefs and folkways of the time would engage in the exorcism of these *Dybbukim.** Perhaps the very nature of the Besht prompted him to travel, in his mind, between the natural and the divine, between the physical and the metaphysical, between empirical reality and a "miracle of God." The Besht is quoted as saying: "If a man clings closely to the *Shekhinah* and thinks of himself in such a circumstance in the Higher World, he is in an instant transplanted into the Higher World, for where a man thinks himself to be, there he is, and if he were not in the Higher World, his thinking could not attain to it." Apparently the Besht was convinced that the sincere, spiritual devotion of a righteous man could achieve changes in the Higher World, but God did not always alter His decrees according to the wishes of the pious; on one occasion, a wonder would occur; on another, the divine decree remained unalterable; sometimes the prophecies of the righteous were fulfilled; at other times, they came to naught. *Hasidic* legend itself tells that the Besht once realized he could not restore a wealthy man's son to health. Observing that the parents were about to castigate the Besht, the latter disappeared with phenomenal speed lest "this incident harm his reputation elsewhere."

If the Besht was unable to cure a person who was either physically or psychologically ill, he would sometimes explain to the patient's kinsfolk that Satan had intruded and interrupted his efforts; on other occasions he would affirm he had heard a voice from heaven announcing that an irrevocable judgment had been decreed against the afflicted one's recovery. The Besht seems to have been careful to avoid families that resorted to either physicians or to gypsies who practiced magic. Once when a non-Jewish physician inquired whence the Besht had derived his skill, he replied with sincerity: "The Lord, praised be He, was my teacher."

* "cleaving spirits."

Like other *Baalei Shem*, the Besht would take a metal container, insert a slip of parchment inscribed with the Secret Names of God, and place it beneath the garments of a sick person. Such amulets were said to be efficacious for women giving birth, or in other extremities that required the warding off of evil spirits. Associated with these amulets was the gift of money for the "Redemption of the Soul" (*Pidyon ha-Nefesh*), usually in the amount (in small or large coins) of the numerical value of the Hebrew word *hay*, or eighteen.

The resort to amulets naturally brought the Besht into disfavor in Talmudic and medical circles. On one occasion, Rabbi Yitzhak of Drohobycz queried the Besht regarding his use of them. The Master opened one of the amulets and showed the doubter that on the parchment nothing was inscribed but his own name and that of his mother, namely, "Israel ben Sarah." In other words, the amulet itself did not possess magical power and was nothing "but a sign and pledge of the personal bond between the helper and the one who is given help, a bond based on trust . . . The amulet is the permanent symbol of his direct influence at the given moment. It contains his name and thus represents him. And through this pledge of personal connection, the soul of the recipient is 'lifted.' " Thus Martin Buber explains the role of the Besht as healer.

In spite of this contemporary rationalization of the Besht's practices, the fact remains that he was "a man of his age," and, with respect to his activity as a healer, he deserves no more tolerant treatment than Jewish and non-Jewish practitioners of the nineteenth and twentieth centuries. The Besht as a "wonder rabbi" exemplified the tendencies of his particular period, and we must no more condemn him than we do the physicians who employed leeches and blood-letting (as the Besht likewise did) in conformity with the medical knowledge prevalent during the eighteenth century.

In 1752 the Besht undertook a journey with his daughter and Rabbi Hersch (Zevi), his secretary, to the Holy Land. Though they reached Stamboul, numerous vicissitudes compelled them, to their disappointment, to return without reaching their goal.

Seven years later, in 1759, the Besht was one of three Talmudist delegates to the disputation with the followers of Jacob Frank, a pseudo-Messiah who later converted to Christianity.

The Master fell ill from overexertion and died on the first day of *Shavuot*, 1760.

Character of His Message

In what way did the Besht transcend the function of the ordinary Baal Shem? What was it that made him the leader of the great movement which in his lifetime and thereafter exerted so profound and widespread an influence? The answer lies in a description of the many-sided teachings of the Besht which went far beyond his profession as a "faith-healer." The character, message, and institutions of the movement known as *Hasidism* are the Besht's true monument in history. From the first moment of his career as a teacher throughout the years of his ever-mounting fame and in the years of his fruition as a Master of hosts of disciples, he acted upon the central theme of his mission, namely, that communion with God is not confined to a select and aristocratic few, but is the possession of all of His creatures. The motivating idea and the very name of the *Hasidic* movement is derived from the rabbinic statement attributed to Hillel: "an ignorant man cannot be pious." In order to provide an antidote for the arrogance and aloofness among many scholars of his day, the Besht encouraged the commoners to believe in their faculty for authentic religious feeling. His very masquerade in his youth as an *am ha-aretz* was undertaken to bring him closer to the ordinary folk of the villages, farms, and cities—the teamsters, water-carriers, tailors, bakers, peasants, carpenters, servants, storekeepers—so that they might realize they were not excluded from fellowship with the All-Compassionate, All-Loving, Omnipresent, Universal Father on High.

Thus, the shepherd boy blows his whistle at *Neilah* services in a mood of spiritual fervor, to the delight of the Besht; another lad recites the letters of the alphabet as a prayer, having forgotten the words of the prayer book. When a pious man deplores his failure to attain improvement, the Besht solaces him by the reminder that to recognize his lack of worth is an accomplishment. A stocking-maker, accustomed to recite the psalms while at work, was praised for thus laying "the cornerstone which will uphold the Temple until Messiah comes." A man so busy that he must recite his prayers in a by-street is very dear to the Lord, and his "prayer pierces the firmament." Said the Besht: "The lowest of the low you can think of is dearer to me than your only son is to you."

Scholarship as such was not condemned by the Besht, but he believed that excessive concentration on Talmudic texts often proved a barrier to genuine inwardness (*Kavanah*). He once remarked of a famous sage: "I envy him his scholarship. But what am I to do? I have no time to study because I am under the compulsion to serve my Maker." While the Besht did not specialize in rabbinic learning, nevertheless he had a genius for illustrating his ethical and spiritual lessons with items which ordinary folk could comprehend and appreciate. In a parable concerning two petitioners, he declared: "Even if we do not behold the king face to face, we may view his treasures in his palace; namely, we may study God's Torah and thereby at least be near His presence." Using a simile of the maiden who declined a prince's admiration until he had developed an affection for learning, the Besht remarked that the Lord instils within us a desire for a long life, but He tells us we may not enjoy it until we have learned Torah. He defended the minority in Torah interpretations, saying they were the "kindlers of the lamps." Later the *Zaddikim* (righteous ones), among them the Mezeritzer and Rabbi Schneour Zalman of Ladi, sought to achieve a synthesis between Rabbinism and *Hasidism*, but the pristine emphasis upon simplicity in learning and in piety remained. Thus, the fable, the anecdote, and the parable drawn from the daily experience of his adherents always engaged the Besht. He quoted Psalm 14:15: "The simple believeth every word"; and Psalm 116:16: "The Lord preserveth the simple." He declared that just as coarse food proves as helpful as fine food to the defenders when a castle is besieged, "likewise, my friends, store in your memory those common tales I narrate to you, as well as the teachings which seem to you profound. In your work among the people, everything will prove useful." Sometimes a man feels remote from God, even as a child, learning to walk, is sometimes left alone by his father so that he may walk unaided. Just as a father takes delight in the stumbling words of his child, so God does not object if a man misunderstands what he is studying, provided he aspires to learn.

Role of Joy in Hasidism

Joy and good cheer were heartily recommended by the Besht and became a leitmotif of *Hasidism.* Asceticism and mortification of the flesh were abhorrent to the Master. He believed such practices led to melancholy and depression. "Only where there is joy do God's dictates prevail. For it has been explicitly commanded: 'Thou shalt not hide thyself from thine own flesh.'" "Asceticism," he said, "should be practiced only at the commencement of a man's self-discipline, until his evil inclinations are subdued. Later he should conduct himself in a normal way and be in communication with his comrades. Otherwise he will fall into pride." "The strength thou wert willing to lose through fasting devote to the Torah and to worship," he counselled. Once the Besht answered some disputants, saying: "It is the aim and essence of my pilgrimage on earth to show my brethren by living demonstration how one may serve God with merriment and rejoicing. For he who is full of joy is full of love for men and his fellow-creatures."

Once a Jew in great tribulation asked the Besht: "How many days have I to fast, to make atonement for a grievous sin?" The Besht replied: "Not through fasting is the ire of God averted, but through the joy of which the psalms are harbingers. Say the psalms with inward rejoicing and you will be quit of your sin." Again he said: "Weeping is evil indeed, for man should serve God with joy. But if one weeps from joy, tears are commendable." He cordially praised a rabbi who read the *Yom Kippur* prayers in most cheerful tones, comparing him to a royal servant who sings a merry song while he sweeps the forecourt free of dirt, "for he does what he is doing to gladden the king."

In the way of life recommended by the Besht he gave a practical application of his ideals. He emphasized again and again the importance of good health and normal activity, saying: "Do not consider the time you spend for eating and sleeping wasted. The soul within you is rested during these intervals, and is enabled to renew its holy work with fresh enthusiasm . . . You may be free from sin, but if your body is not strong, your soul will be too weak to serve God aright. Maintain your health and preserve your strength." He laid great stress upon the ritual bath and immersion. Music played a decisive role in the community life which the Besht helped fashion. The drinking of wine, adding merriment and gaiety to the *Hasidic* way of life, was approved by the Besht though it later brought the *Hasidim* under strenuous rabbinical reproof. In speaking of the beauty of womankind, the Besht said: "When you admire beauty in a woman, remember that her beauty is but a reflection of the Supreme Source of Beauty–the Lord." The Besht explained the *Shalosh Shelishit* as follows: "The *Hasidic* custom of eating the Third Sabbath Meal in company with comrades is founded upon the following reason: among good Jews it is eminently desirable that a man offer up his soul in the presence of ten Jews. At the conclusion of the last Sabbath meal, we offer up our Super-Soul (*Neshamah Yeteiarah*) received by us on the Sabbath. We desire to do this in congenial company."

The dance, of course, was a major interest of the *Hasidim* in their effort to express joy in worship. Once on *Simhat Torah*, the Besht danced with his disciples. "He took the scroll of the Torah in his hand and danced with it. Then he laid the scroll aside and danced without it. At this moment one of his disciples who was intimately acquainted with his gestures, said to his companions: 'Now our Master has laid aside the visible dimensional teachings and has taken the spiritual teachings unto himself.' " Out of the *Hasidic* dances intricate and decorative art forms have developed which have found their way into the theaters of the nations.

Religious Ideas

The religious system enunciated by the Besht revolves, of course, about the concept of God. The Besht's interpretation of God was in strongly pantheistic terms, even so-called evil itself existing in the nature of the deity. Cleaving to the Lord (*Deveikut*) was a paramount virtue in the eyes of the Besht. "Thou art righteous," he said, "only when thou feelest more joy in cleaving unto the Lord than in any material pleasure." On another occasion he said: "Some seek God as if He were far removed from us, and surrounded by many walls . . . Had they been wise, however, they would have known that 'no space is free of Him.' They can find Him in everything and everywhere, and they should understand that 'one who attaches himself to any part of God is as if he were attached to the All in All.' "

Concentration (*Kavanah*) in the endeavor to cleave unto God is essential. "When it is desired to solder a piece of silver to a silver vessel, the edge of the piece must be cleansed so that no foreign substance may intervene. Likewise when a man wishes to cleave to God, he must purify himself of every foreign thought beforehand." "Most tribulations," the Besht said, "come to those who are wavering in their beliefs and resolutions, whether they concern matters of substance or spirit." Not only is concentration required in work for pleasure or wealth, but also in labor which will bring you into "communion with the Lord and His holiness." In another parable the Besht contrasted two farmers, one indolent, the other diligent, to illustrate the point that one man collects many *mitzvot* without proper attention to his prayers; another performs fewer *mitzvot* but displays concentration and sincerity. "It is desirable that a man should frequently interrupt his occupation, sacred as well as secular, for a moment, whatever it may be, and concentrate his mind upon the fear of the Lord." "Mind," said the Besht, "is the foundation of man. If the foundation is solid, the building is secure. By the same token, if a man's mind is filled with holy thoughts, his action will be sound. But if his mind is occupied with selfish thoughts, even his good actions are unsound, being built on a weak foundation."

The love of God and its counterpart, the fear of God or reverence before Him, are linked with concentration or inwardness in worship of the divine. Once when the spirit of the Besht was so downcast that it seemed to him he would have no share in the world-to-come, he said to himself: "What need have I of a world-to-come, if I truly love God? . . . Our love of God should be more like the love between brother and sister, or between a mother and her child, than the love between man and wife or between lovers. The first may show their love both in private and public, whereas the latter may do so in private only. We should not imitate those who say that our love of God should be demonstrated only in the synagogue or the home, but should not be shown on the street or in public places."

In the spiritual system of the Besht, the concept of the fear of God was associated with the idea of repentance and also of attachment or cleaving to God (*Deveikut*). While he underscored the love of God, the Besht appreciated the value of *Yir'ah*, namely, reverence or fear before God. To him there were two kinds of fear of the Lord, one outer, the other inner. "The outer is fear of punishment, and induces a man to repent. The penitent may then gain the inner fear, namely, the fear of displeasing his beloved Father in Heaven, and thus he will have no further need of the outer fear."

In accordance with his humane and tender attitude toward mankind and the world, the Besht declined to believe in "absolute evil," saying: "When the good man perceives evil-doers, he rejoices in goodness." In speaking of the "sediment of evil inclinations," the Besht remarked: "When a man squeezes wine-grapes into a vessel, he must first use a sieve with large holes to strain it; later he uses a cheese cloth. But no matter how many times he strains it, some sediment still remains. It is the same with the *Zaddik*. He must rid himself of his evil inclinations and continue to do so his entire life. But there are always a few dregs left over." Thus while the Besht was mindful of the unceasing struggle for moral perfection, at the same time he recognized man's capacity to enthrone goodness in his soul.

One of his best-known parables called "The Bird's Nest" describes the effort by the king's strong men to capture a migratory bird of rare beauty. To do so the courtiers formed a human ladder; but when one weakened, the entire structure crumbled to the ground. In the same way, he said, the man of holiness depends on the support of lesser and even lowlier men; but when one man weakens, the structure totters and falls, and even the *Zaddik* must begin anew.

Though the Besht was venerated by his contemporaries, he tolerated no deification of himself, nor did he pretend to the Messianic role. He shared in the traditional Hebraic concept of the Messiah and the Messianic age, emphasizing the individual Jew's responsibility to usher in the redeemer's reign. In this connection he speaks of the "pangs of the Messiah," saying: "before the coming of the Messiah there will be a period of prosperity and Jews will become wealthy. They will grow accustomed to extravagant living and forget all their habits of frugality. Later, a terrible depression will arise, and the means of livelihood will be scarce. Poverty will descend upon those who no longer know how to live sparingly." Not only did the Besht oppose the Messianic pretensions of Jacob Frank, but he also commented in a derogatory way on Sabbatai Zevi, the pseudo-Messiah of Smyrna: "Many have trodden the same steep path, and have attained the same fortunate goal. He, too, had a holy spark in his being; he fell, however, into the net of Samuel, the false deceiver, who thrust him into the role of a redeemer. This overtook him only because of his arrogance." The Besht's insistence upon the virtue of humility served as a safeguard against any overweening ambitions within himself.

Importance of Love

Filled with a love of man, the Besht was strongly opposed to sermons which excoriated sinners. Once he said to a *Zaddik*, accustomed to vituperative, castigating discourses: "What do you know about admonishing? You yourself have remained unacquainted with sin all the days of your life, and you have had nothing to do with the people around you. How should you know what sinning is?" On another occasion he said:

> A prince was banished from his father's realm. Two servants were assigned to him, commissioned to report on his conduct. One servant made a dry report of facts unfavorable to the prince. The other made the same report, but added that the youth's misconduct resulted from his exile, and his sense of disgrace and melancholy. The father took compassion upon his son, restored him to the palace, and rewarded the loyal servant. In the same fashion, when a sage or a preacher reproves Israel, let him always employ the method of the second servant. It is in this way that he will surely please the Father in heaven.

In recommending loving rebuke, the Besht said:

> One who sees faults in another and dislikes him for them is surely possessed of some of these very faults in his own person. The pure and good man can see only the goodness in others. We read (Leviticus 19:17): "Thou shalt not hate thy brother in thy heart; thou shalt surely rebuke thy neighbor, and not bear sin because of him." This teaches us: rebuke thyself first for seeing faults, and

thus being to a degree impure; then thou shalt not hate thy brother, but feel love towards him. If thou rebukest him, it will be in the spirit of love. He will become attached to thee, joining the goodness within him to thine own goodness, and all his faults will disappear. If he should refuse to listen to thee, and to admit his fault and abuse thee, he shall lose thereby his goodness to thee, and remain wholly evil. Thus through a loving rebuke, either of these two courses is open: both of ye shall join in love, and both of ye shall attain improvement. Or if there is hatred left, it shall be in his heart, not thine.

Love, in the judgment of the Besht, is the cardinal thing. When asked: "What is the chief point in service to the Lord if it be true that fasting and self-chastisement are sinful?" he replied: "The main thing is to encompass oneself in the love of God, the love of Israel, and the love of the Torah. A man may attain this if he secures enough nourishment to preserve his health, and if he makes use of his strength to battle against evil inclinations."

The Master's love of Israel is illustrated by his words of comfort to a stricken mother who had lost her only child at the age of two. He narrated to her the tale of the prince who had become a Jew and whose soul had entered the mother's beloved child for its two years on earth. From the commandment to love one's fellow man as oneself he learned the Talmudic commandment to judge one's fellow man on the scale of merit. "Since thou always findest excuses for thine own misdeeds, make excuses also for thy fellow man." When a Jew was exposed as a thief, the Besht said to him: "God pardons and helps. But you must promise me never to commit another transgression of this kind in the future." A few years later when the same Jew came to Rabbi Jacob Joseph of Polonnoye to complain of business difficulties, Rabbi Jacob exclaimed: "Do penance!" The Jew exclaimed: "Alas, would that the Holy Baal Shem Tov were still living . . . He knew that I was a receiver of stolen goods and yet he spoke to me with kindness. You, however, address me angrily and demand penance from me, before I have stolen anything at all."

The love which the Besht displayed toward God and the universe expressed itself also in his love for God's dumb creatures, the domain of nature, and human beings in their arduous social relationships. For example, when a father complained that his son had forsaken God, and asked what he should do, the Besht answered: "Love him more than ever!" On every side there is evidence of the keen psychological and human insight which the Besht displayed throughout his entire life.

The Master always sought to make repentance easily accessible if the offender were sincere in his appeal for pardon. "If a man sins purposely, how can he know whether his intentional repentance can overcome his intentional sin? The remedy lies in maintaining his mood of repentance for a long time until he is confident his sins have been forgiven." "The chief joy of the Satan," said the Besht, "is when he succeeds in persuading a man that an evil deed is a *mitzvah*. For when a man is weak and commits an offense, knowing it to be a sin, he is likely to repent of it. But when he believes it to be a good deed, does it stand to reason that he will repent of performing a *mitzvah?*"

The Besht compared the tactics of the evil impulse to those of a man who secured permission to drive a nail into the wall of a householder, and ended up by marring the entire wall. In his recommendation of self-discipline, the Master showed his disciples an acrobat at a fair walking a high tightrope. He commented: "I reflected that if men would submit their soul to such discipline as that to which he has submitted his body, what deep abysses might they not cross upon the tenuous cord of life!"

Ethical Virtues

Sincere humility contrasted with pride and hypocritical self-abasement engaged the Besht's attention among his disciples. He declared that a man who serves God has no leisure for pride, and the world's respect or disrespect does not concern him. "He is then able to perform any good deed without feeling pride in doing it." In an eloquent parable the Besht said: "A king was told that a man of humility is endowed with a long life. He attired himself in old garments, took up his residence in a small hut, and forbade anyone to show reverence before him. But when he honestly examined himself, the king found himself to be prouder of his seeming humility than ever before. A philosopher thereupon remarked to him: 'Dress like a king; live like a king; allow the people to show due respect to you. But be humble in your inmost heart.' " The Besht affirmed that a gifted man is inclined to attain to pride before he is aware of it; he is like a traveler who falls asleep in a stagecoach while it ascends to the summit of a hill; only when a descent is made, after a smooth ride downhill, does he realize how high he has been. The Besht also told of a man who studied humility so earnestly that when someone failed to show him deference, he became incensed and cried out: "Don't you know that since I have learned humility, I am a man of perfect character?" He believed that God was even with the sinner who considers himself base, for He "dwelleth with him in the midst of their uncleanness" (Leviticus 16:16); from the Gemarah, however, we learn concerning the man who prides himself that he is unburdened by sin: "There is not enough room in the world for myself and him."

Needless to say, the Besht lost no opportunity to convey to others his disdain for luxury and ostentation. He once taught his little son concerning the silver objects of a well-to-do scholar: "The silver truly stands in the wrong place, but not because it is not ours. It should rather be given away as charity, instead of glittering here as futile ornaments." In describing the four dispositions with reference to charity, the Master remarked: "The uncharitable man is the chair upon which the charitable sits." In speaking of ethical virtues in everyday living, the Besht declared that a boy before he becomes thirteen cultivates a taste for *mitzvot* without the necessity of battling the evil impulse. "It is like a man who enters a new confectionery store and is offered a free sample of a new condiment. If he finds it sweet and wishes more of it, he is asked to pay. The adult may taste the sweetness of the *mitzvot* only after he has triumphed over his inclinations."

Role of Zaddik

The Besht recognized the important role of the *Zaddik* or righteous man, described in the Book of Proverbs as "the foundation of the universe." Though he believed the wealth of the world exists because sometimes the *Zaddik* may find comfort in it, nevertheless the Master always urged that a man rely upon his own personal efforts to secure moral improvement. The verse (Psalms 52:13), "Also unto Thee, O Lord, belongeth mercy; for Thou renderest to every man according to his work," was applied by the Besht to teach that God makes it possible for man to perform good deeds. "Man's work is of slight merit, yet He rewards man as if he achieved it by his own unaided efforts."

In similar vein the Master taught:

> The lion became enraged at his subjects, the animals of the forest. They asked the fox to placate the king of beasts by relating to him an appropriate fable. The fox replied, however, that fear had caused him to forget his fables. Hence the beasts were compelled to wait on the lion themselves. In the same fashion, on the Awesome Days, the people of the congregation should not depend upon their rabbi to pray in their behalf. Each man should do so by and for himself.

The Legacy of Hasidism

The Besht's message has been transmitted not by his own writings but by those of his disciples and their followers. Though the Master's activity covered a period of more than twenty-five years, his literary work consists of only a few letters. He did not write down his doctrines, but communicated them by word of mouth to his pupils and friends. He was accustomed to write special prayers which are preserved in a *Siddur*, regarded as a veritable Holy Gospel by the Besht's followers. In recent years scholars have occupied themselves with a new Genizah or "hidden collection" of the letters of the Besht and his disciples. Many of these letters are palpable falsifications, and though considerable effort has been expended to distinguish the authentic from the apocryphal material, the reliability of some of the documents has not yet been determined.

The *Shivhei ha-Besht*, namely "The Legends (Praises) of the Baal Shem Tov," was published in Kopyss in 1815 by Israel Joffe; in the same year another edition appeared in Berditschev under the name of the author, Dov Baer ben R. Samuel, *shohet* of the community in Linetz, and son-in-law of the Besht's secretary, Alexander. This is regarded by the *Hasidim* as a holy book, the teachings of which bring healing to the body and soul. A considerable number of similar works, intended for distribution among the masses, finally moulded the personality and work of the Besht into a monumental entity, based partly on truth, but chiefly on psychologically correct legends.

The *Hasidic* movement, evolving in many forms and tendencies, gained immense popularity, in spite of the hostility of the *Mitnagdim* or the "Opponents." During the nineteenth century, it crystallized into a distinctive system and became institutionalized. Unfortunately, the veneration shown the *Zaddikim* in their respective communities and areas of influence encouraged the very ostentation and pride which the Master had opposed. Some of them became selfish potentates, and their gullible adherents only encouraged their regrettable ways.*

The Nazi catastrophe during World War II resulted in the annihilation of communities where *Hasidism* had flourished. But a few *Zaddikim* with some of their followers found refuge outside of Eastern Europe, including the United States.

In recent years, as a consequence of the activity of Chaim Bloch, Martin Buber, Simon Dubnow, S. A. Horodetzky and others in Europe; and of Jacob S. Minkin, Maurice S. Friedman and others in the United States, *Hasidic* literature has enjoyed an extensive vogue. There is a close affinity between the direct, simple approach of *Hasidism* and the ideals of modern Judaism as expressed in the United States. The parables, folk-tales and biblical interpretations of the Besht and his disciples have proved helpful to contemporary preachers, both Jewish and Christian. The literature on *Hasidism* is steadily increasing, and the contemporary world seems to be discovering in the teachings of the Besht and his disciples a warmth, an enthusiasm, and a vitality which the ultra-rationalistic philosophic and religious systems are believed to lack.

The legacy of the Besht for the modern world cannot be easily appraised. Without doubt, his reliance upon seemingly magical methods of healing, while deserving of study by persons interested in the power of mind over body, cannot be approved by the advocates of medicine, surgery, and psychiatry. We must go beyond this phase of the Besht's activity, and understand him in the role he sought most to fulfill, namely, that of an ethical and religious teacher and mentor. The concern of searching men and women today for an interpretation of the universe and of

* I. J. Singer in *Yoshe Kalb* has presented a vivid picture of the *Zaddik* who tended to give *Hasidism* a negative reputation in many quarters of Jewish life.

society in terms of "dialogue," of a close relationship to God, leads them, as it has Martin Buber, to a preoccupation with *Hasidism* and with the Besht, its progenitor and supreme exponent.

6 . *Moses Mendelssohn*

[1729-1786]

ALFRED JOSPE

ONE day in 1743, a weak and deformed boy of fourteen knocked at one of the gates leading into the city of Berlin, the capital of the Kingdom of Prussia. A Jewish watchman, whose special task it was to screen every Jew seeking admission and to turn away all arriving without means of support, harshly questioned the pale and crippled boy, who managed to tell him stammeringly that he was from Dessau and that he had come to enroll in the Talmudic Academy of the renowned rabbi of Berlin, David Fränkel.

Eventually the boy was admitted. He was Moses Mendelssohn. That knock at the Rosenthaler Gate, the only gate through which Jews could enter Berlin, was one of the dramatic turning points in Jewish history. It signaled the entry of Judaism into the modern world. Today the train trip from Dessau to Berlin takes two hours. In Mendelssohn's time, the trip required several days on foot. But in Jewish history, it represented a journey across several centuries—from the Jewish Middle Ages to modernity. Mendelssohn was the bridge that led from the ghetto to Europe.

Mendelssohn's greatness lies in the perception and boldness with which he set two tasks for himself. He wanted to end the cultural isolation and backwardness of the medieval ghetto and make the culture of the world acceptable to the Jew. And he wanted to make Jews acceptable to Christians as their fellow citizens. He wanted to bring about nothing less than the inner liberation of Jews through cultural enlightenment and their outer liberation through civil emancipation.

Mendelssohn was a fascinating and colorful man. Small, homely, humpbacked, afflicted with a slight stammer, he managed to gain acclaim for the charm of his language, the elegance of his style, the clarity of his thought. A timid and retiring person, he found himself in the forefront of numerous controversies and battles to win respect and recognition for Jews and Judaism. Though not a brilliant philosopher, he became one of the fashionable thinkers of his time. He was no profound theologian yet was the first to define the crucial question which has confronted the modern Jew ever since the Emancipation: how to harmonize Jewish tradition with contemporary thought? How to reconcile the supernaturalism of an ancient faith with the demands of reason and modern science?

Nor was he the first to advocate enlightenment for Jews. Long before Mendelssohn's time there had been Jewish physicians, scientists, writers, musicians who had played distinguished roles in the general European culture. Jewish diplomats and financiers had enjoyed great prestige and influence. Moses Luzzatto, a sensitive intellect in Italy, wrote poems and plays on secular themes in masterful Hebrew. Azariah de Rossi first applied the principles of modern historiography to the study of the traditional texts of Judaism. Individual Jews had achieved prominence in the culture of the world long before Mendelssohn's time. But Mendelssohn was the first to make a deliberate effort not to acquire European culture solely for himself but also to bring enlightenment and modern culture to his fellow Jews. Though the emancipation of the German Jews was not the achievement of any single man, Mendelssohn became the key figure in the struggle to tear down the intellectual, social, and cultural barriers separating Jews from the outside world and to prepare the way toward their civic and cultural equality.

Early Years in Dessau

Mendelssohn was born in Dessau, capital of the German state of Anhalt, on September 6, 1729. Throughout his life, he was known to his fellow Jews as Moses Dessau. He himself preferred the name of Mendelssohn, which was derived from the name of his father, Menachem Mendel, who earned a precarious living as a *sofer*, a scribe of Torah scrolls and other Hebrew documents. Before his sixth year, Moses was enrolled in the *heder*, the traditional Jewish elementary school of the time. The story is told that his father, anxious not to have his son miss a single lesson, wrapped the boy in an old coat on winter mornings and carried him through the darkness and cold to the *heder*. Moses soon showed such brilliance in his study of the traditional Hebrew texts that he attracted the attention of the rabbi of Dessau, David Fränkel, the author of a well-known commentary on the Jerusalem Talmud. Under Rabbi Fränkel's guidance, the boy continued his studies of Bible and Talmud; he became an accomplished Hebraist and by the age of thirteen was working in material far beyond his years. He had discovered the world of medieval Jewish philosophy and was entranced by it, especially by Maimonides' *Moreh Nevukhim* (*Guide for the Perplexed*).

The World of German Jewry

In 1743, when Fränkel accepted a call to become rabbi of the Jewish community of Berlin, Mendelssohn, then fourteen years old, followed his teacher. In Berlin Mendelssohn entered a different world, a world of strange contrasts. The capital of Prussia was a different place from the small provincial ghetto in which he had been born. Jews had lived in the province of Brandenburg since 1247, and in Berlin, its largest city, since 1295. Since then, Jewish life had been a tragic seesaw of flight and return. Expelled from Brandenburg in 1446, Jews were readmitted in 1509, driven out again in 1573, this time "for eternity." But soon they reappeared, and in 1650 the Great Elector legalized their residence in a decree permitting Jews to engage in trade and commerce for seven years. Twenty years later, another edict brought additional Jewish settlers; fifty of the wealthiest families of Austrian Jewry, who had been expelled by the Austrian empress, received permission to settle in Berlin provided they brought their wealth along and invested it in the country's commerce.

But the number of these privileged Jews was small. The

Jewish masses were still subject to medieval limitations and restrictions. Some of them were self-imposed. The ghetto knew no modern language. People spoke a dialect akin to the Yiddish of Eastern Europe. The standards of Jewish learning had declined sharply. There was no native rabbinical leadership; spiritual leaders and teachers had to be imported from the Talmudic academies of the East. The rabbis, fearful that knowledge of even the superficial aspects of German culture would weaken the loyalty of their congregants, discouraged the use of the German language. It was a serious offense to read a German book. Mendelssohn himself tells how the Jewish communal authorities made short shrift with a boy whom he had asked to get a German book for him; when caught carrying (not reading!) it, the boy was expelled from Berlin.

Other restrictions were imposed from without. The walls of the ghetto were still standing, and few Jews could escape. Freedom of movement was severely restricted since many localities excluded or expelled Jews altogether. Where they were allowed to live, their rights of residence were sharply circumscribed. A few wealthy Jews were able to attain the status of "*Schutzjuden*" (privileged Jews); they had the right of domicile in the cities of Prussia. But this right was transferable only to the eldest son in each family. Other children were merely "tolerated" and had to seek new homes as they came of age. People often were desperately poor, restricted in their occupations, burdened with heavy taxes, packed together in overcrowded quarters, and not even allowed to marry except by permission of the government.

There was little Jews themselves could do to find release from their legal disabilities. But many, rebellious against the burdens of the ghetto, were anxious to improve their condition. Their hopes for freedom were encouraged by the changing patterns of German society and thought.

A wealthy upper class was beginning to emerge within German Jewry, especially in Berlin. The status of the Jew improved in direct relationship to his wealth (money has always been the great equalizer). In spite of the economic restrictions to which Jews were subjected, a handful of Jews succeeded in rising to positions of wealth and influence in commerce and industry—as contractors, purveyors, bankers, court agents. Their prosperity opened doors heretofore barred by bigotry. They had attractive, often luxurious homes. They spoke German, not Yiddish; they had social contact with Gentiles, sent their children to German schools, read the fashionable novels, became patrons of art and literature, went to concerts, frequented the theater. In 1779, a visitor to Berlin reported that on Saturday nights most orchestra seats in the theaters were occupied by Jews.

As the wealthy Jew moved from the ghetto into the world, however, he became more and more attracted by the host culture. He discovered that Jewish life had little of that beauty, art, and worldly sophistication that made Gentile civilization graceful and attractive. The Jewish religion involved a body of beliefs which seemed outmoded or contrary to reason; and Jewish religious law expected the individual to practice a daily regimen of rituals and customs which were inconvenient and set him apart from his fellow citizens.

It was inevitable that the Jew should begin to ask questions. If the world refused to complete the process of liberation, could it be that the fault was with the Jew himself? The Jew had to earn his self-emancipation through his enlightenment. As long as he insisted on being different, on maintaining certain habits which were strange and inexplicable to the Gentile world, had he a right to expect full acceptance?

The temptation to break with the past was therefore great. In order to win the approval of the Gentile world and clear the way for securing equal rights, some Jews began to feel that they had to "modernize" Judaism—or even forsake it altogether so that they could no longer be distinguished from their Gentile neighbors.

A second factor which nourished the rebellion of many sensitive young Jews against the limitations of the ghetto was the spirit of rationalism permeating the thought and literature of the time. Kant had defined rationalism by admonishing his contemporaries, "*Sapere aude*"—"dare to use your reason." Reason was the supreme judge and arbiter of all human affairs. The churches and their doctrines were boldly criticized, and French critics like Voltaire and d'Holbach went so far as to assert that religion was ignorance and illogical stupidity; that worship was weakness and self-delusion; and that the earth would come into its own only when heaven was destroyed. These were extreme views. Other thinkers retained a belief in a universal God but they, too, maintained that man's reason was the ultimate test of what was true and good; that the laws governing man had not been made by God but by man himself; that the essential purpose of human institutions and social arrangements was to promote the welfare and happiness of all men regardless of nationality and creed; and that only ignorance, which would soon be overcome, barred mankind from achieving utopia on earth.

These new ideas penetrated even the walls of the ghetto. The insistence of the Enlightenment on the use of reason, its demand for freedom and the equality of all people, its rejection of dogma, and its belief in progress found a ready response. Jews could not anticipate that this rationalism would eventually threaten to undermine the very foundations of their existence as they had known it. The keystone of Jewish tradition had been faith in God as the creator of the universe, the source of all life, the giver of all law, the center of authority and meaning. How could this faith be reconciled with the demands of reason? What would happen if the keystone were removed? Was there anything else that could take its place?

Study in Berlin

These were the ideas and problems that agitated the world which Mendelssohn entered on his arrival in Berlin. Without funds or the right of domicile, he found a place to live in the garret of a Jewish merchant and managed to earn a meager living by copying letters for his landlord. He enrolled in Rabbi Fränkel's academy, but his thirst for knowledge was no longer satisfied with study of the Talmud. There were other fields he wanted to explore. He studied the German language and mastered it in a short time. He read voraciously. He was aware that it was a break with tradition and a violation of his religious duties when he, who had been brought up solely on the Hebrew language and its literature, read a German book.

But Mendelssohn would not turn back. One of the first German books which fell into his hand was a volume on the early history of Protestantism—which opened a new world for him. Until then, he had not had the slightest notion of the existence of a Christian theology or of a philosophy which went beyond Maimonides. He was even more impressed by Locke's famous essay "Concerning Human Understanding," which he read in Latin. Its common sense and insistence on reasonableness in all things influenced him deeply.

Mendelssohn sought more knowledge, extending his studies into other fields. A brilliant Polish Jew, Israel Zamoscz, taught him the fundamentals of mathematics and introduced him to Euclidean geometry. Abraham Kisch, a Jewish physician who had come to Berlin from Prague, taught him Latin and encouraged him to take up French and English on his own. Another doctor, Aaron Gumpertz, member of a prominent Berlin family who had received a medical degree from the University of Frankfurt (Oder) (an unprecedented achievement for a Jew at that time), introduced Mendelssohn to the world of the great contemporary philosophers, especially Leibnitz and Christian Wolff.

Mendelssohn's poverty was great; often he could not afford the books he wanted to read. At times, his only food for days was bread. But he did not allow hardships to deter him from his studies, and he made rapid progress.

When he was about twenty, Mendelssohn left Fränkel's academy. In order to support himself he accepted a position in the home of a silk manufacturer, Isaac Bernhard, a "privileged" Jew, whose children he tutored in Hebrew and mathematics. A few years later he became head bookkeeper and finally a partner in Bernhard's firm. This association gave Mendelssohn security and some of the leisure which he needed for his studies. During the day he was a businessman; in the evening he dwelled in the world of ideas.

Mendelssohn and Lessing

Mendelssohn's first impulse to write came from the brilliant German critic and dramatist, Gotthold Ephraim Lessing. The two men met during the course of a chess game at the home of a friend one afternoon in 1754. Lessing was immensely impressed by the young Jew. Though only a few months older than Mendelssohn, he himself was already well known in the German literary world. A few years earlier, he had written a drama *Die*

Juden (*The Jews*), in which he had pilloried the bigotry and ignorance of the Christian world vis-à-vis the Jew, whom he had idealized as a man of integrity, selflessness, and nobility of character. Lessing was delighted to discover in Mendelssohn a Jew who personified the virtues with which he had endowed the hero of his play—his brilliant intellect, his moral integrity and questing for truth, his modesty and gentleness, his love for people. In a letter to the friend who had brought them together Lessing wrote that he saw in Mendelssohn "a second Spinoza lacking only his errors to be his equal," and he described his excitement about having met "a real Jew . . . who will bring great honor to his people provided his fellow Jews, who have always liked to persecute people of his kind, will allow him to develop his talents and personality fully."

Mendelssohn, on his part, found in Lessing a kindred spirit, a man whom he could admire as much for his brilliant style of writing and mastery of German literature as for his liberal convictions and courageous defense of freedom of thought and of a persecuted people. The two men became close friends; Mendelssohn inspired Lessing's portrait of the Jew in his most important play, *Nathan the Wise*, a powerful plea for religious tolerance. Their friendship ended only with Lessing's death in 1781.

Literary Success

Under Lessing's influence, Mendelssohn turned to the study of German literature and literary criticism. He worked hard to improve his mastery of the German language, and rapidly learned to use the vernacular with a facility which made him a leading figure on the German literary scene. His first German essay was a vigorous defense of Lessing's drama *The Jews* against an attack by a professor of theology, Johann David Michaelis, who had asserted that Lessing's hero, who combined integrity with nobility of spirit, could not be true to life. Passionately, Mendelssohn expressed his anguish. "Is it not enough that we must suffer the cruel hatred of the Christian world in countless ways? Must calumny and slander be added and our character be defamed in order to justify the injustices committed against us?"

Other writings followed in rapid succession. Mendelssohn's

interests covered many fields. He wrote a philosophic essay, *Philosophische Gespräche* (Philosophic Discourses), which Lessing arranged to have printed without Mendelssohn's knowledge as a surprise for his friend. Collaborating with Lessing, he also published a study on the English poet Alexander Pope.

His works impressed the literary world even more by the gracefulness of his style than by the lucidity of his arguments. It was something extraordinary that a Jew should be able to master the German language as completely and write as beautifully as Mendelssohn did. His literary contributions were eagerly sought. When the scholarly publisher Friedrich Nicolai founded a journal for studies in literature and the arts, Mendelssohn became a contributor and published numerous essays on the philosophy of beauty and principles of esthetics. He again collaborated with Lessing in the publication of the *Literatur Briefe*, devoted chiefly to literary criticism. Nor did he neglect his first love, philosophy; in 1767 he won the prize of the Prussian Academy for an essay on the *Evidenz der metaphysischen Wissenschaften,* in which he attempted to show that metaphysical truths (i.e., truths proclaimed by religion) were not contrary to reason and could be proved as logically as the tenets of science. His thesis has long been outdated but his achievement was spectacular in view of the fact that one of the other contestants was the future "king" of German philosophy, Immanuel Kant.

Mendelssohn's essay was published by the Academy and translated into Latin and French. He thus became a figure of national fame and stature and was ranked as one of the leading minds and writers of Germany. About that time, he married Fromet Guggenheim of Hamburg, and their home soon became a meeting place for writers, artists, and thinkers.

Mendelssohn's success, however, did not protect him against the indignities to which Jews were exposed at that time. On a trip to Dresden, he could not enter the city until he had paid a head tax levied upon Jews and cattle. When he took an evening walk with his wife and children in Berlin, Gentile boys would yell "Jew" and even throw stones at them. As an "immigrant" from Dessau, he was permitted to live in Berlin only because he was employed by a "*Schutzjude*," and could be expelled at any time. The uncertainty of his residence status was finally ended through the effort of the Marquis d'Argens, one of his admirers at the court of Frederick the Great. The Marquis supported Mendelssohn's application for the privilege of permanent residence with the laconic comment, "A philosopher who is a bad Catholic begs a philosopher who is a bad Protestant to grant the privilege to a philosopher who is a bad Jew. There is too much philosophy in all this for justice not to be on the side of this application." Though Mendelssohn was anything but a "bad" Jew, the adroit phrase was effective. Mendelssohn received his permit as "*Schutzjude*" though only for himself; it could not be transferred to his children. Later, when his name was proposed for membership in the Berlin Academy of Sciences, the king vetoed the proposal; Queen Catherine of Russia also was a candidate and Frederick did not want to offend her by having her name on a membership list which included the name of a Jew.

For the indignities which he had to sustain, Mendelssohn found compensation in his work and in the recognition he won among the intellectual elite. He reached the height of his fame and popularity with the publication of his *Phädon*, which, modeled on Plato's famous dialogue *Phaedo*, defended the belief in the immortality of the soul against the skeptics of the time.

Mendelssohn felt there were compelling proofs for the immortality of the soul. Like Leibnitz before him, he thought that existing things which perish do not pass into nothingness but are only dissolved into their elements. The soul, according to Mendelssohn, is a perfectly simple substance. It has no elements into which it can dissolve. Hence it must be imperishable. But there was another, even more forceful reason. God had implanted in man the idea that his soul was immortal. How could it be compatible with the goodness and justice of God to suppose that such an idea was deceptive? "I feel I cannot reject the notion of the immortality of the soul without destroying my faith in everything I have always believed to be true and good. If our souls were mortal, then reason would be a dream . . . we would be like animals destined only to seek food and perish."

The book seemed to meet a need of the time and was immediately successful. Reprinted a number of times and translated into several languages, it was widely read throughout Europe. Its author was called the "Jewish Plato," whose home was a mecca for many visitors to the Prussian capital.

Yet in spite of the success of his works, Mendelssohn influenced his time far more by the impact of his personality than by his contributions to German philosophy and literature. His *Phädon* was outdated a mere twenty years after it had appeared. Though Mendelssohn has a place in the history of philosophy, he was overshadowed by Kant, Fichte, Hegel, and other thinkers who followed him. Nevertheless, the influence of the "Jewish philosopher" was exceptional. The world was intrigued by this man who was a loyal and strictly observant Jew and yet at the same time a leading citizen of the world of European culture. The public admired his personality which combined in a unique way a capacity to think clearly with a keen sensitivity to beauty and a deep-grained integrity in personal conduct.

Controversy with Lavater

Mendelssohn had always carried his Jewishness with dignity and had openly associated himself with the life of his people. He felt keenly about the continuing indignities of Jewish life. But he still felt that his own experiences and success showed the best way to improve the condition of the Jews: not by pleading with the mighty but by winning their respect through distinguished acts and the acquisition of German culture and refinement. In a letter to Herz Homberg he wrote, "There must arise among us more and more men who without noise should come to the front and perform valuable services to humanity. Recognition to our people will then follow."

Mendelssohn might not have changed his thinking and might have made no contribution to Judaism had he not been challenged by a Christian admirer, who regretted that Mendelssohn was not a Christian and was eager to convert him. Johann Kasper Lavater, a Swiss preacher, had visited Mendelssohn several times to discuss religious questions with him. In 1769, he translated a French book by Charles Bonnet of Geneva into German and published it under the title, *An Examination of the Proofs for Christianity*. Lavater dedicated the translation to Mendelssohn and in his preface challenged him either to refute

Bonnet's arguments or to do "what truth and honesty demanded and what a Socrates would have done had he read the book and found it irrefutable"—abandon his religion and accept Christianity.

Mendelssohn hated controversy of any kind and was reluctant to be drawn into a public dispute about the comparative merits of Judaism and Christianity. He did not want to give offense to Christians but felt he would be accused of fear or evasiveness if he let this challenge to his religion and personal faith go unanswered. He responded in a letter in which he defended his loyalty to Judaism tactfully but forcefully. "I cannot see what could possibly have kept me tied to so severe and generally despised a religion if in my heart I had not been convinced of its truth. If I ever became convinced that my religion was not the true one I would feel compelled to leave it. . . . And if I were indifferent to my religion, what could have prevented me from changing it in order to better myself? Fear of my fellow Jews? Certainly not. Their power is nil. Stubbornness? Inertia? A blind clinging to tradition? I have spent part of my life in the study of my religion and hope no one expects that such personal foibles would make me surrender the results of my studies."

Mendelssohn frankly conceded that his religion was not free of certain human additions and abuses. But he was firmly convinced of the irrefutable truth and superiority of Judaism as a religion. Rebuking Lavater for his ill-considered zeal, he pointed out that Judaism was tolerant of the convictions of others; it had never sent out missionaries to make converts; and, unlike Christianity, Judaism maintained that even the unbeliever was in God's care and could attain salvation if he was a man of moral stature.

In Defense of Jewish Rights

Mendelssohn's answer was effective and brought a letter of apology from Lavater. But the incident convinced him of the need to devote more time and energy to the welfare of his people. Having become the leading Jewish personality in Europe, he was looked upon as the man to whom other Jews in need or danger could turn for aid. Opportunities for action were not lacking. The first appeal came from the Swiss villages of Endingen and Lenglau, where the authorities had denied Jews the right to marry; Mendelssohn was urged to persuade Lavater to intervene on their behalf. Distasteful as it was to resume his contact with Lavater, Mendelssohn complied with the request, and the ban was eventually rescinded. Through his friendship with Von Ferber, the privy councillor of Saxony, he was also able to secure the withdrawal of an order directing the expulsion of hundreds of Jews from Dresden. Upon the request of the Chief Rabbi of Berlin, he compiled a compendium of all Jewish laws concerning marriage, wills, and inheritance for the use of the Royal Ministry of Justice; and he drafted a new oath for use in the courts which replaced a medieval Yiddish oath whose language and content he found degrading to his coreligionists.

Mendelssohn was soon drawn into other battles for Jewish rights. In 1779, the Jews of Alsace were viciously attacked in a pamphlet written by a French judge. The leaders of the Jewish communities, wanting to appeal to the French government for relief from their intolerable conditions, turned to Mendelssohn to draft an appropriate petition. Not wanting to undertake the task himself, he persuaded Christian Wilhelm Dohm, a young publicist and liberal spirit, to undertake the defense of Alsatian Jewry. In response to Mendelssohn's request Dohm wrote the first systematic argument by a non-Jew in favor of Jewish emancipation, *Über die bürgerliche Verbesserung der Juden* (Concerning the Civil Amelioration of the Jews, 1781). Dealing with the position of Jews not only in Alsace but throughout Germany, Dohm pointed out that they possessed all the necessary qualifications for citizenship. His recommendation was that Jews should be granted civic rights ("*bürgerliche Rechte*") rather than citizenship rights ("*Bürgerrechte*"). They were not to hold public office or engage in political affairs, but to retain their own communal autonomy under government supervision, including the right to discipline recalcitrant members of the community and to maintain their own rabbinical courts for the disposal of civil cases in which both litigants were Jews.

Dohm's plea did not have immediate practical results but it placed the question of Jewish rights into the center of public discussion. Numerous statements were published in the press, some supporting Dohm, and others opposing and attacking his views. It was clear that a centuries-old tradition of prejudice could not be silenced by a single courageous voice. Additional efforts were needed, and Mendelssohn induced another friend, the physician Marcus Herz, to publish a German translation of *Vindiciae Judaeorum*, by Menasseh ben Israel, a seventeenth-century Amsterdam rabbi, whose defense of the Jews addressed to Oliver Cromwell in 1656 had helped to persuade that ruler to readmit Jews to England.

This time Mendelssohn did not hesitate to become personally involved. He wrote an extensive introduction to the translation. He wanted to add his voice to that of Dohm and press home the attack against bigotry. But he also wanted to correct certain views of Dohm which, while well-intentioned, had been misconceived. His impression was that Dohm himself was not wholly free from prejudice as revealed, for example, in his expressed view that Jews were not yet ready to receive the full rights of citizenship. Mendelssohn was also critical of Dohm's proposal that the Jewish community should have the right to punish members for religious infractions or dissent. This proposal was incompatible with Mendelssohn's concept of religious freedom. In his view, pure religion should not be coercive. Jews should be as free to believe and act as Christians were. Nothing less than complete freedom of conscience and equality was acceptable to Mendelssohn.

Mendelssohn, in a passionate dissent, put the responsibility where he felt it belonged: upon the prejudices and cruelty of the world. He showed how bigotry changed its face in every century. In the Middle Ages the Jews had been accused of using blood, desecrating the host, or poisoning wells. In Mendelssohn's time, Jews were accused of having an aversion to manual labor, an antipathy to science and culture, a preference for trade, a concern for money. "People continue to keep us away from all contacts with the arts and sciences or with trades and occupations which are useful and have dignity. They bar all roads leading to increased usefulness and then use our lack of culture to justify our continued oppression. They tie our hands and then reproach us that we do not use them. . . ."

Quest for Inner Renewal

Mendelssohn's plea was a moving appeal to the conscience of the world for Jewish dignity and human rights. But he knew that more than the liberation of the Jew from the political and civic restrictions of ghetto life was needed if the barriers which separated him from the non-Jew were to be demolished. The acquisition of external freedom had to be accompanied by renewal from within; political emancipation had to be accompanied by cultural emancipation. The world had to revise its attitude toward the Jew; but the Jew, too, had to change his attitude toward the world. For centuries, he had cut himself off deliberately, had isolated himself from the world not only in speech and dress, habits and manners, but also in cultural affairs. When he read, he confined himself to stories of rabbinic lore, pious legends designed to instruct or edify, or tales springing from the fertile imagination of the *Kabbalists*. When he studied, he concentrated his intellectual energies on the clarification of some intricate and often obscure Talmudic passage and neglected the Bible. The thought and culture of the world were rejected. Mendelssohn felt that intellectually the Jew still lived in the Middle Ages while the world had progressed. But he was confident that the cultural and spiritual level of German Jews would be raised if the treasures of German thought and literature could be opened to them. The first step was to teach them German. And the best way to teach them German was through a German translation of the Bible.

Mendelssohn had already started a translation in order to prepare a textbook for the instruction of his son. The boy was not sufficiently fluent in Hebrew, and Mendelssohn taught him the Bible in German in order to make it easier for him to understand the text and the nuances of the Hebrew language. Solomon Dubno, a Polish Hebraist whom he had engaged to teach Hebrew grammar to his son, urged Mendelssohn to have that translation published so that other children could also profit from his efforts. Dubno's suggestion coincided with Mendelssohn's own thinking. He disliked intensely Yiddish, which was still the vernacular in the ghettos of Germany. He knew the doors to German culture would never open to the Jewish masses unless the barrier of language was torn down. And he hoped that the introduction of Jews to German language and culture would secure for them as a group the same welcome and acceptance which he had received as an individual.

Translation of the Bible

In 1778 he issued a prospectus in order to solicit subscriptions for the Bible translation which he called *Alim li Terufah* (Healing Leaves), a title which referred to the need for healing the cultural ills of German Jewry. The first volume, Genesis, came off the press in 1780, the others following rapidly. The translation, in beautiful German prose, was printed in Hebrew letters, with which Jewish readers were more familiar; each volume contained not only the German text but also a commentary called *Biur*, designed to provide a better understanding of the text. This translation was entirely Mendelssohn's work as were the Hebrew introduction and commentaries on the first part of Genesis and the entire Book of Exodus. Dubno completed the commentary on Genesis, supplied extensive notes on the rules and use of Biblical Hebrew, and supervised, at least initially, the publication of the work as a whole. Other friends and associates also helped. Naftali Herz Wessely wrote the commentary on Leviticus, and Aaron Friedenthal and Herz Homberg composed those on Numbers and Deuteronomy, while Mendelssohn himself prepared the comments on the poetic portions of Deuteronomy.

The impact of the translation was enormous. Orders were received from all parts of Europe. Well-known rabbis welcomed and endorsed the work, among them the famous Gaon of Vilna. Herschel Levin, Chief Rabbi of Berlin, expressed the hope that the translation would achieve what Mendelssohn had set out to do—namely, put an end to the ignorance of German Jewry. Some outstanding spokesmen of traditional Judaism, however, objected to the translation precisely because they were fearful that Mendelssohn's plan would succeed and that a knowledge of German would tempt Jewish youth to neglect their Jewish studies for the pursuit of secular interests. Three leading rabbis issued a ban against the book and threatened to excommunicate those who read it. In some communities, the book was burned publicly as a gesture of protest and warning. But Mendelssohn was able to silence the opposition, especially that of its leading member, Rabbi Raphael Kohn of Altona, by a subtle strategy. Through the intervention of his friend, Councillor von Henning of Copenhagen, he obtained subscriptions for the translation from the King and the Crown Prince of Denmark and other leading personalities. Since Altona belonged to Denmark at that time, Rabbi Kohn's hands were tied: he could take no action against a book that had found the approval of the rulers of the country.

The work, completed in 1783, caused a cultural revolution among German Jews. It provided the bridge on which they could pass from the ghetto to Europe; it ended their use of Yiddish, introduced them to the German language, and gave them the key to the world of literature, science, and philosophy from which they had been cut off until then. The commentary gave them new understanding and appreciation of the grammatical structure of the Hebrew language.

Gradually, the entire structure and control of Jewish education were changed under the impact of the translation. Mendelssohn persuaded some friends to establish a school for Jewish children in Berlin which soon became a model for others. German replaced Yiddish as the language of instruction, and secular subjects supplemented the traditional Jewish studies. Religious instruction included not only the reading of Hebrew texts but also study of the principles of Judaism. In addition, boys received vocational guidance and training, especially in manual occupations.

The influence of Mendelssohn's translation went beyond the borders of Germany. It gave Russian and Polish Jews who read German a new insight into the literary and linguistic structure of the Bible, and the graceful Hebrew of the *Biur* was one of the forces that contributed to the renaissance of Hebrew, the language in which Jews of Eastern Europe pursued enlightenment and sought to acquire the culture of the world. Mendelssohn also encouraged Wessely and other scholars to found a

Hebrew journal, *Ha-Measseph* (The Gatherer), which published articles on religious and secular subjects in order to bring the best fruits of contemporary thought and culture to its readers.

Jerusalem

While Mendelssohn was still occupied with his translation, he could not withdraw completely from the discussions and controversies which his preface to Herz's translation of the *Vindiciae Judaeorum* had started. His views were harshly questioned in numerous handbills and pamphlets. Some opponents flatly rejected his appeal for civic freedom on behalf of Jews. Germany was a Christian state; the state and the church were coextensive; Christianity was the established religion, and only those who were church members were eligible for citizenship in the Christian state. Others attacked Mendelssohn's view that a man's religion was his personal affair and that no religious authority should be permitted to punish or exclude dissenters. But neither the Christian nor the Jewish authorities were prepared to accept Mendelssohn's reasoning and give up their disciplinary powers, especially the weapon of excommunication. Mendelssohn's views were challenged by a number of writers, one of whom published an anonymous letter under the title "*Das Forschen nach Licht und Recht*" (The Search for Light and Right), in which he argued that Mendelssohn either was a hypocrite or had discarded Judaism. He pointed out that the Jewish religion as laid down in the Torah possessed an elaborate system of rewards and punishments to compel obedience to its laws. How then could Mendelssohn seriously advocate that a man's religion should be his private concern and that the use of religious compulsion be banished? Either his proposal was untenable or he was no longer a real Jew.

Mendelssohn realized that he could not remain silent in the face of these public challenges. He presented his views in a small work which he published in 1783 under the title *Jerusalem, or Religious Power and Judaism.*

Jerusalem consisted of two parts. The first was a powerful restatement of his convictions on freedom of conscience and a fervent plea for religious tolerance. Mendelssohn knew that

Jews could not hope to be admitted to citizenship in a "Christian" state and that genuine freedom of conscience was impossible. Therefore, nearly a hundred years ahead of his time in Europe, he pleaded for the separation of state and church. In broad philosophical terms, he defined and delineated their respective spheres of competence. In sharp contrast to the theories underlying the concept of the Christian state, he showed that their functions and rights were not identical but essentially different. The state governs the relationships between man and man, and therefore has the right to control or regulate the actions of its citizens. It can compel them to obey the law and punish them for infractions even though they may disagree with the wisdom or fairness of the law itself. But the state cannot control or regulate the ideas or convictions of its citizens, and must not be allowed to favor one religion over another or to require its citizens to hold particular beliefs as a condition of citizenship.

The church, on the other hand, is concerned with man's relationship with his God, his faith and thoughts, his beliefs and convictions. But a man's thoughts are free. This was Mendelssohn's personal credo and the heart of his argument. A man's beliefs are his personal affair; he has a right to defy any attempt on the part of state or church to control his thoughts or convictions. The state may force a person to act in a certain way, but not even the church can force him to think or believe in a certain way. The church has the right and, in fact, the duty to seek to influence his ideas by instruction and persuasion. But this is where its power ends. It can neither control his actions, impose its beliefs upon him, nor punish him if he disbelieves. The only judge of man's convictions is reason, and the only yardstick of a man's worth is his actions. "Observe what men do or fail to do, and judge them by their actions. . . . Don't reward or punish them in accordance with their thoughts! Let every man who does not disturb the public welfare, who obeys the law, who acts righteously toward his fellow men, be allowed to speak as he thinks, to pray to God after his own fashion or after the fashion of his fathers, and to seek his eternal salvation where he thinks he can find it."

But were these views of Mendelssohn compatible with the teachings of Judaism? Did not Judaism reject the freedom of conscience which the German philosopher advocated? Were his critics right when they implied that he had broken away from the faith of his fathers?

Mendelssohn used the second part of *Jerusalem* to defend himself against the charge of insincerity and to counter the challenge to his Jewishness by presenting his concept and philosophy of Judaism. First he defined what he meant by religion. Like the rationalists of his time he held that no belief was valid if it was contrary to reason. Reason was the medium through which man could discover what he needed to know in order to achieve happiness on earth. Mendelssohn did not recognize any truth or eternal verities except those which could be comprehended by man's intellect and verified by it.

For Mendelssohn, Judaism was the ideal religion precisely because its basic principles were in harmony with the demands of reason. Unlike Christianity, Judaism had no dogmas which were contrary to reason, no doctrines in which the faithful had to believe in order to attain salvation, no mysteries which men had to accept on faith but could not understand. Judaism offered complete freedom of thought. There were no binding articles of faith choking independent thought. No one was asked to believe what his reason was compelled to reject. Judaism was not concerned with what a man believed; its stress was on what he did and how he acted. According to Mendelssohn's definition, Judaism was not revealed religion; it was revealed law. "Among all the laws and commandments of Moses, there is none saying, 'Thou shalt believe' or 'thou shalt not believe.' They all say, 'Thou shalt do' or 'thou shalt not do.' " Judaism did not address itself to a man's mind and tax his credulity. It addressed itself to his will. It sought to influence and guide his daily actions but did not seek to control his thoughts.

Distinction between Religion and Law

Mendelssohn's distinction between "religion" and "law" is crucial to the understanding of his philosophy. To him, Judaism actually was not a religion in the strict sense of the word at all. What were considered its religious tenets—its belief in the existence and unity of God, His providence, and the immortality of the soul—were not specifically Jewish notions. These teachings were the principles of Deism, the general religion of reason. They were self-evident to reason and required no proof, no mysterious supernatural act of revelation in order to be intelligible to men of reason everywhere. Judaism had not discovered them. Reason had. Judaism merely reaffirmed them.

What was specifically Jewish and distinguished the Jew from the non-Jew was not his religion, those general teachings which were the common property of all men of reason, but rather the unique "laws" and commandments which had been revealed at Sinai. These were valid only for the Jewish people. Their purpose was to distinguish the Jew from the non-Jew, to guide his moral and spiritual conduct, to teach him the acts which were conducive to human happiness, to stimulate his imagination and make him ponder man's nature and destiny in God's world. Above all, the commandments enabled Jews to maintain their identity and integrity as a distinct group that was the carrier of the pure religion of reason.

Mendelssohn hoped to prove the permanent validity and truth of Judaism by defining it as revealed "law" rather than as revealed "religion." What he did not realize was that he had merely discovered that the nature of Judaism had become a problem in his time but that he had not solved it. If reason is the only criterion of what is true, how can God's revelation on Sinai be "true" since it can neither be explained logically nor verified by reason? What Mendelssohn did was simply to take the religion of reason of his time and graft upon it an emasculated Judaism which had been deprived of its rational elements and which consisted solely of customs, rituals, and ceremonial laws. The paradox was that he, the rationalist and man of enlightenment, the thinker for whom no belief was valid if it was contrary to reason, declared that all those concepts and ideas which were rational were not Judaism, and that Judaism consisted solely of elements which were not rational, which reason could neither prove nor understand, which had to be accepted on faith, and which God, therefore, had to disclose to Jews in a mysterious and non-rational act of revelation.

Mendelssohn was not conscious of the paradox of his position. He saw no contradiction. The God of reason and the God of Israel were one and the same God. God was both the benevolent creator and sustainer of the world whom his reason could affirm, and the king and guardian of Israel who had spoken on Sinai and ordained the laws which governed Jewish life. This was the only way in which Mendelssohn could harmonize his deepest feelings and convictions: his insistence on reason and on man's freedom of conscience and thought, and his determination to observe and preserve Jewish law and thus maintain his membership in the congregation of Israel. He was able to bring together in his personal life what his theory of Judaism failed to reconcile philosophically.

Mendelssohn's thinking can be understood only against the background of the causes which commanded his deepest loyalties. His faith in the power of reason was linked with his passion for human equality and his uncompromising attachment to traditional Judaism. If, as he firmly believed, a knowledge of truth was indispensable to the achievement of man's happiness, truth had to be accessible to all people alike without distinction of race, creed, or social status. It was inconceivable to him to believe that God, in His goodness, could capriciously have revealed the truth only to a part of mankind and left the rest of mankind without revelation and therefore without access to happiness. No religion, not even his own Judaism, could be the sole instrument through which God revealed His truth. Truth was indivisible and reason was its source; it belonged to all men.

But it was equally impossible for Mendelssohn to surrender his deep attachment to Jewish life. He found great emotional and intellectual satisfaction in the observance of Jewish law. It was the instrument by which he could translate his convictions into action. It was his great means of self-discipline; it enabled him to perform the acts (*mitzvot*) that bound him to God and united him with his people. Above all, such acts safeguarded the continued existence of the Jewish people. Therefore Mendelssohn insisted time and again on the crucial importance of Law for the Jew. He even proclaimed boldly that if a choice had to be made it would be better that the Jew surrender the benefits of emancipation than his loyalty to Law.

Jerusalem had a powerful impact on the general reading public. Many non-Jews were impressed by its author's compelling analysis of the relationship of state and church, and his courageous defense of man's inalienable right to freedom of thought. Mirabeau, who was soon to become one of the leading spirits of the French Revolution, declared that the book ought to be translated into every European language, while Kant wrote to Mendelssohn that he considered the little volume a masterful statement which would spur a reform from which not only Jews but countless non-Jews would benefit.

The impact of the work upon Mendelssohn's coreligionists, however, was negligible. Mendelssohn's arguments for the preservation of Jewish law, persuasive as they were to individuals like himself, who had been brought up in a completely Jewish environment, had little influence on most of his contemporaries, who preferred the actual or presumed benefits of civic emancipation even if they had to be acquired at the expense of surrendering their distinctive Jewish observances and identity. Mendelssohn's own children were an example. Only one of them, Joseph, remained a Jew, while the others defected shortly after their father's death. One daughter, Dorothea, after leaving her first husband, the Jewish banker Simon Veit, was married to the famous romantic poet Schlegel and turned first Protestant and then, together with her husband, converted to Catholicism. Another daughter, Henriette, who had been trained as a teacher, turned Catholic. Abraham Mendelssohn, father of the famous musician Felix Mendelssohn-Bartholdy, became a Protestant.

Final Years

The completion of *Jerusalem* had left Mendelssohn physically and mentally exhausted. He had never been strong, and the intellectual battles and efforts over the years had drained his limited reservoir of energy. He was aware that a new philosophical literature of vast importance was being published in Germany and that its theses challenged some of his deepest convictions. But he felt too exhausted to read the new works and either challenge their claims or revise his own thinking. He devoted his remaining strength to the religious and philosophical instruction of his son Joseph, and gave a daily lecture on the philosophical proofs for the existence of God to a circle of young people that included his own children and a group of their friends. He did not propound any new ideas; his main argument was the so-called cosmological proof of God which proceeds from the assumption that everything that exists must have a cause. The world exists; hence it must be caused by a power other than itself, and itself "uncaused." This final original cause is God.

The lectures were published in 1784 in a small volume called *Morgenstunden* (Morning Lessons) because they had been given in the morning when he still felt strong enough for the task. The book added little to Mendelssohn's stature. His assumptions and views in philosophy had long been known and had, in the meantime, been effectively refuted by Kant and others.

His final work was an essay addressed to Lessing's friends, in which he attempted to vindicate the memory of his beloved friend by proving that, contrary to an assertion of the philosopher Jacoby, Lessing had never been a follower of Spinoza. Mendelssohn caught a cold while delivering the manuscript of his reply to the publisher. He died a few days later on January 4, 1786, and was mourned by Jews and Christians alike.

Contribution to Jewish Life

The nature and extent of Mendelssohn's contribution to Jewish life have been the subject of a great deal of controversy. Peretz Smolenskin, a Hebrew writer and ardent proponent of Jewish nationalism, denounced him as the father of the German Reform movement which, in his view, had weakened the Jewish people by proclaiming it to be merely a religious group and not a nation. The attack was pointless since, contrary to Reform's repudiation of the divine origin and validity of the Law, Mendelssohn himself strictly observed it and persistently upheld its immutability. Orthodox leaders also continued to denounce him long after his death as a destructive influence, drawing young Jews away from their Talmudic studies and turning their interest to mundane matters and the study of general European culture.

This of course was what Mendelssohn had hoped to achieve. His significance for Jewish life lies in the fact that he was the bridge between the Jewish world and that of Europe. A citizen of both worlds, he had managed to bridge them in his own personality. In his thinking, he was a European; in sentiment and conduct, he was anchored in the Jewish community and identified with its traditions.

Mendelssohn also enabled other Jews through his work and personal example to bridge the same two worlds. His translation of the Pentateuch prepared the way for the cultural emancipation of Jews by placing the treasures of European culture within their reach. His writings and the example of his personality helped to pave the road for civic emancipation as well. As he gained the friendship and admiration of influential Christians, he won allies who associated themselves with the Jewish battle for human rights and created the moral and intellectual climate for the ultimate emergence of Jewish emancipation.

However, Mendelssohn's attempt to bridge the two worlds philosophically as well as culturally and socially did not succeed. He wanted to harmonize the traditional teachings of Judaism with the rational spirit of the age. But how could faith and reason be reconciled? How is it possible to believe in a God whose existence reason cannot prove? To these questions, Mendelssohn had answered that Judaism was compatible with reason because it was not a religion. It was merely revealed law which required certain actions and not an act of faith on the part of the Jew. But Mendelssohn's contemporaries and successors were unable to accept this definition of Judaism. They agreed that Law—customs and ceremonials—was one of Judaism's vital ingredients. Obviously, however, Judaism is more than a mere system of legal prescriptions. The law itself presupposes a belief in God who has given it, who requires its observance, who is the master of man's destiny and the source of all life. This God cannot be "proved" by reason, and therefore the question still remains as to how the faith of biblical Judaism can be harmonized with the demands of reason and the findings of science.

What makes Mendelssohn important to the modern Jew is not his definition of Judaism but the questions which he raised. Standing at the threshold of Jewish modernity in central Europe, he was the first to recognize and formulate the central problems which had begun to trouble his generation and to which, since then, each new Jewish generation has had to find a meaningful answer: how to live as a Jew without surrendering the values of Judaism to the values of the modern world, or the wisdom of the world to the claims of Judaism.

7 . *Sholom Aleichem*

[*1859-1916*]

LOUIS FALSTEIN

SHOLOM Aleichem died on May 13, 1916. A correspondent from the *New York Sun*, sent to the modest apartment on Kelly Street in the Bronx where the writer's body lay in state, surrounded by an honor guard of distinguished Yiddish writers, described the scene as follows:

> To one who stood in the tiny room with six candles and the body of Sholom Aleichem, there was shown that the death of a jester who had touched the hearts of the people is a matter of greater grief than the death of a king. For the men and women, old and young, rich and poor, who turned from the face of the dead to the light of the outside day, there were few whose eyes were not moist . . . Some women, under the stress of extreme grief, broke into hysterics. . . .

What the reporter found incredible was "a grief so universal that it could bring tears to the eyes of full-grown men . . . men who had never before looked upon Sholom Aleichem, but knew him only through his books." All day long, the walk opposite the apartment building was crowded with mourners who overflowed into the street, causing all traffic to be rerouted. Though some wept, the great mass of people stared in silence at the shaded windows of the second-floor apartment. Later in the day and toward evening, delegations began arriving from Philadelphia, Pittsburgh, the Middle West, and Canada. Messages of condolence poured in from the Pacific Coast, England, and the Continent.

"When has a man died in poverty," asked the *Literary Digest* in a glowing summation of the writer's life, "and on the next day brought out more than thirty thousand mourners to his bier?"

The thirty thousand who escorted Sholom Aleichem to his final rest and the countless thousands throughout the world who lamented his passing had not the vaguest notion of the grinding poverty that was the writer's lot before his death. Those who mourned were bereaved because in his passing something of themselves had died. Sholom Aleichem had been the singer of their inarticulate desires, shattered dreams, small triumphs, and fragile hopes. No Yiddish writer had identified himself so completely with the masses of the Pale of Settlement who lived in the *shtetlach* (small towns) crowded together as "tightly as herring in a barrel." He had touched the heart of the Jewish idiom, coming closer to it than any other writer. He did not attempt to poetize or alter the language which was rich in tenderness, intimacy, and affection. In his hands, vernacular Yiddish had seemed a perfect tool, as though it had been fashioned for his purpose. He was the first writer of stature—with the exception of Mendele Mocher Sephorim, whom he venerated—to work in the Yiddish language, and the most popular. He wrote no towering novels. Most of his works were short stories, monologues, and now and then a play—but they attained full epic stature because they embraced the fullness of life.

The World of Sholom Aleichem

The world of Sholom Aleichem was the impoverished *shtetl* of Eastern Europe. The towns were vast slums, congested, dirty, the roads impassable after a rain. The people lived in cramped, rickety wooden shacks—all but the wealthy—with thatched or tin roofs over their heads and mud floors under their feet. Sewerage was unknown. The market place was the town's hub, the source of bread. The synagogue was the spiritual as well as social center. The most crowded place was the cemetery, where many had lain since before Columbus sailed for America—Jews who had died natural deaths as well as those killed in pogroms.

With few exceptions, the people spoke Yiddish, the "mother

tongue." "Anyone with a sound reading and writing knowledge of Russian was a suspicious character; he was on the road to assimilation, to shortening of the beard and gaberdine, removal of earlocks, consumption of forbidden meats, and the final horror of apostasy."*

A large number of *maskilim* in the towns held Yiddish in low esteem, and instead corresponded in Hebrew, read Hebrew books, and frowned on the pious. There were also in the *shtetlach*, later made famous by Sholom Aleichem by such laughter-provoking names as Kasrilevka, Mazepovka, and Kozodoevka, some who clipped their beards and wore the short coats of Gentiles. But, by and large, those communities were strongholds of old Jewish ways. The Sabbath was a day of rest and renewal. Religion was the sun around which their lives revolved. The children crowded the *heders;* the bright boys went on to study in *yeshivot*, the fortunate among them being snatched up by in-laws of means who enabled them to pursue their studies without having to worry about filling their stomachs.

Learning was held in high esteem. One of Sholom Aleichem's most humorous stories describes a large household, the head of which took inordinate pride in his learned sons-in-law. The only son-in-law whose praises the man failed to sing was the one who worked to support the others and made it possible for them to study.

On occasion, there was a pogrom, with the acquiescence of the authorities. But the people managed to get along. They believed in miracles; indeed their survival from one Sabbath to the next was a miracle. Hordes of beggars marched from house to house. The difference between the beggars and the givers was often nonexistent.

The towns, for the most part, were *Hasidic* strongholds, where rabbis ruled like feudal princes, the movement of *Hasidism* having lost its spiritual purity by Sholom Aleichem's time. Hereditary priesthood was enthroned. Rivalries flourished among wonder-working rabbis whose courts were little islands of prosperity and opulence surrounded by a sea of wretchedness.

Jews without residence permits were excluded from the large cities, a great many obtaining such permits by bribing officials. Those who were desperate and could not scrape together a liveli-

* Maurice Samuel in *The World of Sholom Aleichem,* the most delightful of works.

hood in the small towns clung to the cities without permits, changing their residences often, and keeping one step ahead of the Czar's police. Notwithstanding the many obstacles placed in their path, Jews became doctors, lawyers, engineers, well-to-do merchants, and revolutionaries. There were even a few who attained great wealth and whose names inspired almost as much awe among Jews in the *shtetlach* as the mention of Rothschild.

The May Laws of 1881, following the assassination of Czar Alexander II, let loose a reign of terror. Jews were further restricted, driven from the countryside, and forced to flee the large cities as well. Anti-Semitism became an unsheathed sword. The population of the over-crowded Jewish towns increased, as did the ranks of *luftmenschen.** This was the world Sholom Aleichem mirrored in his stories.

Growing up in "Kasrilevka"

Sholom Aleichem—his real name was Rabinowitz—was born on February 18, 1859, in the small Ukrainian town of Pereyaslav, in the Poltava region. "Of children there were a goodly number," he wrote many years later in his autobiography, *Fun'm Yarid*, "over a dozen; of all sizes and colors, black-haired, blond and yellow." The family moved to Voronko, a town smaller still than his birthplace, and which, not a quarter of a century later, Sholom transmuted into the famed Kasrilevka of his many stories.

In *heder*, where Sholom spent all his waking hours, he was the brightest if not the most diligent student. His rich fantasy life—he dreamt often of hidden treasures—frequently brought him into conflict with the *rebbe*. However, he suffered no humility from the canings, assured that the offended parts would "heal before one walked under the marriage canopy."

Sholom's father, Nahum Vevik's, a well-to-do merchant by Voronko standards, was a curious combination: a *maskil* and philosopher who at the same time was a follower of a *Hasidic* rabbi; a pious Jew who defied family tradition and sent Sholom to a school where he received a modern education. The chores

* See page 104.

of rearing the large family and taking care of the store fell to the mother.

As a boy, Sholom believed firmly that Voronko was the center of the universe and its Jews the select of God; at the very summit stood his father, whose seat was near the east wall, second only to the rabbi's. In Sholom's opinion there was not a home in Voronko or elsewhere more resplendent, a father more distinguished.

Unfortunately, Nahum Vevik's lost his business, and the family was forced to move back to Pereyaslav. Reb Nahum opened a small unattractive inn. The family fell upon evil times and eventually all their jewelry and silverware had to be pawned. But Sholom's gloom was dispelled by Pereyaslav's broad streets and wooden sidewalks. Soon after their arrival, his display of scholarship earned him the nickname of "Bible boy."

After a great deal of soul-searching on the part of his father, Sholom was entered in the county school, where he came in contact for the first time with the world of Gentiles. Although his Russian was far from adequate, he accomplished the unprecedented feat—for a Jewish boy—of winning a prize of 120 rubles for being a brilliant student. This event created a furor among the town's Jews, who streamed to the Rabinowitz house in great numbers to verify the truth of the rumor. Uncle Pinney, the most pious of the three Rabinowitz brothers, was bitterly opposed to the fuss made over the boy. He argued that "many of the Jewish boys attending the county school, instead of the *yeshiva*, where they belonged, departed so far from the ways of piety, they carried handkerchiefs on the Sabbath and conversed in Russian."

During those days epidemics sweeping through the countryside took their heaviest toll among the Jews crowded into small towns. The cholera epidemic that struck Pereyaslav claimed Sholom's mother among its many victims. "We did ourselves proud," Sholom Aleichem recalls in his autobiography, "when the six of us said *kaddish*. One of the visiting relatives said with envy: 'How could you not go straight to paradise with such *kaddish* readers?' "

After a decent interval, Sholom's father remarried. The new mother possessed a "hot temperament and a rich Berdichev stepmother vernacular." In dealing out punishment, "she did not favor her own children," treating all alike with scrupulous impartiality.

Although Sholom was pressed into service by his stepmother—his job was to stand outside the inn and coax passers-by to stop with them—he found time to read books, journals, and newspapers in both Russian and Hebrew. The first novel he read was in Hebrew, the language favored by the Pereyaslav intelligentsia. It was a famous work *The Love of Zion* written by Abraham Mapu, a modern Hebrew novelist from Lithuania, who was in great vogue among the "emancipated" youth. The boy read in the garret, away from the suspicious and prying eyes of his stepmother. He enjoyed the book thoroughly, weeping for the hero, and embracing the heroine.

With the few kopecks he had put by, Sholom bought a ream of paper, ruled the pages on both sides, and began himself to write a novel entitled *The Daughter of Zion.* He wrote at night, by lamplight. One evening his stepmother apprehended him in the attic. "She immediately created such a furor, the whole household woke in fright." He was forbidden, henceforth, to waste precious kerosene and to indulge in such idle and unbecoming pastimes. His father "confiscated" the unfinished novel, but instead of destroying it, as Sholom had feared, showed it to a friend. "Reb Nahum, you don't know what you have here!" the friend said prophetically. "This boy is going to be a somebody." Reb Nahum's friend insisted that Sholom must become a writer. In this he was echoed by others of the inner circle, the men who drank tea and played chess with the innkeeper.

Sholom liked the notion of becoming a writer. The question was whether to write in Hebrew or Russian. Yiddish was not even considered a possibility; it was for speaking, but writing in what was called "jargon" and "*ivretaitch*" was "fit for women" and out of the question. A person who even carried Yiddish books might be ridiculed.

Sholom's first literary endeavor was a lexicon of his stepmother's invective, compiled and arranged in alphabetical order. Soon he was forced to interrupt his writing to give private lessons. After tutoring for a short time in Pereyaslav, Sholom, who had then turned seventeen, was engaged by a leather merchant from a nearby town to educate his children. But in view of the fact that his duties also included minding a newborn infant at night and performing other chores, he soon sought a livelihood elsewhere.

After several unfortunate experiences, the wandering half-starved young tutor was introduced to a wealthy Jewish land-owner, Elimelech Loieff, who was looking for a teacher for his thirteen-year-old daughter. Reb Loieff, who possessed "the voice of a lion and the bearing of a field-marshall," put Sholom through a gruelling examination before consenting to hire him. He tested Sholom's Russian and Hebrew as well as his knowledge of Rashi's *Commentaries*.

The next three years, passed in the village of Sofievka, on the large estate of his employer, were the happiest of Sholom's life. "I lived like a prince," he later wrote. Reb Loieff, who treated him as one of the family, was generous and wealthy. Sholom's life was transformed, as if by magic, from one of privation to abundance. It was as though one of his own boyhood reveries had borne fruit.

Romance in the Shtetl

In his three decades as a writer, Sholom Aleichem's plots were as varied as the types he portrayed. But the most wildly improbable, tenderly romantic plot was one he did not write; he lived it. Olga, Reb Loieff's only daughter—and after the death of her brother his only child—was Sholom's constant companion. Together they read Shakespeare, Dickens, Goethe, Schiller, Gogol, and sentimental French novels. During this period he wrote a great deal: novels that were "heart-rending," "noisy dramas," and "inextricable tragedies." As soon as he had finished a work, he read it to Olga. Both hailed each composition as a masterpiece. But as soon as a new manuscript appeared, they enthusiastically crowned it as Sholom's glory, burning the previous one in the oven.

In one of his novels, *Yoselle Nightingale*, Sholom Aleichem dramatized the plight of two young lovers unable to consummate their romance in marriage. In the case of Sholom and Olga, it was Reb Elimelech who presented the final obstacle. Upon discovering that the two were in love, he dismissed Sholom and took Olga on a long journey. Although he was fond of the young tutor, Reb Loieff did not approve of his daughter's carrying on a romance without his knowledge and approval.

From Sofievka, the lovelorn, impecunious Sholom went to Kiev, where "eminent novelists and poets blessed by God" dwelled in great numbers. He arrived in Kiev without the residence permit required of Jews. During his first night in the great city, which later appeared in his stories as Yehupetz, the police raided the inn where Sholom stopped; he hid in the attic with other non-resident Jews.

Unable to obtain a residence permit, penniless, and disillusioned, he left Kiev and subsequently settled in the small town of Luben, where he served briefly as a government rabbi. Meanwhile, in Sofievka, Reb Loieff withdrew his opposition to Sholom as a son-in-law, and his marriage with Olga took place in 1883. The couple lived on the father's estate, with Sholom serving as its general manager. Reb Elimelech, of whom Sholom Aleichem wrote a masterful sketch in his autobiography, died in 1885 leaving his daughter a quarter of a million rubles. The young couple gave up Sofievka and moved to Kiev. Their money enabled them to obtain a resident permit without difficulty.

Writer in the Making

In Kiev, Sholom assumed a role in which he was sorely miscast, that of speculator on the stock exchange. Eventually he lost Olga's inheritance—but Yiddish literature gained by it. How else could he have written about the immortal character Menachem Mendl? It was during this period, while he was still in business, first as a speculator, broker, and later as a merchant, that the author assumed the pen name Sholom Aleichem (in Hebrew, "peace be unto you," and used as a greeting). The use of the pseudonym was in part due to his desire to keep his business colleagues from finding out about his literary avocation; moreover, he probably did not take his initial thrusts at Yiddish literature very seriously at the start.

Sholom Aleichem first broke into print in 1879, writing local correspondence for the Hebrew weekly *Ha-Tzephirah*. This was followed, in 1882, by articles on Jewish education in another Hebrew weekly *Ha-Melitz.* During this period of literary apprenticeship, he also wrote in Russian for *Yevreyskoie Obozrenie* (1884) and *Kievlianin* (1885).

Inspired by the phenomenal success of Mendele Mocher Sephorim, Sholom Aleichem also wrote a Yiddish tale, his first, called "Two Stones," which appeared in *Yiddishes Folksblatt* in 1883, and brought the author instantaneous recognition. "Penknife," a children's story, one of his best, came next. Other stories followed, rich in humor, compassion, and gentle irony. He won praise from eminent writers such as Mendele and later from Gorki and Tolstoy. His name was linked with Gogol, Dickens, and Mark Twain.

Temporary wealth enabled Sholom Aleichem to found a Jewish annual, *Die Yiddishe Folksbibliotek* (1888), a publication of high literary merit. To attract authors of distinction and talent, he paid large fees for contributions. Isaac Leib Peretz, who wrote in Hebrew but like Sholom Aleichem was inspired by Mendele's success to try his hand in Yiddish, appeared in the *Folksbibliotek* with his celebrated poem "Monish." Peretz and Sholom Aleichem remained friends long after the annual was discontinued for lack of funds.

After losing his wealth, Sholom Aleichem decided to move from Kiev to the more congenial climate of Odessa, where he planned to devote all his time to writing. In Odessa he was near Mendele Mocher Sephorim, whom he considered his master, and who exerted a powerful influence on him. On one occasion when "Grandfather," as the younger man had nicknamed Mendele, visited his home in Odessa, Sholom Aleichem gave the master a newly completed manuscript to read. After a brief lapse of time, Mendele lifted his eyes from a page he was reading and inquired of the host whether there was a fire in the oven. Sholom Aleichem, trembling lest his distinguished guest was hungry, replied in the affirmative, assuring him that a meal would soon be forthcoming. "If the oven is going," Mendele said calmly, handing Sholom his manuscript, "throw this in. This is not your genre." Years later, at a banquet celebrating the seventy-fifth birthday of Mendele, Sholom Aleichem publicly thanked "Grandfather" for his sound advice.

In Odessa, Sholom Aleichem became the center of a group of prominent Jewish writers. Among them were E. L. Levinski, who wrote a Utopian volume about a visit to Palestine a hundred years hence; Ben Ami, who wrote in Russian; J. H. Ravnitzki, a collaborator with Bialik on several anthologies; and M. L. Lilienblum, writer and philosopher. Unable to earn a livelihood in Odessa, Sholom Aleichem returned to Kiev, his mind alive with business schemes, determined once again to storm the battlements that had repulsed him in the past. But he forsook commerce finally and irrevocably in 1900, admitting failure. Henceforth he determined to stick to his last as a professional writer in Yiddish. During this period in Kiev, Sholom Aleichem did some of his best writing. Tevyeh, Sholom Aleichem's famous character, appeared in 1895. Kasrilevka, Yehupetz, and Boiberik were soon household words. But even though the name of Sholom Aleichem was becoming increasingly famous, he struggled desperately "not to let the world know how difficult things were," and how he was often forced to seek means other than writing to care for his wife and six children.

First Visit to America

The Kiev pogroms of 1905 profoundly shocked Sholom Aleichem. As a protest against a regime that permitted such atrocities, he left Russia. After settling his family in Switzerland, the writer toured Western Europe, lecturing before Jewish audiences. Later on, the dapper little man with the long hair, the merry twinkle in his eye, the velvet waistcoat, and flowing tie became a familiar figure on the American lecture platform as well. America enchanted and bewildered him. Unlike other countries he had visited, America was not completely strange. There were in its large cities many thousands of Jews originally from the *shtetlach*. Sholom Aleichem listened to their tales, rejoiced in their triumphs, and grieved over their defeats. He lamented the loss of traditional values on the part of many of his former "little people." Some of them who achieved the status of *all-rightnik* (*nouveau riche*) placed material success above the spiritual. According to Sholom Aleichem, the *all-rightniks* looked upon the coming of the Messiah as a great catastrophe because they would have to abandon all their American material acquisitions and migrate to Palestine. Subsequently, a new element appeared in his stories: America as the one place on earth where Jews suffered no pogroms and spent all their energies "making a living."

Sholom Aleichem and Bialik

Sholom Aleichem returned to Europe in 1907 and went to The Hague as an American delegate to the Zionist Congress. There he met Hayyim Nahman Bialik. The two embraced as though they were old friends. In Sholom Aleichem's account of his brief but pleasant stay in Holland's capital, a good deal was said about the joyous occasion of his meeting with the great Hebrew poet, their conversations, long walks, and reveries, but nothing about the Congress. Beyond the esteem each had for the other as a creative person, both dealt in their writings with the changing pattern of Jewish life in Russia, and revealed a strong attachment to the traditional ways of their people. Bailik wrote in Hebrew as a poet, on an intellectual plane, while Sholom Aleichem wrote in Yiddish on the level of the common man.

Before returning to Russia, Bialik visited his new friend in Switzerland. They talked, reminisced, and planned for the future, and sometimes they were joined by Mendele Mocher Sephorim, who, like Sholom Aleichem, was also a voluntary exile from the Czar's domain.

In 1907, Sholom Aleichem began writing one of his most humorous works, the saga of Mottel Peissi, the cantor's son. Sholom Aleichem continued writing about Mottel even after he became ill with tuberculosis and did not have enough money for rent. "When I look at the calendar," he wrote a friend, "and see the date when I have to pay rent, and my wallet is as dry as a desert, it is bad. It is my jubilee of twenty-five years as a writer. So Jews in Russia have scraped together their pennies and there is already a special fund for me of a hundred rubles . . ."

His illness alarmed many of his friends, among them Peretz, who wrote often to urge Sholom Aleichem to take care of himself and achieve a quick recovery. He was at a German resort, surrounded by his large and growing family (two sons-in-law having been added), when World War I broke out.

Threatened with internment as an enemy alien, Sholom Aleichem fled to Denmark. In Copenhagen, he was struck down by diabetes, a malady that two years later claimed his life. Writing to a friend in Warsaw, Sholom Aleichem quipped: "Having been told I have diabetes, I no longer fear of dying from hunger. I'll most likely die from thirst."

Last Years in America

Sholom Aleichem arrived in the United States on December 3, 1914. Pardoxically, his arrival was reported more fully in the *New York Times* than in any of New York's five Yiddish dailies. In his first public appearance at Cooper Union, arranged by the Committee of One Hundred that had brought him and his family to the United States, Sholom Aleichem said:

> I came to America the first time in 1905. This is my second time. Both times I came in the wake of a catastrophe. My first visit here followed the bloody excesses of 1905 in Russia. This time I'm here because of the insanity, the war in Europe. If ever it becomes necessary for me to come a third time, I'm hard put to it to imagine after what kind of catastrophe that will be. The worst, it seems to me, has already happened.

Although Yiddish-speaking residents of New York, where he settled, came in large numbers to hear Sholom Aleichem whenever he spoke, and read his works, the Yiddish newspapers devoted little space to him. After he became a contributor for one of the dailies, *Der Tog* (*The Day*), the four competing Yiddish papers ceased printing his name altogether.

Ignored, neglected, suffering from poverty and ill-health, and grieving over the loss of Jewish lives in the war, Sholom Aleichem nonetheless continued writing. There were still many Mottel tales to be told—Mottel in America, growing up and "making a living." There was also his own autobiography. "My friends have often insisted," Sholom Aleichem wrote not long before his death,

> that I should recount the story of my life. The time has come, they said, and it may even be interesting. I tried to listen to their advice. Several times I put the pen aside until . . . until finally

> the right time came. Before I had reached the age of fifty, I had the honor of meeting his majesty, the Angel of Death, face to face. I was almost dispatched to that place whence one cannot write letters nor even send a greeting by messenger. In short, having been practically gathered unto my forefathers, I said to myself, "Now the time has come. Snatch the opportunity and write, for no one knows what tomorrow will bring! You may die suddenly. People who think they knew you and understood you will turn up with cock-and-bull stories about you. What will you gain by it? Better do the job yourself, for nobody knows you as well as you know yourself . . ."

Thus began the introduction to his final and, in many respects, his most significant work—the summing up, the autobiography, or, as he called it, "the return from the fair" (*Fun'm Yarid*). Unfortunately, he did not live long enough to complete this work. But the episodes he committed to paper, sections of which are available in English as *The Great Fair* (translated by the author's granddaughter, Tamara Kahana), are eloquent proof of the great loss suffered by Yiddish as well as world literature when Sholom Aleichem put down his pen for the last time.

Tevyeh the Milkman

Among Sholom Aleichem's major character creations is Tevyeh, about whom the author was writing as late as 1914, and who had a little of every Jew in him. A pauper with a philosophical bent, whose emaciated nag crawled along the dusty road between Anatevka and Boiberik, delivering milk, cheese, and butter to the summer homes of the wealthy Jews from Yehupetz, Tevyeh was the immedately recognizable symbol of the wretched Jew who refused to accept defeat. As though being a Jew was not in itself a sufficient liability in the Czar's domain, Tevyeh's business was bad, his horse old and stubborn, his wife ailing. Moreover, he was the father of seven marriageable daughters.

"Tevyeh the Dairyman" is not properly speaking a story. It is a catalogue of disasters, told in monologue form. Notwithstanding the fact that Tevyeh's tribulations were endless, he was astonishingly resilient. He believed implicitly in God, addressing Him intimately, sometimes imprudently, but always hopefully.

> Blessed are they that dwell in Thy house (Right! I take it O Lord, that Thy house is somewhat more spacious than my hovel!) . . . I will extol Thee my God, O King (what good would it do me if I didn't?) . . . The Lord is good to all (and suppose He forgets somebody now and again, good Lord, hasn't He enough on His mind?) . . . The Lord upholdeth all that fall, and raiseth up all that are bowed down (Father in heaven, loving Father, surely it's my turn now, I can't fall any lower) . . . Thou openest Thy hand and satisfiest every living thing (so You do, Father in heaven, You give with an open hand; one gets a box on the ear, another a roast chicken, and neither my wife nor I nor my daughters have even smelt a roast chicken since the days of creation) . . . (cited by Maurice Samuel)

Although he provokes laughter, Tevyeh is not a comedian. The millions of Jews who read the Tevyeh episodes as they appeared in Yiddish newspapers and between the covers of books laughed because they identified themselves with the milkman's dilemmas and his unique way of articulating them. Tevyeh, who misquoted the Holy Books liberally, was a traditional Jew, like any pious Kasrilevkite, but his contacts with the outside world were broader and he was more tolerant of those who did not believe as he did. Deriving from the old stable Jewish life, he was witness to the cataclysmic changes taking place in Russia and among the Jews. He was more than a witness. He was an unwilling participant. One of his daughters married a revolutionist whom she followed to Siberia and exile, with Tevyeh's acquiescence; another took a Gentile for a husband and became an apostate and was disowned by her parents. His wife died and the peasants of Anatevka, his former friends, descended on his hut during the incitements against the Jews in 1881 for the purpose of staging a pogrom. But Tevyeh survived.

Tevyeh was Sholom Aleichem's resounding answer to those who questioned the capacity and ability of the Jew to survive. Although not an observant Jew, the author knew better than anyone that Tevyeh could not have endured without his faith.

Menachem Mendl, the Luftmensch

As a character, Tevyeh was completely passive (what could a Jew do?), reacting to each catastrophe as it befell him. Menachem Mendl, on the other hand, was a person to whom action was imperative. Not that his action ever resulted in anything. Cane in hand, Menachem Mendl and his fellow-*luftmenschen* in the Jewish towns of the Pale literally became adepts at necromancy, trying to coax a living out of thin air. Denied access to the soil, excluded from the guilds, barred from the large cities, they were reduced to "deal in things you can't put your hands on." Sholom Aleichem introduces Menachem Mendl to the reader through a series of letters exchanged between the character and his wife, Sheineh Sheindl. Menachem Mendl writes from Yehupetz or Odessa, where he is playing the stock market with his wife's inheritance. His letters home are full of characteristic optimism and enthusiasm for the propects at hand. His wife's replies, just as characteristic, are heavy with skepticism; she has been married to Menachem Mendl for many years—there are hungry children in the house—and she finds little reason for optimism, since Menachem Mendl has never been successful in earning a living. He had tried a great many things, but the ruble always eluded him. As a marriage broker he once virtually consummated a match, but it turned out that both parties were of the same sex. So eager had he been to close the deal, he had failed to make a proper check. The luck of a *luftmensch!*

Menachem Mendl was not a fool. But his judgment was impaired after living too long on a merry-go-round that failed to stop. He was Sholom Aleichem's most tragic character. Unlike Tevyeh, who had his faith to sustain him, Menachem Mendl existed largely by self-delusion.

To many readers of Sholom Aleichem's tales, Menachem Mendl was not a fictitious character. Copied straight from life, he was someone they knew, were related to, met daily in the market place.

Tales about Children

Some of his saddest and, at the same time, most exuberant tales were about children. Sholom Aleichem retained until the day of his death the freshness of a child's viewpoint. He was the first Yiddish author to write about children. "Penknife," one of his earliest and most celebrated tales, dealt with a boy who stole a knife he desired more than anything else in life, only to find his days poisoned by feelings of guilt. In his final work, *Fun'm Yarid*, Sholom Aleichem returned to his childhood, to a world he loved and never really abandoned for any length of time during his three decades of creative writing.

There is a universality in Sholom Aleichem's youthful characters, though their reveries are different from those of Gentile neighbors. The Jewish boys about whom he wrote felt more kinship with the *Kabbalah* than with God's green fields and swift rivers. The fantasy life of these boys and girls never strayed far from the spirit of the Jewish people. The Kasrilevka boys, Sholom and Shmulik, searched for a hidden treasure. In this they were no different from Gentile boys, but it was the manner in which they proposed to find the treasure that differed: they meant to use the *Kabbalah* as a magic key that would unlock all secrets and lead them directly to their object. "Why do you think God created the *Kabbalah?*" Shmulik, the expert, inquired. The *Kabbalists* could do anything they pleased. Even Sholom, the skeptic, could see at a glance the incomparable advantage of being a Jew. The only complicating factor, the single obstacle preventing them from going to the spot where the treasure was buried and loading their pockets full of precious stones, was the ritual which must be observed. According to Shmulik, it was necessary to fast forty days and forty nights and recite forty chapters from the Psalms on each of these days before the mystery revealed itself. Sholom was prepared for this arduous ritual—but then Shmulik left town and never returned.

Sholom Aleichem's children were steeped in Bible lore. In a story titled "Song of Songs," ten-year-old Shimek said to the little girl, Buzie, whom he fancied: "Come, my beloved, let us go forth into the fields. Let us lodge in the villages. Let us get up early to the vineyards. Let us see if the vine flourish, whether the tender grape appear, and the pomegranates bud forth . . ."

The Jewish boys dreamt of romance fully and passionately, but they had their own unique ways of expressing their love. "And it came to pass," a boy wrote to a girl who captivated his heart, "that a Jew named Mordecai, who is Motelle in real life, and dwelt in the city of the Kingdom of Ahasuerus, called Shushan, which is none other than our own city . . . and the maiden was fair and beautiful, and she found favor in the eyes of Mordecai. But Mordecai instructed Esther to reveal no word thereof to any man . . ."

One of Sholom Aleichem's best-loved characters is little Mottel Peissi, the cantor's son. "Hurrah, I'm an orphan!" Mottel exclaimed after his father, who had been ailing for a long time, finally passed away. As an orphan, Mottel fancied himself the center of attention and the object of sympathy. Like Sholom Aleichem's grown-up Jews, Mottel did not realize how badly off he was. Being a child, he took his pleasures where he found them.

Mottel, Jewish to the core, possessed the universal child's sense of wonder and novelty in all the things he touched and experienced both in the *shtetl*, where he was born, and in America, where he finally went to live. Mottel, the child whose spirit was as free as a bird in flight, was Sholom Aleichem's perfect vehicle for his irrepressible humor. Mottel also served as a bridge between Russia and America. Sholom Aleichem was composing new Mottel episodes a few days before he died.

Genius of Sholom Aleichem

In all his creative life, Sholom Aleichem strove and succeeded to remain at one with the people about whom he wrote. On two occasions when he departed from the pattern—in his novels *Sender Blank* and *The Storm*—the results were not successful. *Sender Blank* (1888) explored the life of a parvenu and snob, a Jew who, having lost the traditional ways of his fathers, ends up as a miserable usurer. *The Storm*, written in 1907, after the defeat of the revolution in Russia and the disillusionment following in its wake, dealt with a group of young Jewish revolutionaries, among whom was Yashka Vorona, an apostate and stool pigeon. Sholom Aleichem, the man of compassion and gentle irony, made no attempt to conceal his hatred both for Sender Blank, who betrayed his heritage as a Jew, and for Yashka Vorona, who betrayed his fellow-Jews to the Czarist police. Although both these novels were important social studies, they were not his genre, as Mendele had said of another of Sholom Aleichem's works. Hatred was not his forte.

Sholom Aleichem was at his best as an indefatigable chronicler. He strikes the reader as a listener rather than a writer, an omnipresent eavesdropper, notebook and pencil in hand, wandering among the Jews of the small towns of the Pale, riding along on the temperamental narrow-gauge train known as the *ledig geyer* (loafer) that crawls interminably through endless Ukrainian steppes and towns, through Berdichev, Vinnitsa, Nemirov, Gaisin—and all the way to Kamenka on the Dnestr River. During the course of the journey, lasting a week—one or two days should have been sufficient—Sholom Aleichem talked with and listened to hundreds of Jews, each one of them with a tale as long as the Exile. Talk was not proscribed. The right to act having been taken away from them long ago, Sholom Aleichem's Jews were the world's most prodigious talkers.

Sholom Aleichem was a patient listener. He listened to all, and in particular to the poor, toward whom he was partial. The rich fared less well; he satirized and pitilessly "exposed" them in the manner of Balzac.

Before Sholom Aleichem's death and for many years afterward, critics debated his place among the famous triumvirate of acknowledged masters of Yiddish literature. Like Peretz, Sholom Aleichem became a folk hero while still alive. In addition to mirroring the lives of poor Jews in Russia—and this meant the vast majority—he was an active partisan in their ceaseless struggle to survive as a people. Like Mendele, he wrote about the *shtetl*. Sholom Aleichem's genre was humor, while Mendele excelled in satire. Peretz eschewed realism and achieved fame through his mystical tales of *Hasidism*. Each was supreme in his genre.

Some critics maintain that Sholom Aleichem's characters are not as complex as those of Mendele, that he was not as profound as Peretz, that he did not probe deeply, and that Tevyeh, Menachem Mendl, and Mottel were types who lack the dimensions of full-blooded fictional persons. What must be kept in mind is that this may have been Sholom Aleichem's intent; in recreating a prosaic and commonplace world, as contrasted with Peretz's mystic and exotic one, he sought the representational and familiar. His readers were the same people about whom he wrote. Were all history books of that era to vanish, Sholom Aleichem's tales could offer a complete and faithful picture of life among Russian Jews in the latter part of the nineteenth and beginning of the twentieth centuries.

Sholom Aleichem became the most popular of writers among the mass of Yiddish readers because his tales were simple, direct, and free of abstruse symbolism. He spoke to the heart and without circumlocution. Readers found his voice gentle and compassionate. More important still, he taught people to laugh at their own predicaments. He made them take pride in their virtues and laugh at their foibles. He taught them to be optimistic—in the face of a repressive, pogrom-ridden government that plotted their spiritual if not their physical extinction. He often romanticized the characters he created—though he did not neglect their weaknesses—portraying his "little people" not only as they were but as he might like them to be.

The jester, the mimic, the folk humorist who "discovered the liberating power of laughter" has taken his rightful place among the immortals in world literature. Sholom Aleichem's greatness as a man lay in his broad humanity; his greatness as a Jew lay in complete self-identification with his people; his greatness as a writer lay in his ability to encompass in his works the manifold aspects of Jewish life in the Pale of Settlement. A pioneer in a new literature, he led a successful crusade on behalf of Yiddish, thus opening fresh vistas to writers of talent as well as to thousands of readers.

Sholom Aleichem's legacy to the world was his simple philosophy, an optimism that permeated his stories, faith in the inconquerable spirit of man, and hatred of tyranny. For Jews, his stories open a window on the world of their fathers, on values and traditions that were centuries in the making. He is thus a link with a tragic but proud, heroic past.

8 . *Hayyim Nahman Bialik*

[1872-1934]

M. Z. FRANK

HAYYIM Nahman Bialik is considered to be the greatest Hebrew poet in a thousand years and in some respects the most important Jewish literary figure since the writers of the Bible. In his lifetime he was called the "national poet of the Jewish people," the "Jewish poet laureate," and even "the modern prophet," designations which are still meaningful today. Wherever modern Hebrew literature is studied—in the schools of Israel and elsewhere—Bialik's works occupy almost the same importance as do Shakespeare's plays in the English-speaking world. Since Bialik's death in 1934, innumerable articles and books have been published which record the poet's conversations, explain his vocabulary and Hebrew style, comment on his poems, or interpret hitherto unknown letters and biographical details. His works have been translated into twenty-five languages, including Japanese, and are included in most anthologies of modern poetry.

Childhood in the Ukraine

Hayyim Nahman Bialik was the youngest child of Reb Yitzhok Yoissef and Dinah-Priveh, both of whom had had children by previous marriages. Reb Yitzhok Yoissef was a pious scholar and an unsuccessful member of a fairly prosperous merchant family whose main business was timber.

Hayyim Nahman was born in December, 1872 in the little Ukrainian village of Radi, where his father managed one of the family's enterprises, a flour mill, while also looking after some lumber business nearby.

Hayyim was left almost entirely to himself. In that village there was one other Jewish family, with a young daughter who was Bialik's only playmate. His mother was busy all day and had little time for the boy, while the father was at home only for the Sabbath, which he spent in prayer and study. Reb Yitzhok Yoissef had little patience with his son; he was an unhappy sullen man, full of resentment against his treatment at the hands of his brothers and brothers-in-law, on whom he was dependent economically for his livelihood. Being an imaginative child, full of spirits, Hayyim grew up without much guidance. He roamed the beautiful sunny countryside and found his playmates in nature: "any bird that flies, any tree with a shadow, any shrub in the woods, the face of the moon timidly glowing into the window . . . any bramble growing behind a broken fence, any taut golden ray reaching my eyes from the sun . . ." ("Radiance"). Whenever he darted into the woods or into a pool, Hayyim Nahman felt himself accompanied by "myriads of invisible sprites."

As Bialik relates in his autobiographical prose story *Wild Growth,* that first world was a happy and carefree one.

> That pristine world of my existence which I brought with me from the village and which still lives on in a secret compartment of my being—that strange, marvelous singular world—that, it seems to be, knew no autumn or winter. I can see the village of my childhood as made out of solid summer stuff. The sky, the earth, the vegetation, the animals—all are summer. Even little Feigele, my only playmate in the village, appears as a summer creature . . .

The golden summer of Hayyim Nahman's early childhood suddenly gave way to dreary winter when his father decided to defy his relatives and go into business for himself. He moved the family to Zhitomir, the provincial capital, where he opened a tavern in an outlying section called the Tarmakers' Suburb. To be a barkeeper was an occupation far less suitable to a pious scholar than the respected timber trade in which Reb Yitzhok Yoissef's family engaged. In a poem entitled "My Father"

Bialik later recalled his father's face "floating above the smoke of the tavern as he stood behind the counter, immersed in some religious volume, as if seeking to insulate himself from the unclean surroundings of drinking and brawling, and leaving his book only now and then to serve a drink or to prevent a fight from getting out of hand. The sensitive child would nestle up to his father and, raising his eyes, would often see a tear running down the older man's face.

Unfortunately the business did not prosper. The poverty of the household was described by Bialik in a poem called "My Song."

> On Friday nights our Sabbath festival profaned by want:
> The table lacking the sacramental wine and even the Sabbath loaves;
> The candlesticks pawned, and in their stead mud
> Holding the few lean and wretched candles,
> Their smoking flames sending the walls a-dancing weirdly;
> While seven hungry sleepy children sat at the table,
> As mother sadly listened to their chanting welcome
> For the ministering angels of the Sabbath.
> Father, with a guilty mien, in a dejected mood,
> Cutting a dry small morsel of black bread with a blunt knife
> And then a tail of a herring for the Sabbath fish—
> And as, in misery and humiliation, we chewed upon
> Our tear-soaked stale and tasteless crumb
> We joined our father in the singing of the Sabbath hymns,
> Singing on a hungry crying stomach, on a desolate heart,
> The cricket then would join our mournful choir
> Hailing, he, too, the Sabbath from his dismal crevice in the dark.

The transition from village to town proved difficult for the boy. As soon as the family moved to town, Hayyim Nahman was sent to the *heder* where the teacher, like so many ghetto teachers recorded in Jewish literature, had little sensitivity, imagination, or pedagogical skill. An assistant called for the children and brought them home, often carrying them through the town's mud, and drilled them in the Hebrew alphabet. Both master and apprentice, as Bialik recorded in *Wild Growth*,

> knew only how to hurt, each one in his own way: The *rebbe* used to hit with a whip, with his fist, with his elbow, with his

wife's rolling pin or with anything else that could cause pain, but his assistant, whenever my answer to his question was wrong, would advance toward me, with the fingers of his palm distended and bent before my face and seize me by my throat. He would look to me then like a leopard or a tiger or some other such wild beast and I would be in mortal dread. I was afraid he would gouge out my eyes with his dirty fingernails and the fear would paralyze my mind so that I forgot everything I had learned the previous day.

Life with Grandfather

When Hayyim Nahman was seven, his father succumbed to illness and died. The four oldest of the seven children were sent off to live with relatives or were apprenticed to artisans. Bialik's mother was left with her "three little striplings," for whom she had to provide as best she could, working all day and half the night, peddling, sewing, washing, and mending. The task being beyond her, she decided to give Hayyim Nahman, the youngest and brightest of the three, into the care of his well-to-do grandfather. She bundled up the boy's few belongings, prepared his favorite muffins, and then led him to the other end of Zhitomir, to the suburb of the Timber Merchants, where his grandfather lived.

Reb Yaakov Moishe Bialik was a widower of about seventy, retired from active business and devoting his time to prayer and study. The old man was annoyed at first at this disturbance in his peaceful existence, but soon grew fond of the boy, even though, like most pious Jews, he seldom showed any outward signs of affection.

The *heder* which Hayyim Nahman now attended offered better instruction than those most boys of his age were able to attend. Reb Meir, who headed it, was a good teacher and endowed with a dramatic flair. He was able to make the stories of the Bible come alive, drawing or building models of Noah's ark or of Moses' tabernacle; he called the pupils' attention to the beauty of the Hebrew language, and, in the summertime, he held classes outdoors under the trees.

In this new atmosphere, the sensitive boy began to perceive the inner light and warmth that shone through what had hitherto been to him only the exacting discipline of the Jewish tradition. In a later poem, Bialik was to describe a winter evening at his grandfather's home when the *dayan* (assistant rabbi) of the neighborhood came to study; the two scholars would engage in a discussion of a point of Law, with the folio of the Talmud and other volumes before them on the table. The oven was hot; the kerosene lamp shone brightly. The grandfather's second wife sat in a corner, knitting a stocking and nodding her head. Though there was a strong wind outside tearing at the shutters, the little boy had a feeling they were all in a strong fortress, protected by the power of the Torah from the storms raging outside.

Living in his grandfather's house opened to young Bialik the world of Jewish learning and the spirit of Judaism, which were to provide so much inspiration for his future writings. One of the greatest influences was the old man's library, where the boy was able to delve into a large selection of Hebrew books.

Early Doubts

These books in his grandfather's library were nearly all of a religious nature. Only here and there he found a book dealing with the rules of Hebrew grammar, a story written for its own sake, or a book of philosophy. The latter type of book was not supposed to be taken seriously since it was not considered proper for a young boy.

Yet it was precisely such "frivolous" books that Hayyim Nahman bought secretly with his own few pennies, which he managed to save. Some of the titles would have shocked his grandfather: books written in the "holy tongue" which questioned and even ridiculed the very notions which pious Jews for centuries had held sacred and immutable; books of poetry extolling love and nature; novels, including translations from the French by Eugene Sue (*Mysteries of Paris*) which dealt with the Gentiles and their underworld. In Bialik's days those were books Jewish scholars read secretly or kept under their large folios of the Talmud, hidden from the eyes of the pure.

At the age of thirteen he began to have doubts about the value of the traditional Jewish way of life, with its total emphasis on piety and religious scholarship to the exclusion of secular knowledge, with its disdain for the arts and sciences, its complete regulation of conduct, even of thinking and feeling, and its toleration of so many superstitions.

The doubts which arose in the boy's mind resulted not only from the influences exerted by secular books and by friends who recommended such books to him, but also from the life around him, which had changed since grandfather was a boy. The district in Zhitomir where the Bialiks had lived did not happen to be inhabited by Jews afflicted with a strong spiritual thirst either for the old Jewish heritage or for the new Western civilization which had at last penetrated the Russian provinces, or even for the budding Russian literature which was just then coming into its own. On the contrary, the Jews of the Tar-makers' Suburb, as described in some of Bialik's short stories ("Big Man Arieh," "Behind the Fence"), were "pennyworth people with pennyworth souls." Yet, somehow, cultural influences stirred the air. Somewhere, it was said, there were Jewish young men who went to Russian high schools and universities or went to study abroad, in Germany, France, or Switzerland. Somewhere there were Jews who shaved their beards, cut their earlocks, wore European clothes—Jews who lived a richer, fuller life, so different from the constricted life in the ghetto which was hemmed in by innumerable regulations, fears, and prohibitions, and was so narrow in its horizons.

And yet the old Jewish way of life had its fascination too. The traditional sing-song of Talmud study was so sweet, the old beliefs so heartwarming. So much blood had been shed to keep Judaism alive—was it all in vain? The old tradition commanded Bialik's loyalties all the more because so few of the Jews in the Tarmakers' Suburb in Zhitomir—or in the whole town, for that matter—kept the old fire of studying Torah alive. Hayyim Nahman was the only boy of his age who continued his study in the house of worship in his neighborhood, where once there had been many. He was a solace to the older men who frequented the *bet-midrash*. In later years one of them was to recall nostalgically "the nightingale" Hayyim Nahman, whose sweet cantillations as he studied the Talmud had given them hope.

Volozhin: Pull of the Larger World

When he was fifteen years old, Bialik had a dream of going to Berlin to study at a modern rabbinical seminary, where loyalty to Judaism and Jewish scholarship could be wedded to knowledge of the larger world. But he did not dare breathe this thought to his grandfather. Instead, he ventured a far less daring suggestion: that he go to study at the famous *yeshiva* of Volozhin, established in 1803, in the province of Vilna in White Russia. In those days, the best Talmudic academies were to be found in Lithuania and White Russia. Each *yeshiva* had its own tradition and methods, and attracted students from all over Europe and even from other parts of the world.

At first, the old man would not agree to young Bialik's going to Volozhin because he knew that *yeshiva* to be a stronghold of opposition to *Hasidism*, of which he, like most Jews in the Ukraine, was a strong adherent. However, when the grandfather accidentally discovered that the boy had little faith in the *Hasidic* rabbis, he agreed to let him go to Volozhin; he hoped that would at least help to keep the skeptic young Hayyim Nahman within the fold of observant Jews.

The red-headed boy from Volhynia (he was called, in the fashion of the time, "*Der Zhitomirer*," the student from Zhitomir) presented a curious spectacle in Volozhin: he wore the long coat and earlocks, blue stockings, and sandals of the Ukrainian *Hasidim*. The "Litvak" *Mitnagdim* of Volozhin wore shorter earlocks, shorter coats, and more somber dress. In temperament, too, they were more sedate. Their method of studying Talmud also differed; the "Litvaks," especially at Volozhin, stressed thoroughness rather than quantity, and rational discussion rather than flights into mysticism. However, since many students came to Volozhin from other parts of the world, a certain tolerant attitude existed toward "outlandish" figures.

Bialik arrived at Volozhin at a tumultuous time in its history. The students were demanding that they be taught secular subjects, while the Russian governmental authorities were stipulating that the Russian language be taught. There were student strikes, mild riots, sabotage. Much time was consumed in the struggle, and a number of students studied Russian in secret or read forbidden Hebrew books. Bialik, one of the culprits, began also to learn Russian and joined a secret society of religious Zionists, which entrusted him with the task of drawing up its program.

During his first few months at Volozhin, Bialik managed to attain a high degree of scholarship according to its exacting standards. But, after a while, he grew tired of the confined life at the *yeshiva*, where the students' every hour was controlled and supervised, their letters censored, outside reading prohibited, and all study limited to the Talmud.

Yet there were certain features of the regime at Volozhin which made a lasting impression and engendered fond memories for Bialik. The methods of teaching were in some respects those of the most advanced colleges and modern universities—through seminars rather than ordinary lectures. Each student selected his own assignments, with the approval of the dean. The most memorable aspect of *yeshiva* life was the constant din in the study halls—a din which to the Talmudic scholars was more in the nature of heavenly music than the most solemn chanting in the synagogue.

Bialik spent his final months at Volozhin roaming the woods and the fields, watching the Byelorussian peasants at work, dreaming of Zion, and writing Hebrew verses. Finally, after a year and a half at the *yeshiva*, he decided to run away to Odessa. A hundred of his fellow students accompanied him to the stagecoach, singing Hebrew songs, and predicting future greatness for their friend Hayyim Nahman of Zhitomir.

Odessa: Launching of the Poet

Bialik hoped to find in Odessa what he had once dreamed of finding in Berlin—a synthesis of Judaism and modern European culture. Odessa, Russia's main port on the Black Sea, built by Catherine the Great, was perhaps the most cosmopolitan city in Russia, inhabited by Russians, Ukrainians, Greeks, Armenians, Tartars, Germans, and Jews from Germany, Galicia, and other parts of Russia. To Orthodox Jews of the smaller towns, Odessa was a den of iniquity, a godless city, where Jews did not obey the Law, dressed like Gentiles, and spoke Russian. During the latter part of the nineteenth century, the city had become the main center of modern Hebrew literature. It was the home of Ahad Ha-am (Asher Ginzberg), the great Hebrew essayist and philosopher whose ideas had been much discussed at Volozhin. Bialik had been very much influenced by him—perhaps no less for the unusual felicity of Ahad Ha-am's Hebrew prose as for his ideas. In fact, Bialik's flight to Odessa was in a sense a pilgrimage to see the writer, who was one of his heroes.

A rabbi in Odessa, the father of a classmate at Volozhin, had given Bialik a letter to Ahad Ha-am. When Bialik showed the great man one of his Hebrew poems, Ahad Ha-am arranged for its publication in a magazine. Entitled "Welcome to the Bird," the poem had a freshness of Hebrew style which commanded attention.

Do you bring me friendly greetings
From my brothers there in Zion
Brothers far yet near?
O the happy! O the blessed!
Do they guess what heavy sorrows
I must suffer here?

The success of this first poem did not assure Bialik of any immediate triumphs as a writer, nor did it provide him with food and shelter. Bialik suffered hunger and cold, and whenever he went to the homes where he had been engaged as a private tutor in Hebrew, he kept his torn trousers covered by his overcoat. But he managed to improve his Russian and to learn the rudiments of German. He stayed in Odessa only a few months.

From the World of Business to Education

When Bialik's grandfather was on his deathbed, the poet returned to Zhitomir. Shortly after his grandfather's death, Bialik married into a family of lumber merchants in the province of Kiev and became a businessman. Except for the circumstance that there were no children, Bialik's marriage with Mania Averbach was an eminently happy one, and so were the poet's relations with his father-in-law Reb Shevach Averbach. But his venture into business proved catastrophic financially, wiping out his wife's dowry. The years spent by Bialik in the woods where timber was being cut, however, produced some of the best-known poems in the Hebrew language, many of which were first scribbled on the backs of receipts, bills of lading, and other such documents, or written in the middle of the night, while singing, much to the bewilderment of the night watchman.

But Bialik was no businessman. After his failure in that endeavor he was forced to accept a teaching engagement in a town in Russian Poland on the German border. There, too, he tried his hand at business, as a coal merchant, and there again his principal achievement was producing poetry.

Eventually Bialik was offered a position in Odessa, teaching in a modern Hebrew school conducted by Zionists. The poet now had the opportunity to introduce improvements in an area of Jewish life in which he had suffered so much as a child. In the Odessa school he taught children to speak Hebrew, using a simple vocabulary before they began the study of Bible. In collaboration with his colleagues, Bialik compiled children's readers in Hebrew, an activity which led him into a career as publisher—starting with school textbooks—which he was to continue to the end of his days.

Conflict of Cultures

When Bialik returned to Odessa in 1900, he was twenty-eight years old and already recognized as the leading Hebrew poet of the age. Most of the poems he had written in the decade since his first visit to Odessa expressed nostalgia for the traditional house of study (*bet hamidrash*), Talmudic literature, and the inner conflict of the Talmudic student.

The generation of Jewish intellectuals in Russia and nearby East European countries (Galicia and Bukovina in the Austrian-Hungarian Empire, and Rumania) consisted, in large measure, of former students at the *bet hamidrash* or the *yeshiva*. This was a generation which had to move from one culture into another, a transition which, in most cases, was accompanied by loss of faith and abandonment of religious observance. In nearly all cases it was a painful process. Such young men were torn by two strong opposing sentiments: on the one hand, the pull of the old Talmudic Orthodox civilization, with its haunting melodies, its habits of thinking and feeling, and the consciousness that there was an ancient civilization which preserved Judaism through the ages; and, on the other hand, the lure of the modern Western world, with its arts and sciences, the rule of reason, and the promise of a better life.

Bialik struck a responsive chord in the hearts of his contemporaries with his description of the *bet hamidrash*:

> The spring whence strength of soul was drawn in evil days
> By those who gladly walked to meet their death . . .
> climbing to the stake,
>
> The stronghold where your fathers
> Salvaged their soul's desire and held the Law
> Holy above all holies to be saved,
>
> The biding spirit that kept
> Their mighty spirit and its essence pure.
> "On the Threshold of the House of Prayer"
> translated by Harry A. Fein.

But the *bet hamidrash* was now abandoned, with few left to guard it:

> A miserable remnant . . . a few stray sheaves of much lost,
> some shrivelled Jews . . . who lose their pain in faded Talmud
> page . . .
>
> Abandoned in the nest, the fledglings gone
> Like shadows vanished in the lofty trees.

The most important of Bialik's poems of that period is "*Ha-Matmid.*" ("The Talmud Student"), a long poem of some twenty pages, written over a period of seven years. The most emotional of Bialik's poems, it deals not only with the specific problem of the conflict of cultures in the Jewish world but also touches on the universal conflict between the hunger for life and the hunger for self-dedication. Many tears were shed by former Talmud students as they read the poem, which appeared in installments in *Ha-Shiloah*, a Hebrew magazine.

The poem dealt with the recluse scholar, the *matmid*, who was not necessarily the brightest but by far the most dedicated scholar, and who refused to take advantage even of the limited time permitted at the *yeshiva* for rest and recreation in order to devote every possible moment to study the Talmud.

> A prisoner, self-guarded, self-condemned
> Self-sacrificed to study of the Law.

Bialik echoed what was in the hearts of thousands of his contemporaries:

> I, in my boyhood, was a listener
> Among the voices, and my youth was passed
> Among these wan sufferers, whose wrinkled brows
> And staring eyes implore the world's compassion.
>
> The heart in me cries out: Lord of the world!
> To what end is this mighty sacrifice?

This last question apparently is unanswerable. But there is an affirmative note in the final lines of the long poem:

> . . . How strong, how sturdy
> The seed must be that withers in those fields,
> How rich would be the blessing if one beam
> Of living sunlight could break through to you;
> How great the harvest to be reaped in joy,
> If once the wind of life should pass through you.

An even more vigorously affirmative note on the value of such devoted study is found in the last lines of "On the Threshold of the House of Prayer."

> Thou shalt not fall, Shem's tent, I'll build thee fast;
> From heaps of dust thy walls I'll resurrect.
> All palaces shalt thou alone outlast!
>
> With clouds dispersed, God's glory there will bide
> All flesh shall then behold that God holds sway;
> Buds fade, grass withers . . . God endures for aye.

Bialik espoused the Jewish attitude whereby man refuses to accept fate as inevitable but makes an intelligent effort to control his destiny. He based one of his most majestic poems, "The Dead of the Wilderness," on an ancient Talmudic legend about giant warriors who, in spite of divine injunction to wait, attacked the enemy as they were proceeding to the Promised Land, and their bodies are said to lie intact, still buried in the desert sands. Once every few centuries, they rise to renew their challenge to divine procrastination.

We are the mighty!
The last generation of slaves and the first generation of free men!
Alone in our hands is our strength.

Yea, on the tops of the crags in the thickness of clouds,
With the eagles of heaven we drank from the fountains of freedom.
Even now, though the God of vengeance has shut the desert upon us,
A song of strength and revolt has reached upon us, and we rise.

Forward despite the heavens and the wrath thereof.

A year or so later, Bialik was very much moved by the pogrom in Kishinev, in which about two score Jews were killed. He wrote "The City of Slaughter," a poem in which he preached not an abstract doctrine against a philosophical kind of passivity, but a concrete form of revolt against the habit which Jews had developed, in centuries of oppression, of running away, hiding without offering a fight, and praying and weeping:

Come now, and I will bring thee to their lairs
The privies, jakes and pigpens where the heirs
Of Hasmoneans lay, with trembling knees,
Concealed and cowering—the sons of Maccabees!
The seed of saints, the scions of the lions!

It was the flight of mice they fled,
The scurrying of roaches was their flight;
They died like dogs and they were dead!

For great is the anguish, great the shame on the brow:
But which of these is greater, son of man, say thou. . . .

The traditional Jewish response to calamity was to view it as a punishment for sins, to repent, to pray for forgiveness, and, sometimes, to tighten control on the community or to look for culprits as scapegoats. The prevalent attitude was acceptance, which, Bialik felt, by the time of the Kishinev pogrom had lost whatever tragic grandeur it had once had. The poet seemed to hear the divine voice bidding him carry this message:

> Wherefore their cries imploring, their supplicating din?
> Speak to them, bid them rage!
> Let them against Me raise their outraged hand,—
> Let them demand!
> Demand the retribution for the shamed
> Of all the centuries and every age!
> Let fists be flung like stone
> Against the heavens and the heavenly throne!

As soon as "The City of Slaughter" appeared, Vladimir Jabotinsky translated it into Russian and Bialik himself translated it into Yiddish. In the three languages the poem became the rallying call of Jewish self-defense and its author was hailed as "prophet." It had a more far-reaching effect than any other poem in Jewish literature.

> Arise and go now to the city of slaughter;
> Into its courtyard wind thy way;
> There with thine own hand touch, and with the eyes of thine head,
> Behold on tree, on stone, on fence, on mural clay,
> The spattered blood and dried brains of the dead. . . .

The day that poem was written, states Jacob Fichman, a leading Hebrew poet and literary essayist, "was perhaps the most important date in the history of modern Hebrew poetry . . . In that poem of pain and shame Bialik attained the stature of a mentor and a chastiser of his people, the like of which was unknown in Hebrew poetry since the days of the Bible."

To "The City of Slaughter" is credited the fact that a year later, when a similar pogrom took place in Homel, White Russia, a formation of 450 young Jews fought off their attackers and put them to flight in spite of the encouragement the rioters had from the Russian police. In 1907, in Jaffa, Palestine, a number of veterans of such Jewish self-defense groups in Russia, including the leader of the group in Homel, met in the room of Itzhak Ben Zvi (later President of Israel) and formed the first military unit to defend Jewish life and property in the country. Out of that unit (called *Hashomer*, "The Guard") in time grew the Hagannah, the Jewish militia in Palestine, which, in turn, eventually became the present Israel Army.

Many of Bialik's "prophetic" poems are written in the mood recurrent in Jeremiah—the complaint by the messenger of God's word that the people fail to heed the divine message. Bialik saw the problem as the Jews' lack of courage, dignity, regard for their own historic heritage, or an earnest desire to reconstruct their national life on sound foundations. One of the most powerful of such poems was written by Bialik in Yiddish, presumably in order to reach wider masses. "The Last Word," still today the favorite of Yiddish school recitations, begins with the lines: "I have been sent to you by God . . ."

"The Scroll of Fire"

In "The Scroll of Fire," a long prose poem written in 1905, Bialik developed a philosophy of Jewish history. The central idea is that with the loss of their political independence and exile from their homeland, Jews can preserve their heritage only at the cost of foregoing the wholesome and normal enjoyment of life; and periodically they revolt against the heavy burden. Based on a Talmudic legend pertaining to the destruction of the Temple and the ensuing captivity by the Romans of hundreds of Jewish youths and maidens, this poem merges the story of Bialik's own life with the story of the Jewish people. The Biblical period is the happy years of the people's childhood —like Bialik's own in the Volhynia countryside. The austere Talmudic law imposed on the Jewish people is personified by an old man reminiscent of Bialik's grandfather or the dean at the Volozhin *yeshiva*. In the following passage, a solitary youth who managed to escape the Romans says to the maiden:

Tall standing corn and choicest fields blessed by childhood
And flourishing groves and the branches of the cypress trees took me into their secret.
And I loved the God of the earth, the God of the mountains and the valleys,
And revered the God of the heavens.
And one day a hoary-headed man of Judea

Found me flung down among the mountains with dawn
And the man was garbed in a cloak and his hair was wild
As he walked darkly and angrily.

And the aged man had compassion on me,
And he planted me in the innermost shelter of his tent,
And with the shade of his trembling white beard he covered me.
And he taught me his ways and caused me to worship his God,
And he restrained my soul from all delight and taught me to look to the heavens,
And all the blossoms of my youth he plucked forth one by one.

And my days became fasts as were his days,
And my nights became prayers as were his nights.
And I feared the old man exceedingly
As the flower fears the autumn.
My face grew thin and my forehead blanched from day to day.

See now, the heavens have mocked me
And with a cruel lie encircled me.
My youth, my everything, have they taken from me.
And nothing have they given me in return.

"The Scroll of Fire" is not the best-known of Bialik's poems, though it seems to be one of his most ambitious. The poet's purpose seems to have been to produce the equivalent of Dante's *Divine Comedy*, Milton's *Paradise Lost*, Goethe's *Faust*, Pushkin's *Eugene Onegin*, Mickiewicz's *Pan Tadeusz*—or, to use an example from medieval Hebrew literature, Gabirol's *Crown of Glory*. In other words, the poem was to give expression to the spirit of a whole age, a people, or a total philosophy. But whereas all the foregoing poems took years to produce, Bialik wrote his "Scroll of Fire" in one month. Had he worked at it for seven years as he did in the case of "*The Matmid*," "The Scroll of Fire" might perhaps have become Bialik's magnum opus.

Career as Editor and Publisher

Except for an interruption of two years, Bialik lived in Odessa, from 1900 until he left Russia shortly after the Russian Revolution. During this period and until his death in 1934, editing and publishing remained his chief occupation, first in Odessa, then later for a brief period in Berlin, and finally in Tel Aviv. But his publishing career was more than a business venture: it was closely linked to a vast project of historic cultural significance which Bialik in time came to consider as far more important than his own poetry.

The project which Bialik evolved and which today, over thirty years after his death, is still far from being carried out is comparable to the work of those who in centuries gone by edited the Bible and the Talmud. In each case, scattered expressions of the Jewish spirit covering many generations were examined, sifted, winnowed, and edited, and finally brought together in one great collection as an authentic body of literature representing the basis of Jewish culture. What Bialik had in mind was a new collection, edited in the spirit of modern secular Jewish nationalism, but with more modest pretensions to authority than the Bible, Mishnah, or Talmud.

With two colleagues, Bialik at first undertook to issue an abridged Bible for school children. This immediately aroused a controversy; not only the Orthodox but many irreligious Jews as well objected to any tampering with the Bible in its traditional form.

After the completion of the Bible series came a Talmud series, with special emphasis on the *Aggadah*, that part of the Talmud and Talmudic literature which deals with legend, folklore, and proverbs. Out of the *Aggadah* compilation for school use grew also a similar collection for adults. The Bialik *Book of the Aggadah* remains the standard modernized text, with the original Hebrew left intact as found in the old sources, and the Aramaic portions translated into the same style of Hebrew.

Bialik never tired of advocating what he called *Kinnus*, literally "ingathering" or "collection." His aim was the publication of a sort of Hebrew equivalent in Jewish literature of the Harvard Classics, including works written in Hebrew as well as translations from other languages. Among Hebrew works the first to claim his attention were the poems produced by the literary giants of the Golden Age in Spain—Solomon ibn Gabirol, Judah Halevi, and the two Ibn Ezras—though he actually succeeded in publishing only the annotated works of Gabirol and Abraham ibn Ezra.

After about 1905 or 1906 Bialik stopped writing poetry, except for an occasional rare piece, at a time when he was seemingly at the height of his poetic productivity. The surprised and disappointed public hoped it was a mere pause and vainly sought for explanations. One theory advanced by some critics (e.g., Jacob Fichman) grew out of Bialik's feeling that modern literature in Hebrew had little future unless the public had an adequate appreciation of the literature of the past. He seemed to consider the task of husbanding the literary heritage of the Jewish people and presenting it in readable Hebrew more important than that of writing his own poetry.

Bialik rendered into Hebrew Cervantes' *Don Quixote*, which he abridged, and Schiller's *Wilhelm Tell*. He translated into Hebrew from the Russian manuscript a play which became most famous in its Yiddish version—S. Ansky's *Dybbuk*. Bialik also gave the first renderings of some of Sholom Aleichem's stories from Yiddish into Hebrew, and collaborated with Mendele Mocher Sephorim in translating his Yiddish books into Hebrew.

Russian Revolution: Departure for Palestine

Bialik's publishing career was interrupted by the victory of the Bolsheviks in Russia in 1917. They declared the Hebrew language to be "counter-revolutionary," and forbade its teaching. All Hebrew schools were closed. The plates in Bialik's printing shop, including those prepared for the publication of Ibn Gabirol's works, were scrapped for metal.

Bialik's life was in danger on several occasions, but his fame as a poet and the prestige in which he was held in Russian literary circles saved him. He often quarrelled with Bolshevik leaders in Odessa, who included some of his most avid readers and admirers. Once he told the leader of the secret police, a Jew named Deutsch: "You are the second great lie in history . . . The first one was two thousand years ago, when, in the name of brotherly love, rivers of blood began to be shed." To his brother-in-law, Jan Gamarnik, a Bolshevik general, he said, "Some day you will die a shameful death at the hands of your own comrades." (Gamarnik really did perish in the first purge in the 1930's at the hands of Stalin's henchmen.)

Finally, as the result of efforts by Maxim Gorki and other great literary figures who were in his good graces, Lenin issued a permit to Bialik and a few other Hebrew writers to leave Russia, on the understanding that they would proceed to Palestine. Some petty Jewish officials in the Communist Party sought to sabotage the implementation of that permit, but the group managed to outwit them and left Russia, making their first stop Berlin. It happened that the German capital was at that time a gathering place for Hebrew writers—some who had lived there before World War I, others who were recent refugees from Soviet Russia or emigrants from Poland. With its facilities for producing books Berlin was for a while a center for Hebrew publishing. Bialik, too, started his Dvir Publishing House there, but even then the books bore the mark "Berlin-Tel Aviv." Within a couple of years Bialik moved to Tel Aviv, his original destination on leaving Russia. The Jewish city on the Mediterranean shared with Berlin and Warsaw the role of successor to Odessa as the center of Hebrew publishing in the world, and has in our time become the main center. Tel Aviv was the natural place for Bialik in which to take up residence. (It already boasted a colony of the leading Hebrew writers in Palestine, including Bialik's revered master, Ahad Ha-am, who had moved to Tel Aviv from London a short time before.) Many of these men taught at the Herzliah, the oldest and largest Hebrew secondary school.

On April 1, 1925, a year after Bialik's arrival in Palestine, when the Hebrew University was opened on Mt. Scopus by Lord Balfour, Bialik delivered the main address.*

Bialik in America

In 1926 Bialik visited America in the company of his friend and associate in the publishing business, Shemaryahu Levin, on a mission to raise money for the Keren Hayesod as well as to interest individuals in the Dvir Publishing House of Tel Aviv. Bialik was given a royal welcome, and his visit left a lasting impression. But he was forced to travel for five months at a dizzying pace all over the country, making two or three

* An English text of the address is to be found in *The Zionist Idea*, edited by Arthur Hertzberg (Doubleday, New York, 1959).

speeches a day, listening to many more in his honor, and hearing himself introduced by chairmen who did not know how to pronounce his name and who did not know whether the man they were honoring was an alto, a soprano, or a cantor's apprentice (the Hebrew word *meshorer*, used also in Yiddish, means both a poet and a singer). Bialik described all his experiences at the end of his trip in a famous letter to Ahad Ha-am, in which he waxed sarcastic about American publicity and campaign methods, deprecated the lack of cultural and spiritual content in American Zionism, but expressed enthusiasm for the vitality and spirit of freedom of American Jewry and faith in its future potentialities. The growth and development of American Jewry within a single generation he termed one of the great marvels of Jewish history.

More than a decade earlier, when the great Yiddish writer Sholom Aleichem and his son-in-law, the Hebrew writer I. D. Berkowitz, first contemplated settling in the United States, Bialik, who was a close friend to both men, had strongly urged them to desist from such a step. There was no room, he argued, for men of talent and sensitivity in that brash, noisy country, with its vulgar plebeian spirit, its low-class Jews (for, after all, no respectable Jew in Russia would think of emigrating to "The Land of the Dollars"), its sensation-seeking Yiddish press, its rapacious and uncouth Jewish publishers.

In his letter to Ahad Ha-am, however, Bialik now showed a more benevolent attitude toward the boisterous nature of American Jewry, the first signs of appreciation of what he called "the miracle of Jewish history" in the rise of American Jewry, and some belief in its future. He frankly confessed that his previous prejudices were irrational and prompted by a fear of the unfamiliar and by the dread of the rustic for modern urban civilization, which, in his mind, was embodied in New York. He realized, he said, that America was a country in the process of becoming, and that what he had previously considered as "American bluff"—the brashness and lack of proportion—in reality represented vigor, "a superabundance of youthful forces"; here, he now felt, was "virgin soil" which some day would be capable of producing "spiritual power of incalculable dimensions."

He found encouragement in many of the meetings he had

with Jews in America, whether those meetings were formal or informal. He met American Jews who had a warm feeling for Judaism and Jewish learning, who "did not throw away the traditional Jewish concern" for Jewish survival. "They remained with that great concern in their new homeland." He came to the conclusion that even though the Jews of America might be overly optimistic about their own position, it was still the best of all Diasporas, and that next to the historic Jewish homeland in Israel America was the country in which the survival of Judaism had the best prospects.

Last Years

Bialik's years in Tel Aviv were the happiest of his life. He became the most beloved figure of the Jewish community of Palestine, attracting large crowds whenever he lectured; he was often seen dancing on the streets and on the beach with *halutzim* (pioneers) and children. In an effort to give fresh meaning to traditional practices, Bialik introduced in Tel Aviv the custom of gathering on Saturday afternoons for discussions on questions relating to Judaism, which he called *Oneg Shabbat*—Sabbath Delight. The name is ancient, but its current widespread application to the Saturday afternoon cultural get-together owes its origin to Bialik.

The *Oneg Shabbat* took place in the Ohel-Shem (Tent of Shem) auditorium and was always filled to capacity: though Bialik was rarely the main speaker, he was nearly always the chairman, and the public, as a rule, was more interested in his comments and remarks than in the main lecture. The meetings usually started and ended with community singing, mostly of traditional and religious songs, with the poet himself, who had a good voice and a good ear for music, as a lusty participant. This institution of *Oneg Shabbat* has since spread far and wide in the Diaspora.

In his last years Bialik underwent several operations to cure an ailment from which he had suffered for a number of years. In Vienna, where he had gone in 1934 for another operation, a blood clot unexpectedly developed which choked him. "My heart," were the last words Bialik uttered. Only a few minutes earlier he had been rereading the Bible from the beginning, and had reached the end of the story of creation before he expired.

The poet was brought back to Tel Aviv to be buried beside Ahad Ha-am. His house numbered 22 has become the Bialik Museum, and the street has been renamed Bialik Street. The library of the Museum contains some thirty thousand volumes in Hebrew on subjects related to Hebrew literature and Judaism —the two subjects nearest the poet's heart.

The Legacy

Bialik was the favorite poet of Chaim Weizmann, Itzhak Ben Zvi, David Ben-Gurion, Moshe Sharett, Vladimir Jabotinsky and the whole generation which fought for the Jewish homeland and created the State of Israel. When men and women of that epoch spoke of themselves or of their children born in the homeland as "the last generation of enslavement, the first generation of freedom," they were using a phrase taken from Bialik's "Dead of the Wilderness." They did not merely derive esthetic enjoyment from his Hebrew verses: they drew inspiration for the great historic task to which they had set their hands. Though Bialik wrote few verses which contained a direct Zionist appeal, he evoked a mood for action as no other poet did.

The tribute Bialik paid Mendele—that he succeeded in blending the various Hebrew styles stemming from different historic periods into one homogenous idiom—applies more to Bialik than to Mendele. His highly developed sense of idiom combined with his profound scholarship and love of the language produced a Hebrew style the like of which had not been known in the past. No one else was as capable of using a Hebrew word or phrase with such a keen sense for its shadings, nuances, and connotations accumulated over the centuries. He was, however, primarily a poet, and his prose lacked the succinctness or unique character of his verse.

Outside of Hebrew, Bialik wrote only in one other language—Yiddish. Though Yiddish was his mother tongue, it was not a language he studied or cultivated. And yet the few poems he did write in that tongue gave Bialik an honored place in Yiddish literature. One such poem describes little boys at the *heder*. In both Hebrew and Yiddish, his poems revealed a genius for language and an uncanny sense of idiom. In each language, he knew how to select the sounds and the idiomatic expressions suitable for the effect he sought to produce.

Somewhat off the main track of Bialik's poetic contributions are his so-called *Songs of the People* and his many children's poems. In both Bialik displayed his genius for articulating motifs which had evolved in the Yiddish idiom in superb Hebrew. Most of his *Songs of the People* are based on motifs found in Yiddish folk songs, as, for example, "Between the Tigris and the Euphrates" and "By My Well," both of which have been translated into English. Bialik's *Children's Poems* still delight youngsters in Israel—as they always delighted children familiar with Hebrew in Europe, in Palestine, and elsewhere.

In general, Bialik defies classification. As an editor and publisher, he was a great affirmer of historic Jewish values. Though his poetry reflects many moods, it is deeply rooted in the past and at the same time is full of meaning for our own times. Bialik remains "the poet laureate" of the Jewish people, and, since the days of the Bible, its most impressive Hebrew writer.

8 . *Theodor Herzl*

[1860-1904]

MARVIN LOWENTHAL

MORE than any other one man, Theodor Herzl changed the course of modern Jewish history. The Jews, he proclaimed in a clear, measured voice that caught the world's ear, were a people and not a sect or a race, and they were one people and not a collection of miscellaneous communities. It followed—so he insisted—that the nations of the world and the Jews themselves must be brought to act in the light of this reality. By speech and deed Herzl elevated a local sore spot, a domestic misery usually met by stopgap measures, into a challenging international issue. He removed the Jewish problem from the waiting rooms of philanthropists and laid it before the chancelleries of European statesmanship. He turned a religious, racial, or parochial set of troubles into a single broad political question to be settled on the highest level of diplomatic negotiation.

Thus Herzl became, in Israel Zangwill's phrase, "the first Jewish statesman since the destruction of Jerusalem." He represented and presented not the cause of the Russian Jews, Galician Jews, or any other segment of Jewry, but the cause of the Jewish people as a whole—a people with a common past and the aspiration toward a common future. He put Zionism, the program of the indivisible people, on the map; and in creating the Zionist organization, he gave the Jewish people an address.

Herzl was a remarkable sort of statesman. To begin with, he was to all intents a man of letters: a journalist, playwright, feuilletonist, and short story writer. He aspired to become a novelist. Then in 1895, while serving as Paris correspondent of the Vienna *Neue Freie Presse*, he conceived the plan of a Jewish state not merely as the reaffirmation of a traditional ideal and not only as the solution to a world-vexing problem, but as something to be created forthwith through the collaboration of the leading European powers. Virtually overnight he found that his idea had catapulted him into statesmanship on an international scale.

After his premature death, Herzl's dream of a Jewish state eventually came true, thanks to the path he cleared, the implements he fashioned, the procedure he developed, and the will he infused into his people. "He who wills something great," Herzl once wrote in perhaps unconscious echo of Montaigne, "is in my eyes a great man—not he who achieves it. For in achievement luck plays a part."

The present State of Israel owes its origin to Herzl—at least in the sense that he was the catalyst who precipitated the modern forces that brought it to birth. Since Moses no single man, no Washington or Bismarck, has been in equal degree the father of a country. Theodor Herzl was in the noblest sense a man who willed something great.

From Budapest to Vienna

Theodor Herzl was born May 2, 1860, in Budapest, where he was reared during an era when things went well with the Hungarian Jews. During his boyhood the essential Jewish customs were observed in the Herzl household, the festivals were celebrated in the traditional manner, particularly Passover and *Hanukkah*, and little Theodor accompanied his father to the Tabakgasse synagogue every Friday evening and Sabbath morning. From the age of six to ten he attended the local Jewish community school—there were no normal public schools—and the reports show that in "Religion" and "Hebrew Subjects" his marks ranged from good to excellent. At eight his father enrolled him as a contributing member of the Chevra Kadishah,* and at thirteen he was confirmed in accordance with time-

* The society found in most Jewish communities which cares for the sick and buries the dead. It was customary for wealthier members of a community to enroll their male children, as contributing members, at an early age.

honored usage, learning enough Hebrew, even if by rote, to read the appropriate "portion" of the Torah and recite the blessings. Later in life, when entering upon a critical new venture, he never failed to ask for the parental blessing—a biblical observance that weathered Johann Strauss' Vienna. The home ceremonies and regular synagogue attendance, with their inevitable exposure to something of the Hebrew language and Jewish spirit, were bound to leave on a sensitive nature impressions which the outer world would blanket but never could efface.

Then there was Grandfather Herzl. He lived a conscientiously Orthodox life in the old Orthodox community of Semlin (now in Yugoslavia); his standing and piety, as well as the requisite art, were such that it fell upon him to blow the *shofar* on New Year's and chant the *Kol Nidre* prayer on the Day of Atonement; he paid an annual visit to Budapest, where he died when Theodor was past nineteen, and held a tender place in the affection of his grandson. He, too, left an impression. When, nearly twenty years afterwards, Herzl remarked a bearded, fur-capped figure in Sofia, he did not comment as a Westerner might on his exotic looks. He took him to be something familiar: "He resembled," Herzl's diaries record, "my grandfather Simon Herzl." Similarly, when he visited the main Paris synagogue for the first time, in 1895, he found the services "once again" solemn and moving. "Much," he noted, "reminded me of my youth and the Tabakgasse synagogue in Pest."

But, on the whole, there was little in his training, interests, or outward circumstances to inspire him with any particular devotion to things Jewish beyond a deep sense of loyalty grounded in self-respect. His immediate family, Central European in origin with a Sephardic strain on his father's side, was sufficiently well-to-do and world-minded to supply him with a German environment, education, and cultural outlook. But, while there was small evidence of any significant Jewish interest, he soon began to evince a pronounced taste for magnificent scheming. At ten, when most boys were content to dream of becoming the engineer of an express train, he planned to be a second De Lesseps and hew out the Panama Canal. He scribbled stories, plays, and verse at an early age, but, later, on the practical advice of his elders, he took up the study of law. His family moved to Vienna when he was eighteen, became decently rich, and lived as part of the "up-town" Jewish community in the Währing quarter.

The Writer in the Making

Soon after Herzl obtained his law degree in 1884, he gave up the law for his earlier love: literature and the theater. He traveled and wrote. By the time he was thirty he had seen something of Germany, Switzerland, France, the Lowlands, England, and Italy, and had on his own reckoning turned out seventeen plays, besides inumerable articles, travel sketches, and short stories.

Herzl's first play to be produced, a one-act drama called *Tabarin*, enjoyed its premiere at the hands of a German troupe in the Star Theater, Broadway and 13th Street, New York, on November 23, 1885. Five other plays saw the boards in Austria, Bohemia, and Germany, with varying success. Vienna and Berlin newspapers opened their columns to his colorful, not very substantial, but scrupulously composed articles, and in 1887, the *Wiener Allgemeine Zeitung* appointed Herzl, for a spell, its literary editor; he had "arrived" as a journalist. He published two volumes of his essays and sketches, the pick of his feuilletons —*Neues von der Venus* (1887) and *Das Buch der Narrheit* (1888)—and earned himself critical esteem if little else. He had become a master of that fragile and evanescent form of journalism, the feuilleton, especially beloved on the continent. He was not yet, to be sure, a young Heine or Schnitzler, and fate determined that he should never become one.

In 1889, confident of his career as a playwright and man of letters, though still impatient at its slow progress—he was already twenty-nine!—he married a bright, golden-haired, blue-eyed young woman, Julie Naschauer, whose family had much the same background as his own, but more wealth. Three children came in rapid succession, two girls and a boy: Pauline, Hans, Margarete.

Almost from the start, however, the marriage ran into heavy seas. Temperamentally, the young couple were not in accord. Julie loved a gay social life, she wanted her husband to succeed and she wanted to enjoy his success, but she was apparently unable to help him earn it by self-effacing sympathy and devotion; and the efforts she made were rendered harder by a mother-in-law problem. Herzl's mother was intelligent and warm-hearted, but, like Herzl's father, she doted on her son jealously and obsessively—the more so in that her only other child, Pauline, a year older than Theodor, had died before reaching twenty. Herzl, in turn, doted on his parents, partly also because he was led to fill the role of son and daughter. When the Zionist cause, along with journalistic obligations, came to monopolize Herzl's life, the estrangement with his wife widened; Julie had no emotional identification with the destiny of the Jews, and she looked on Zion, rightly enough in her eyes, as a husband-snatcher and home-breaker. Only the children, to whom they were both passionately devoted, held them together.

Paris Correspondent

In August of 1891 Herzl set out on a conjugal vacation—an experimental separation from his wife and their troubled domestic existence. He wandered for two months in the Pyrenees, recovering his composure and power of decision, and writing travel sketches of more than customary substance. One of them, describing the village of Luz, "a fine abode for convalescents of all sorts," elicited an invitation from the *Neue Freie Presse* to become its Paris correspondent. This leading Vienna newspaper was one of Europe's most influential liberal organs, and Paris was the prize post for all European journalists. Naturally, Herzl accepted the position—at twelve hundred francs a month, plus expenses and one hundred francs per feuilleton—and, without returning home, settled in the French capital toward the end of October. His wife and children joined him there the following February.

Paris put an end to Herzl's career as an independent man of letters, at liberty to indulge his personal inclinations, and to a free lance's search for a public. He apprenticed himself to the affairs of the world as a responsible newspaperman. He learned politics and politicians at close range in the Chamber of Deputies; he studied statesmen and statecraft at the Quai d'Orsay; he milled about in the election campaigns in town and village; he reported firsthand the investigations, trials, and mad parliamentary debates attendant upon the Panama fiasco. He wrote up anarchist bombings, cabinet rumpuses, and the stabbing of President Sadi-Carnot. Notebook in hand, he "stared at the phenomenon of the crowd," as he later said, "without for a long time understanding it"—not only election crowds, but unemployment riots, anti-Italian riots, and pro-Russian demonstrations (the latter at Toulon, where he suffered a severe attack of malaria and probably began the history of his heart ailment). He turned out dramatic and literary criticism as well as feuilletons on the many sides of life that do not make spot news. Applying his dramatist's talent to the stage of reality, he fascinated his readers and won a wide reputation by writing politics in terms of personalities and by going behind both to the social and economic forces of which they were lime-lighted protagonists. At the end of his Paris experience he incorporated the best of these human yet broadly analytical articles in a volume entitled *Das Palais Bourbon* (1895).

Herzl's journalism brought him inevitably into frequent contact with newsworthy events and experiences related to anti-Semitism. A libel suit against the anti-Semitic Drumont (in 1892), which Herzl later characterized as a prologue to the Panama affair, ended with Drumont crying out before the court, "Down with the German Jews! France for Frenchmen!" and his adherents shouting, without such nice distinction, "Down with the Jews!" The Panama scandals, though they involved virtually no Jews, provoked the introduction of a bill to disbar all Jews from holding public office and won for it 160 votes in the Chamber of Deputies. A series of duels between anti-Semites and Jews who defended the honor of their people reached a climax when a French-Jewish army captain was mortally stabbed. Disorders broke out during the funeral procession, in which fifty thousand sympathizers followed the hearse. Stock market scandals and other incidents brought a constant recurrence of the Jewish theme. Dramas dealt with it frankly, such as Dumas' *La Femme de Claude* and Lavedan's *Prince Aurec*, and led Herzl, in his reviews, to further cogitations on what it was all about.

The Dreyfus Affair

An army captain, Alfred Dreyfus, was arrested October 15, 1894, on the charge of high treason. His military trial, behind closed doors, took place in December, and he was pronounced guilty and sentenced for life to a penal colony in French Guiana; and on January 5, 1895 he was publicly degraded on the parade ground of the Ecole Militaire. Herzl heard as much of the preliminaries to the court-martial as a reporter could, he witnessed the public degradation, and his ears rang with the howl of the mob, "Death to the traitor!"—or, as he remembered it three years later, "Death to the Jews!" He telegraphed long dispatches on the events when they occurred, but no word about Dreyfus appears in the account of how he came to the Zionist idea which he confided to his diary but a few months afterwards.

In truth, there was no Dreyfus Affair to impress him in 1895; there was only the arrest and condemnation of an officer who chanced to be a Jew. It was not until 1896, well after *The Jewish State* had been written, that evidence of foul play began to come to light and the anti-Semitic implications unfold. Even though Herzl expressly stated in 1899 that the Dreyfus case had made him a Zionist, it was at best an appropriate myth, a dramatic foreshortening of the facts.

In other terms, the Dreyfus Affair, which did not yet exist, fairly epitomized the Jewish aspects of Herzl's experiences in Paris and condensed into one salient example his views on anti-Semitism and the Jewish future. If such things could happen, to use his words, "in republican, modern, civilized France, a century after the Declaration of Human Rights," the Jews as a whole had better look to themselves for salvation in a land of their own making.

The Jewish State

An old idea of writing a novel on the Jewish problem which Herzl had long had in mind now came to new life. So he records in the very opening of his *Diary:*

> I have been pounding away for some time at a work of tremendous magnitude. I don't know even now if I will be able to carry it through. It bears the aspects of a mighty dream. For days and weeks it has saturated me to the limits of my consciousness; it goes with me everywhere, hovers behind my ordinary talk, peers at me over the shoulders of my funny little journalistic work, overwhelms and intoxicates me.
>
> What will come of it is still too early to say. However, I have had experience enough to tell me that even as a dream it is remarkable and should be written down—if not as a memorial for mankind, then for my own pleasure and meditation in years to come. Or perhaps as something between these two possibilities—that is, as something for literature. If no action comes out of this romancing, a romance at least will come out of this activity. Title: The Promised Land.

Herzl also embarked at this time on an attempt to win over Baron Maurice de Hirsch, who was, along with the Rothschilds, one of the great multi-millionaires of the nineteenth century, to a constructive, daring plan for founding a Jewish state. He made a series of notes for his conference with Hirsch, but the latter, without hearing him through, summarily rejected the idea. Both men as good as lost their tempers. "Perhaps," Herzl later confessed, "I did not know the right way of handling him."

After that bad half-hour with Baron de Hirsch, Herzl "plunged" to his desk and indulged in a frenzy of note-making. Day in and day out, for weeks, he committed to slips of paper a torrent of ideas, which were inserted a year later into his diary. In all, these notes run to some fifty thousand words—about two hundred pages in the German edition. They were earmarked partly for an "Address" (itself twenty thousand words) which he intended to read before the Rothschilds assembled in family council; partly for a memorandum to be laid before two competent advisors—Chief Rabbi Güdemann of Vienna, and an experienced businessman—both of whom were to tell him how to gather the Rothschilds together; and partly for the eventual book, whether a treatise or novel he was not sure, if, all else failing, the plan had to be made public. In the end, pruned, tamed, and organized, the notes became *The Jewish State*, a booklet which heralded a turning point in modern Jewish history.

It is significant that, even in the first flush of Herzl's imagination, the details of the new society he envisioned, however extravagant (as he admits), were not utopian. He proposed nothing unknown, untoward, or impossible. He merely drafted a perfected *fin de siècle* commonwealth—1895 model. It was a liberal-spirited Viennese version of a decent, righteous order of things, with time out for light opera and pretty women in stylish gowns. Everything in it was plausible, technically feasible, and consonant with the average run of human nature. "Observe," he wrote for his imaginary audience, but with an eye to reassuring himself, "I do not make up fantasies; I deal entirely with real factors—which you can check up for yourselves; the fantasy lies only in the combination."

It is also significant to observe the comparatively minor role played by anti-Semitism in the original stream of notes and in the mood that dictated them. The psychological distress of Western Jews, which Herzl knew firsthand, and the physical misery of the East European Jews, which was common knowledge, haunt the background. Indeed, the *Elend*—the suffering and plight—of Jewry was to supply in Herzl's view, as alas it did in eventual fact, the motive power which would turn the vision into reality. But the dominant mood, a mood Herzl never abandoned, was positive and creative, an exhilaration in planning a new world where men shall lead finer and truer lives. It was akin to the mood of an Amos or an Isaiah. The "burden of the Lord" had fallen on Herzl to announce not so much the curses as the blessings of Jewish destiny.

The restoration of Zion was an age-old religious theme integral to Judaism; it had its source and divine sanction in the Hebrew prophets—beginning with Moses, who led his people from bondage to freedom. In the mid-nineteenth century a German Jew, Moses Hess, gave the ideal a contemporary nationalistic expression; and while he was a voice crying in the wilderness he did not long remain the only voice. In 1882, Leon Pinsker, a Russian Jew, not only restated the ideal but set forth the instruments for its realization in substantially the same terms that Herzl, who knew nothing of Pinsker's brochure called *Auto-Emancipation*, employed over a decade later. Throughout the eighties and early nineties Zionist essays and tracts abounded. The major novelty and force of Herzl's pamphlet lay not in its contents but in its tone—and, as will be seen, in the character of its author.

Pinsker, and many like him, wrote primarily as a Jew addressing himself to other Jews on a subject of intramural concern. Herzl, in contrast, wrote as a Jew who was a man of the world, an experienced political observer, a ranking journalist with international horizons; and his *Jewish State* was directed as much to the Bismarcks and Rothschilds as to the common reader. It had epigrams and eloquence, but in tenor it was the cool exposition of a trained publicist. Bismarck and Rothschild dismissed it, while Bülow and Plehve did not; neither of these reactions mattered so much as the fact that the common reader, who included editors, university men, and other makers of public opinion, heard about Zionism for the first time in language he was accustomed to understand.

But Herzl's *Jewish State* would have remained one more Zionist tract, even if better known than its predecessors, had he been a man content with words. He was, in fact, over and beyond his literary bent, intrinsically a man of action, and action on a grand scale; he was the boy, grown up, who had wanted to build the Panama Canal. He conceived of the Jewish state not as a subject for discourse, but as something to be acted upon by others and first of all by himself. When the idea first coalesced in his mind, he leaped beyond the thought of a novel or a pamphlet, and his almost instantaneous reaction was to exclaim to himself: "What correspondence, meetings, activities I shall have to encompass—what disappointments if I fail, what grim struggles if I succeed!"

No one better foresaw the unceasingly strenuous life that was to be his than Herzl himself. In a compartment of the Orient Express, on the way to lay his scheme before the Grand Duke of Baden—the first of a long series of princes, sultans, emperors, and influential statesmen he was to entreat on behalf of the projected Jewish state, he jotted in his ever-ready diary: "If I had trouble enough keeping a record of things when the Jewish matter began, what will it be like in the future as we pass from the dream into the reality! For it may be expected that every day now will bring its store of interesting experiences, even if I should never get so far as to found the State."

That was in April 1896, and a few weeks later Herzl was on his way to Constantinople, hoping to win over Sultan Abdul Hamid, the suzerain of Palestine. He was simultaneously occupied with putting a dozen irons into as many fires. Max Nordau, Baron Rothschild, newly-made English connections, the old-fashioned "Lovers of Zion" societies with their emphasis on slow, piecemeal settlement in the Holy Land and their incomprehension of political action, the insurgent Zionistic-minded youth champing at the bit, the Armenians in England, the *Hasidim* in Galicia, Prime Minister Salisbury, Papal Nuncio Agliardi, all received attention in the hope of using them for the acquisition of Palestine. These multiple activities were motivated by a single-minded goal: "to concentrate all our strength upon an internationally sanctioned acquisition of Palestine. To achieve this, we require diplomatic negotiations, which I have already begun, and propaganda on the largest scale."

Much of Herzl's efforts went into trying to win over the great bankers of France and England. But when the Rothschilds, Montagues, and their like turned a cold or lukewarm shoulder on anything that smacked of a political recognition of the Jewish people, he resolved to appeal directly to the masses and, what was more original, organize them for political action. Nothing quite like this had ever been attempted among the Jews since ancient times.

Swaying the Multitude

The instrument for political and financial action, as Herzl conceived it, was to be a world-wide Zionist organization, to be inaugurated by a congress—itself a novel and untried experiment in Jewish life. It was a sound idea, but the road from idea to reality—to the Congress finally convened at Basel—was long, complicated, and arduous. Almost anyone but Herzl, a man with a peculiar talent for not giving up, would have despaired.

During the year and more of preparatory labor, Herzl continued his efforts in a score of complementary directions. He interested Ferdinand of Bulgaria in trying to interest the Czar. He sent medical aid to the Turks in their war against the Greeks. He sounded out King Milan of Serbia and sought to gain the ear of Cardinal Rampolla and the Pope. He fought a continuous round of battles with his employers at the *Neue Freie Presse.* The latter were particularly furious when he founded the Zionist weekly, *Die Welt*, and it did not soothe them to learn that a number of leading *Welt* writers were members of their own staff.

Herzl was attacked on all sides, and he was often despondent: "This business takes a strong stomach," he wrote. A little later, when he discovered that he was the victim of a slander campaign conducted by prosperous Jews, he confessed that he was "beginning to have the right to become the world's worst anti-Semite. I often think of Levysohn's prediction: 'Those whom you want to help will start by nailing you rather painfully to the cross.'" And yet the movement continued to gather momentum. In January, 1897, he wrote: "I receive visitors from every corner of the world. The road from Palestine to Paris is beginning to pass through my door. In these past few weeks there were some interesting figures . . . I gave instructions to each of them . . . unless I am mistaken, Zionism is gradually winning the esteem of ordinary men in all sorts of countries. People are beginning to take us seriously."

First Zionist Congress

The First Zionist Congress met at Basel, August 29-31, 1897. It convened in the Stadt Casino, a concert and dance hall on the Steinenberg, adjacent to the Historical Museum. Besides a throng of spectators, the sessions were attended by 197 "delegates" from fifteen countries: Russia, Germany, Austria-Hungary, Rumania, Bulgaria, Holland, Belgium, France, Switzerland, Sweden, England, the United States, Algeria, and Palestine. They represented old Lovers of Zion societies, newly-formed political Zionist groups, and in some cases only themselves; they came from every stratum of society and embodied every shade of contemporary thought: Orthodox, liberal, atheist, culturalist, nationalist, anarchist, socialist, and capitalist minded Jews. "This was not a mere gathering of practical men," Jacob de Haas reported at the time, "nor yet a mere assembly of dreamers; the inward note was that of a gathering of brothers meeting after the long Diaspora."

Congratulatory greetings and endorsements with approximately six thousand signatures of individuals or organizations, as well as 550 telegrams, poured into the Congress office on Freie Strasse. Petitions, which had been circulated at Herzl's suggestion, brought fifty thousand signatures from Rumania alone, and ten thousand from Galicia; the signers declared their readiness to emigrate, and besought the Congress to create the necessary political and economic conditions for a return to Zion.

Almost the first words of Herzl's opening address set forth the purpose of the assembly: "We want to lay the foundation stone of the house which is to shelter the Jewish nation." It received a precise formulation in the Basel Program (largely drafted by Nordau), which became the official platform of the Zionist movement: "Zionism seeks to obtain for the Jewish people a publicly recognized, legally secured homeland in Palestine." Another memorable phrase from Herzl's opening address —"Zionism is a return to the Jewish fold even before it is a return to the Jewish land"—reappeared in the official platform under more abstract guise as one of the methods by which Zionism was to achieve its aim, that is, by "strengthening the Jewish national sentiment and national consciousness."

In addition to formulating its program, the Congress drafted the main lines of a constitution for the newly-born World Zionist Organization, and recommended the creation of a bank and a national fund, the latter specifically for the purchase of land in Palestine.

An exalted mood pervaded the Congress and rendered its sessions an unforgettable experience. One memorable feature was the impression Herzl made upon the delegates and spectators—who saw for the first time a figure that was already becoming a legend.

"A great eagle had suddenly spread its wings and threshed the air about him," recalled Joseph Klausner, the eminent historian who attended the Congress while a university student. In Martin Buber's memory Herzl had "a countenance lit with the glance of the Messiah." Or more soberly, Mordecai Braude recalls Herzl mounting to the dais at the First Congress: "Suddenly a compelling force had arisen, and he dominated us with his extraordinary personality, with his gestures, manner of speech, his ardor and vision."

"A majestic Oriental figure," observed Israel Zangwill, who had come prepared to scoff and remained to pray and cheer,

> not so tall as it appears when he draws himself up and stands dominating the assembly with eyes that brood and glow—you would say one of the Assyrian kings, whose sculptured heads adorn our museums, the very profile of Tiglath Pileser . . . In a congress of impassioned rhetoricians he remains serene, moderate; his voice is for the most part subdued; in its most emotional abandonment there is a dry undertone, almost harsh . . . And yet beneath all this statesman-like prose, touched with the special dryness of a jurist, lurk the romance of the poet and the purposeful vagueness of the modern evolutionist; the fantasy of the Hungarian, the dramatic self-consciousness of the literary artist, the heart of the Jew.

As for Herzl himself, he too found that "the Congress was magnificent." While he confessed, "I felt as though I were being obliged to play thirty-two games of chess simultaneously," he was sure of the ultimate outcome: "If I were to sum up the Congress in a word—which I shall take care not to publish—it would be this: At Basel I founded the Jewish State. If I said this out loud today I would be greeted by universal laughter. In five years perhaps, and certainly in fifty years, everyone will perceive it." He wrote these words in his diary on September 3—almost fifty years to the month before the 1947 decision of the United Nations to sanction the State of Israel.

Building the Zionist Organization

Meanwhile the Zionist revolution—action and not pamphlets, a political and not a philanthropic goal—was working powerfully upon the popular Jewish imagination. The Congress and a world organization, both the creatures of Herzl's mind and boundless energy, were conceived as practical instruments for creating a Jewish state, but their moral effects were more immediate. In the nature of things, only a small minority of Jews formally joined the organization; but a large, perhaps a vast majority thrilled to Herzl's championship of the solidarity and mutual responsibility of all Jews. Through the spirit of these Zionist institutions he rallied and transformed them from a miscellany of individuals and communities into a cohesive, articulate commonalty. Herzl restored their self-confidence and self-respect. He gave them, as he had told Baron de Hirsch he would do, a flag—"and with a flag you can lead people where you will, even into the Promised Land."

The pressing need, naturally, was for funds—to inspire confidence among government circles, to win concessions from Turkey, and, when won, to lay the foundations for large-scale settlement. But funds were hard to come by; as an old banker friend told Herzl, "men only lend money to the rich." At a preliminary conference in Vienna, which laid plans for the Second Congress, Herzl urged that a sales campaign for the contemplated Zionist bank be carried straight to the people: "As it is, we are like the soldiers of the French Revolution who had to take to the field without shoes or stockings."

The Second Zionist Congress was held again at Basel, on August 28-30, 1898. Herzl had no time, according to his diaries, for depicting moods—"everything was action." Among other decisions, the Congress established the bank Herzl had desired—the Jewish Colonial Trust—but left it mainly for him to turn a parliamentary resolution into a reality. On the diplomatic side, a message of greetings to the Sultan elicited a telegraphic acknowledgment, "which," Herzl confessed, "I never counted on." But meanwhile, more promising prospects were in the offing.

Interviews with the Kaiser

Immediately after the Congress sessions, Herzl went to the Lake Constance island of Mainau, where he had a long and fruitful talk with the old Grand Duke of Baden—"a truly magnificent conversation and on a high political plane." The Grand Duke, he learned, had submitted an "exhaustive account" of the Zionist movement to the German Kaiser, who had in turn "thereupon instructed Count Eulenberg to study the matter and report on it." The German government, moreover, had ascertained through its ambassador at Constantinople, that the Sultan viewed the Zionist cause "with favor." Since the Kaiser was to make his famous visit to Constantinople and the Holy Land in October—a visit inspired by political as well as pious motives—Herzl maneuvered successfully to get a rendezvous with him in both places.

On the occasion of his first audience with Wilhelm II, October 18, 1898, Herzl found that his attention wandered somewhat when the Kaiser launched upon the subject—"for I could not help noting the effect of my three years' work in making the obscure word 'Zionism' a *terme reçu* and one that fell naturally from the lips of the German emperor." When less than six years later, death cut short his pioneer negotiations in the foreign ministries and royal audience-chambers of Europe, Zionism had become not only a current expression in the world's forum but an item on the agenda of premiers and princes. Meanwhile, at the moment—and only for the moment—the Kaiser virtually gave his word to urge upon the Sultan a German protectorate for an autonomous Jewish territory in the Holy Land.

The Kaiser's journey to Palestine began as a religious pilgrimage, centering on the dedication of the German-built Church of the Redeemer in Jerusalem; but it turned into a political demonstration. It played a studied role in Germany's strategy to penetrate the Near East—via the proposed Berlin-Baghdad railroad and similar concessions. Herzl was therefore fairly justified, before the event, in believing the Grand Duke and Philip zu Eulenburg, the Kaiser's intimate friend, when they implied that a large Jewish settlement in Palestine under German protection was consonant with German interests and ambitions; and, after the event, that the Kaiser meant what he said.

In 1898 Palestine was a thinly inhabited land. Only eight per cent of its soil was cultivated; its total population probably did not reach five hundred thousand. It contained eighteen Jewish rural settlements, called "colonies," none of them over twenty years old, and only three or four large enough to warrant the name of village. Perhaps forty-five hundred Jews, all told, lived on the land. None of these settlements, moreover, had a legal basis for its existence; permission to reside in Palestine, buy land, or build was obtainable only through bribery or outwitting the laws. About forty-five thousand Jews lived in the cities, chiefly Jerusalem and Jaffa, and the majority of these urban Jews depended for a miserable existence on a world-wide collection of religious alms.

Of the settlements visited by Herzl, Rishon le-Zion (founded in 1882), like most of the others, owed its living and administration to Baron de Rothschild. Rehovot (founded in 1890) was one of the rare Jewish villages that maintained itself without patrons, supervisors, or subsidies. The Mikveh Israel agricultural school had been established in 1870 by the Alliance Israélite Universelle and was gradually training a generation of capable farmers.

As for the second interview with the Kaiser, at Jerusalem, Herzl came away dubious: "he said neither yes nor no." In the months following his return from Palestine, Herzl gradually came to realize that the Kaiser had bowed out of the picture.

The Unceasing Quest

Founding the land company as well as the bank, or Jewish Colonial Trust, Herzl suffered endless difficulties and postponements. Without the backing of capital, political concessions were impossible, and without political concessions, capital was unavailable. "Days of despondency," Herzl wrote on February 11. "The tempo of the movement is slowing down. The catchwords are wearing out. The ideas are becoming themes for declamation, and the declamation is losing its edge."

The Jewish Colonial Trust, though already established, could not begin operations until it had a paid-up capital of two hundred and fifty thousand pounds—which, in fact, it was not able to secure until 1901. Meanwhile, the condition of Russian Jews grew worse, and, in Rumania, a wave of persecution was driving thousands of Jews into a frantic, disorganized emigration. The morale of East European Jewry, together with the Zionist financial instrument which might bring relief, stood in desperate need of some hope or sign of a concession in Palestine, and spurred on Herzl's efforts to reach the Sultan. Several round-about approaches via Great Britain and Russia had so far led nowhere: Lord Salisbury, then Prime Minister of England, remained as inaccessible as the Czar. Germany was engaged upon a deal with Turkey in which Zionism apparently had no role. The Turkish minions of the Sultan, whom Herzl had enlisted at considerable expense, did nothing.

Herzl finally got to see the Sultan, in 1901, and concessions were offered him for the exploitation of mines, the establishment of a pro-government bank, and the creation of a land company for settling Jewish immigrants—but, as expressly stipulated, not in Palestine. He soon had convincing proof that the whole performance was staged in order to play him off against a French financial and political combine, headed by the French Minister of Finance—who also got nowhere, but not quite so fast as Herzl.

Meanwhile, Herzl had made fruitless efforts in Paris and London to secure financial backing for the concessions. For this as well as for political support, contacts were vainly sought with the Péreires, Rothschilds, Carnegie, Cecil Rhodes, Sir Thomas Lipton, Edward VII, President Theodore Roosevelt, and of course the Czar. Max Nordau and others of Herzl's most faithful colleagues deplored the recklessness and nebulous character of his ventures, and he was led to confide his own estimate of himself to the pages of his diary:

> When once the Jewish State exists, all of this will of course look trivial. Perhaps a juster historian will discover that it was still something after all for a Jewish journalist without means, during an era of the most abominable anti-Semitism and when the Jewish people had sunk into the depths, to have converted a rag into a flag, and a degraded multitude into a nation, which rallied, heads erect, around that flag.

The middle of 1902 opened new vistas and ventures. Alarmed by the influx of Jewish refugees from Russia and Rumania, with their presumed threat to the standard of living among English workers, the British government, of which the Prime Minister was Arthur James Balfour, appointed a royal commission to examine the question of alien immigration. A popular demand for restricted immigration was about to prevail over the tradition of free asylum which had been Great Britain's pride. Herzl's friends persuaded the Royal Commission to invite him to appear as an expert witness before the hearings—in spite of the strong opposition of Lord Rothschild, who looked upon Herzl as a demagogue and who had hitherto refused to see him or answer his letters.

Meanwhile, Herzl's novel, *Altneuland*, had appeared. Under the motto, "If you will it, it is no fable," the book depicted life in a flourishing Jewish state, in Palestine, twenty years hence. He sent copies to the Kaiser, Eulenburg, Bülow, Rothschild, and other important personages. What, in large, Herzl thought of the book may be seen in the note he wrote the Grand Duke of Baden when sending him a copy: "It is a story which, as it were, I am telling by the camp-fires to keep up the spirits of my poor people while they are on the march. To hold out is everything."

While in London for the purpose of testifying before the Royal Commission, Herzl managed to lunch with Lord Rothschild, and win from him flattering personal tributes, vague assurances, and little more. But he did better with the British government. Through other English friends, and to Rothschild's astonishment, he persuaded Joseph Chamberlain, the most talked-of as well as one of the most influential figures in the British cabinet, to support a large-scale Jewish settlement in the El Arish region, just south of Palestine. When nothing came of this—ostensibly because of the Egyptian government's refusal to supply water from the Nile—Chamberlain, the following year, procured from the British government an offer of a large area in Uganda, with an arrangement for local autonomous government which recognized the political existence of the Jewish people.

Russia and the "Uganda" Congress

That same year, 1903, a Russian atrocity horrified the world. The Kishinev massacre, during the opening days of Easter week, wreaked murder, pillage, and rape upon a defenseless and unresistant Jewish community while the police stood by with folded arms: this threw a ghastly light on the character of the Jewish problem and the need for a speedy, radical solution.

Herzl bent his efforts in every possible direction. He tried to weave "combinations"—with Portugal for territory in Mozambique, with Belgium for Congo lands, and with Italy for tracts in Tripoli. He reinvigorated his connections at Constantinople.

He also turned to Russia itself, the archenemy, for a number of compelling reasons. His long-cherished plan of persuading Russia to exert influence on Turkey seemed more timely and feasible than ever, now that the Czarist government stood on the defensive before the bar of world opinion. If Russia would do nothing to relax the persecution of Jews at home, it might conceivably be willing to appease the indignation of an outraged humanity by helping secure for them an asylum abroad —which meant Palestine. In addition, the Zionist movement in Russia was threatened with suppression, and his colleagues there sought his intercession.

After several futile efforts to establish contact with the Czar or other influential authorities, Herzl succeeded in obtaining an appointment for an audience with Vyacheslav Plehve, the Minister of the Interior, and therefore answerable for the Kishinev massacre and, by common report, the sponsor of it. Herzl chose to ignore the record of Plehve and Russia. He was not undertaking to act as an historian, a moralist, or an indignant tribune. As a statesman he considered it his duty to negotiate for a solution of the Jewish problem with anyone in whose hands a solution might lay. There must be, he felt, some answer to Kishinev.

"Alas, what I saw in Vilna!" Herzl kept repeating after his journey to Russia. The cry was not merely the reaction to a personal experience; it voiced a sense of the Russian tragedy which had gripped the whole Jewish people and aroused the concern of civilized men everywhere. It gave a precious though illusory value to the letter he bore from Plehve—with its assurance of Russian aid in securing Palestine—and which he was carrying to the forthcoming Zionist Congress (August 22-28).

The Russian tragedy also gave immediate and poignant urgency to a spacious offer on the part of Great Britain to create the Jewish state in Uganda—which turned out to be not Uganda at all, but a district east of the Mau Mau escarpment in what is now Kenya.

The British offer evoked debates and demonstrations which made the Sixth Congress memorable in Zionist history. At the outset, Herzl stressed that the East Africa project was emphatically not Zion: "It is only an auxiliary colonization—but, be it noted, on a national and state foundation." Palestine, he declared, remained the unalterable goal. The vote was proportionally five to three in favor of an investigation. At once the entire body of nay-voters walked out of the Congress hall. For them the mere examination of a tract in East Africa meant the abandonment of Zion; gathering in another room, they argued, fumed, and wept—some of them sat on the floor mourning as people mourn for the dead.

Herzl went to them with pleas and reassurances. Also with reproaches: the Congresses which were generous with sentiments, tears, and pledges, gave him neither the money nor the disciplined political support to carry out the Basel program on which the movement was founded and to which they all remained true. Eventually, the dissidents were won back to the sessions, though not to a change in their vote.

The aftermath—conclaves of rebels in Russia and Austria, painful scenes of protest, threat, rebellion, and negotiation—continued many months. In December, during a Zionist ball in Paris, a half-crazed Russian Zionist fired a revolver at Nordau. And a bitter irony enveloped the entire affair when it became apparent, by the end of the year, that no suitable territory could be found in East Africa.

The only real victim was Herzl. Although the mass of Zionists, in Russia no less than elsewhere, never wavered in their support of him, the six months of strain and wrangling depleted his physical reserves and hastened his untimely death. Years before, Herzl had written apropos of a play by Björnson: "Why is it that the best men fall? Because the reason that they are the best is that they exceed their strength."

Last Days

Shortly after the middle of January 1904, Herzl set out for Italy, with Venice as his first stop. Within the space of a few days he met and sought to win the regnant figures in the Vatican and Italian governments. It is fairly safe to say that Herzl's buoyant humor throughout the Italian journey, and the sparkle it left in his diary, was due not only to the charms of

Italy, but also to a sense of respite from the Russian Zionist leaders, with whom he had been tussling these many months. It soon became apparent that Italy, like Germany and Russia, had joined the list of major powers which at the start were willing and in the end inactive.

Herzl kept on negotiating, writing letters, and trying to win over statesmen and bankers: the Foreign Minister of Austria, Jacob Schiff, and others. But his health rapidly worsened. He returned home, and then on June 3, 1904 he left for Edlach in the Semmering mountains. Behind, on the desk in his study, lay a sheet of paper on which he had written in English: "In the midst of life there is death."

On July 1 Herzl's heart began to function with marked irregularity, breathing became hard and painful, and a bronchial catarrh set in bringing violent and bloody coughing fits. "Give them all my greetings," he told a friend who had journeyed to his bedside, "and tell them that I gave my blood for my people."

During spells of semi-delirium he presided again at the Congress he had created, beating the bed-quilt with a phantom gavel and calling out, "*Ad loca! Ad loca!*" Or, at another moment, he was executing his vision of a redeemed Palestine: "These three tracts of land must be bought. Did you make a note of it? These three tracts!"

Pneumonia settled in his left lung. His mother and children were summoned. Shortly after their arrival, on the afternoon of July 3, 1904, he died—at the age of forty-four years and two months.

In his will Herzl asked that his body be buried in Vienna, next to that of his father, "to remain there until the Jewish people will carry my remains to Palestine." On August 16, 1949, his coffin was flown to the State of Israel and, the next day, laid to rest on a ridge facing Jerusalem from the west and honored with the name of Mount Herzl.

The Man and the Legend

The posture of world affairs prevented Herzl from achieving his ends while he lived; his heirs, working under more propitious circumstances, finished the task; and though they merit the fullest appreciation for their consummate skill, they are comparable to the architects who brought Michelangelo's great church to completion.

The men whom Herzl attracted to the executive body of the Zionist movement, some of them young enough to be nearly lifelong Lovers of Zion, learned from him the techniques of statesmanship, without which Zion was doomed to remain only an intangible object of emotion and belief. Above all, they learned from him the possibility of statesmanship and the self-assurance to avail themselves of it.

"To all of us," said Chaim Weizmann, the coming leader among Herzl's successors, an habitual critic of Herzl's policy, and the first president of the State of Israel, "he was first and foremost a great teacher of organization and politics . . . we hearkened to his maxims and teaching with joy."

Herzl went further than providing young Weizmann and other Zionist leaders with precept and lesson. He broke open the roads they followed to success; it was almost literally in his footsteps that they walked into the Quai d'Orsay, the Quirinal, and No. 10 Downing Street.

The same Balfour who as Foreign Secretary signed the famous Declaration in 1917 was Prime Minister in 1903, when Herzl secured the British offer of territory in East Africa—an offer couched in terms which, to quote Weizmann, re-established "the identity, the legal personality of the Jewish people." And in 1906, when he first met Weizmann, Balfour was still arguing on behalf of the East Africa scheme. Lloyd George, who headed the cabinet which issued the Balfour Declaration, had drawn up for Herzl the draft charter for a quasi-autonomous regime in East Africa and had advocated the Zionist standpoint during the Parliamentary debate on the offer in 1904. Lord Cromer, Sir Edward Grey, and Lord Milner, all of whom proved helpful to Weizmann in procuring the 1917 Declaration, had been politically inclined toward Zionism by Herzl and his agents in the course of the El Arish and East Africa negotiation. "Our negotiations with the British government," Weizmann cheerfully attested in 1923, "were simple compared with the unending, intense, tiresome, heartrending negotiations which he [Herzl] conducted." Weizmann's labors were far from easy, but they were rendered simpler because of Herzl.

Under Herzl's leadership, the anomalous denizens of the ghetto together with the drifting Jews of the West, above all the youth, set forth on their march to the rank of a nation conscious of its destiny. A new literature and art, a revival of the Hebrew language, received fresh encouragement and gave fresh stimulation in its wake. Herzl once described what he was doing in a homely comparison: "I am a good cooper and I understand how to make one whole cask out of many different staves. . . . I shall bind the cask with the hoops of our common past and future, and I shall fill it with our national ideals of right and justice."

Energy and a genius for organization go far toward accounting for these achievements. It was characteristic of Herzl to awake at dawn and "as customary plan out everything beforehand," and by the day's end do what he had planned.

But this was not the whole secret. Herzl's advent on the scene struck his contemporaries as something unfamiliar and indefinable that embodied a new spirit. There was in his deep, lambent, magnetic eyes, his imperial nose, his stature and bearing, a blend of the Hebrew prophet and the Assyrian monarch, beside which the Hirsches, Rothschilds, Bülows, Chamberlains, Grand Dukes, and Sultans looked like nonentities, plain or fancy. The contrast must have unconsciously contributed to his self-assurance. Physically, he imposed.

But his world was not succumbing to the looks of a man. Perhaps it was his innate knightliness that made him, as well it might, seem mysterious and extraordinary. Genuine knights are rare in any age and among any people. Of course, Chaucer notwithstanding, no knight has ever been perfect. The flaws in Herzl's character—his petty jealousies, undue suspicions, and over-sensitive *amour-propre*—are obvious, even today, because in his writings he had the honesty not to cloak them. His "legend" in fact grew so rapidly and "the cloud in which he walked" became so dense with incense and pious adulation that it is a happy relief to discover in his portrait of himself in his diaries a palpable man with common follies and shortcomings.

Yet the same confessions unconsciously disclose Herzl's

knightliness. It was this that enabled him to surmount with a touch of the magnificent and a flourish of *panache* obstacles enough to daunt the stoutest heart: the recurrent failure of his fellow-workers to understand what statesmanship meant, the purblind opposition of the Lovers of Zion to the actual re-establishment of Zion, the discovery that the kind of money which talks was deaf, the impotence of the masses, the hostility of the publishers upon whom his livelihood depended, the mockery or indifference of his own social and intellectual world, and at almost every turn the refusal to lift a finger on the part of men whose help would have counted most.

Zion ruled Herzl as fate governed a Greek hero or as the burden of the Lord weighed on a Hebrew prophet, and kept him fighting when he knew that the opposing odds were overwhelming and, worse, when he knew that the tactics and human figures in the battle were on occasion tawdry. He was tragic not because he was a Don Quixote winning our indulgent sympathies, but because he was a Don Quixote who recognized his own Quixotism and yet, in obedience to the ideal, never lowered his lance—and drove himself to an untimely grave.

This same knightliness had led Herzl, against the grain of his times, to the sacrifice of his own and his family's fortune to an enterprise which could earn them only moral returns. It imbued his vision of the future Jewish state, the old-new land, with something beyond the embodiment of righteous social principles, or even, when he came to know them, traditional Jewish values; he strove for a state and a people that would become in the truest sense noble. For he could have said of himself, as Heine did, *ich selber bin ein solcher Ritter von dem heil'gen Geist*—"I too am a knight of the Holy Spirit."

He liked to recall the remark an old fisherman once made to him: "The most remarkable of all things is when a man never gives up." The words could have been the emblazoned motto, as they were the perfect expression, of Herzl's life.

10 . *Louis D. Brandeis*

[1856-1941]

MILTON R. KONVITZ

Louis Brandeis was a great Jewish personality in a unique way. He was not representative of Jewish leaders of the past. He was the product and expression of a free democratic society —in which a man was free to be a Jew, and a Jew was free to be a man and citizen. His life and work were those of a civilized man who came to cherish Judaism, and those of a Jew who cherished humanity. Brandeis found his world to be a oneness and a manyness: a world big enough for many nations, many religions, many groups, many loyalties, many systems of values—and yet one world where there was interdependence, and need for cross-fertilization, common respect, and understanding. What the poet Keats wrote in a letter would have been acceptable to Brandeis: "I do not live in this world alone, but in a thousand worlds."

In 1654 a tiny vessel, the St. Charles, deposited twenty-three Jews at New York, the Dutch colony on the Hudson. While individual Jews had probably arrived earlier, the landing of this group marked the beginning of Jewish immigration to the United States. By 1848 the Jewish population was about twenty thousand, most of them immigrants from Western Europe. Some of these men and women, touched by the Emancipation and the Enlightenment, came because the failure of the 1848 revolution in Central Europe had convinced them that only in the United States would they find freedom and equality of opportunity.

Among the "Forty-Eighters" was Adolph Brandeis, a native

of Prague, who would have fought in the 1848 revolution had he not been stricken by typhoid fever. Instead, in the fall of that year, he migrated to the United States. Adolph, fascinated by America, promptly applied for naturalization. "I already love our country so much," he wrote to Frederika Dembitz, his fiancee, "that I rejoice when I can sing its praises." In 1849 the steamship Washington brought twenty-six members of the Brandeis, Dembitz, and Wehle families. Adolph and Frederika were soon married, and settled in Madison, Indiana; after two years they moved to Louisville, Kentucky, where their son Louis Dembitz was born on November 13, 1856.

Adolph Brandeis prospered as a grain merchant. After Louis was graduated from high school, the family went to Europe for three years, part of which time Louis spent at school in Dresden. When they returned to the United States, Louis, then nineteen, entered Harvard Law School, and achieved a scholastic record for excellence that became a legend—a record that no student has since equalled. On graduation Brandeis went to St. Louis, but two years later he opened a law office in Boston in partnership with Samuel D. Warren, Jr., a former classmate at Harvard. The firm did well. At the age of twenty-six Brandeis was successful in raising a fund sufficient to install Oliver Wendell Holmes, Jr., in a law professorship at Harvard Law School. At about the same time he himself accepted an invitation to teach a course in legal evidence at Harvard, but the next year refused the offer of an assistant professorship—he preferred to remain in active law practice. He organized the Harvard Law School Association, and for this as well as other notable contributions to his alma mater, Harvard awarded him an M.A. degree in 1891. By this time he enjoyed an annual income of fifty thousand dollars—a fabulous amount at that time (by 1907 Brandeis had earned a million dollars, and ten years later was a millionaire twice over). His reputation as a leading corporation lawyer was firmly established.

Brandeis' financial independence enabled him to work without compensation for public causes that interested him. Early in life he had begun to seek out such causes, and soon many such causes sought him. He was a rare phenomenon: a successful corporation lawyer with a keen social conscience and an irrepressible desire to work for a better world. Although never opposed to capitalism, Brandeis was one of the first successful Americans to propose measures against the social and moral abuses of aggressive capitalism. He was among the first also to insist on representation of the public interest at legislative hearings. He wanted government to stay out of business, but even more he wanted business to stay out of government.

Early Concern with Social Problems

Brandeis pioneered for the idea of collective bargaining between employers and labor unions. He maintained that unions should not be branded and persecuted as criminal conspiracies; big business made big unions necessary. If unions acted arbitrarily, unreasonably, or criminally, their evil acts or tendencies should be repressed, but their existence and legitimate interests should be encouraged and protected. As early as 1911 he favored legislation restricting the use of the injunction in labor disputes. Earlier in 1904, he had urged stabilization and full employment policies. He had advised management to open its books for inspection by unions so that a proper factual basis for collective bargaining with respect to wages could be established, thus anticipating a decision of the Supreme Court made in 1956. He saw the labor unions as a great conservative force, a bulwark against radicalism and socialism. Though he opposed the closed shop as a restriction on the rights of workers, he favored a union in every shop. The right to combine, he maintained, was absolute, even among public employees; the right to strike, however, was not absolute. In sum, Brandeis was a pathfinder: he projected social policies that later were embodied in the Norris-LaGuardia Act of 1932, the Wagner Act of 1935, the Employment Act of 1946, and the Taft-Hartley Act of 1947.

According to Brandeis himself, it was the Homestead Strike of 1892 that set him to thinking seriously about the labor problem. At Homestead, Pennsylvania, the scene of one of the most bitterly fought labor disputes in American history, the manager of one of the largest steel plants in the United States had hired about three hundred men of the Pinkerton private detective agency to protect company property as well as the non-union men who had been hired during the strike. An armed battle broke out between the Pinkerton men and the strikers in which sixty men were wounded and ten killed. The governor of Pennsylvania called out the National Guard, under whose protection the company kept the non-union employees at work and broke the strike. It took the shock of that battle, said Brandeis, "to turn my mind definitely toward a searching study of the relations of labor to industry." While other American leaders were also shocked by the happenings at Homestead, Brandeis was one of the very few who proceeded to study the causes of the evil and search for remedies.

Brandeis also tackled other pressing social problems. He exposed the industrial life insurance racket and agitated on behalf of insurance by savings banks instead of by insurance companies. (Three states—Massachusetts, Connecticut, and New York—have since enacted laws that permit the Brandeis form of insurance.) Indeed, whenever he had an opportunity, Brandeis fought against monopolies. He saw a threat to the average person in the large trusts, holding companies, cartels, interlocking corporate directorships—in big business in general. Without economic opportunity and economic democracy for individuals, Brandeis argued, political democracy would be ineffective. He therefore raised his voice against every form of absolutism, whether in government, business, or organized labor. He did not consider monopolies a necessary evil that should or could be regulated by government, and opposed regulated monopoly; he wanted instead regulated competition among business and industrial units that would not engage in monopolistic practices.

Contribution to American Labor History

In the first several decades of the twentieth century both the employers and workers in the garment industry in New York City were predominantly Jewish immigrants. The International Ladies' Garment Workers' Union was demanding the closed shop while the employers attacked the union as a Marxist conspiracy. A state of anarchy existed. In 1910 there was a general strike that engendered much bitterness on both sides. Neither party was willing to make concessions or consider compromises. Following the intervention of certain civic leaders, all agreed that the only hope of bringing the dispute to an end lay in empowering Brandeis to confer with both labor and management and submit a plan of negotiation.

This was done; and it is related that in the course of the bitter arguments between garment workers and their "bosses," Brandeis at times heard a man shout in Yiddish: "*Ihr darft sich shemen! Passt dos far a Idn?*" ("Shame! Is this worthy of a Jew?") On one occasion he heard a shopworker confront his employer with a quotation in Hebrew from the prophet Isaiah (3:14-15):

> It is you who have devoured the vineyard, the spoil of the poor is in your houses.
> What do you mean by crushing My people, by grinding the face of the poor? says the Lord God of hosts.

Brandeis was deeply moved by such incidents.

At Brandeis' insistence, the union waived the closed shop, which led to a temporary split in the ranks of the workers. At a peace conference of union representatives and employers, Brandeis stated that his interest was not only in getting them to reach an accord that would end the strike, but also, and of greater significance, to create a relationship that would make future strikes unnecessary. As the basis for industrial peace, Brandeis proposed the preferential union shop, whereby the employer would have the right to select employees on the basis of their qualifications, but with preference for qualified union members. Union shop standards were to prevail in the industry. This proposal was attacked by extremists as a sell-out to the other side; and Jacob Schiff* and Louis Marshall** tried to placate both parties. After months of wrangling and negotiations, the protocol, as Brandeis called it, was accepted and signed by all concerned.

This agreement has played a notable role in American labor history as one of the first important collective bargaining agreements. It marked, on the one hand, a departure by organized labor from its persistent demand for total union security, that

* Financier and philanthropist (1847-1920), and virtual lay head of American Jewry.

** Jurist and Jewish communal leader (1856-1929), eminent as an appellate lawyer and defender of civil liberties as well as in Jewish affairs.

is, the closed shop, and, on the other hand, a departure by employers from their obstinate refusal to concede recognition to labor unions. The protocol also introduced into a disorganized industry a form of self-policing and self-government by setting up an inspection board to standardize and maintain proper working conditions. The protocol also proceeded on the principle, now universally followed, that the agreement is only the initial step in achieving and maintaining industrial peace and democracy; accordingly, it provided for a grievance board with authority to settle disputes arising out of the agreement; if this agency failed to achieve a dispute settlement, the grievance was to be submitted to a board of arbitrators. Lockouts and strikes were not to take place. For its day, the introduction of arbitration for the settlement of grievances was a pioneering step—one which set the pattern for the future.

Efforts for Scientific Management

Shortly after the protocol was signed, Brandeis turned his attention to scientific management, which attracted national attention to the inefficient methods prevailing in American industry. At the end of 1910 the Interstate Commerce Commission conducted public hearings on proposed increases in railroad freight charges. Brandeis, testifying on behalf of the public interest, opposed the increases on the ground that the public should not be compelled to subsidize the inefficient operation of the carriers. Brandeis charged the railroads with engaging in practices that victimized the consumer and the small businessman—particularly, increasing rates constantly in order to meet higher costs. With scientific management, Brandeis maintained, the carriers could pay higher wages without raising rates. By introducing efficiency methods, he argued, they could add a million dollars a day to their income.

These statements by Brandeis created a sensation, and the subjects of business efficiency and scientific management were widely discussed by the public for the first time. Though the railroads attacked Brandeis, within a decade industrialists, including railroad executives, admitted the legitimacy of his claims on behalf of the application of scientific methods to industrial management.

What seemed radical in the first decade of the twentieth century has since become an accepted truth. Just as he worked to make industrial management scientific, Brandeis also sought for ways to make business a profession. In this effort, too, he was a pioneer: today schools of business administration are integral divisions of many universities throughout the country.

In these various ways, Brandeis contributed greatly to an awareness and understanding of social problems. One can easily see his influence in the policies of Samuel Gompers, Sidney Hillman, David Dubinsky, Walter Reuther, and other leaders of American organized labor. Brandeis helped direct American thought and institutions away from the class-struggle ideologies and toward union-employer cooperation, expressed in thousands of collective bargaining agreements and in basic social legislation. Not utopianism, but constant improvement through practical measures was the aim of Brandeis' reformism—a philosophy he derived from Benjamin Franklin, Jefferson, Emerson, and William James, which eventually linked itself with the New Freedom, the New Deal, and the Fair Deal.

Contribution to American Law

Notable and enduring as was Brandeis' impact on American liberal thought and the country's social and economic institutions, his contribution to American law and legal institutions was even greater. In his work as a legal reformer he was, on the whole, a solitary pathfinder: his work was daring and original. And here, too, his effort was not to destroy but to preserve and to give new direction and new life.

In 1908 Brandeis introduced the economic or "Brandeis" brief into the Supreme Court, an act of adventurous courage which alone would have won him distinction in American jurisprudence. In *Muller v. Oregon* the Supreme Court had before it a state statute that limited to ten the number of hours for women workers. At the request of the State of Oregon, Brandeis wrote the brief in defense of the statute, devoting most of it to economic and statistical data and to arguments drawn from official reports which showed that long hours of work were dangerous to women's health, morals, and welfare. This approach—putting the main weight of the argument on economic and sociological factual studies, rather than on dry logic or *a priori* arguments—was bold and new. No lawyer had ever before dared to argue a law case in this way. The Supreme Court was won over by Brandeis and his brief: the Oregon statute was held to be constitutional, and the Court openly complimented Brandeis for bringing before it facts and opinions showing that the act was not unreasonable.

After this sensational success, Brandeis continued to file similar briefs in state and federal cases; a pattern was thus established that lawyers and judges no longer question. The later struggle to validate, constitutionally, social legislation enacted by Congress and by the state legislatures, which was won in 1937, when the Supreme Court began to uphold New Deal legislation, could never have been resolved were it not for the deep and pervasive influence of the Brandeis approach to constitutional questions affecting social legislation. The American people enjoy today the fruit of ideas planted by Brandeis as far back as 1908.

Justice of the Supreme Court

It was against the background of such monumental achievements that Brandeis was nominated for the United States Supreme Court by President Woodrow Wilson early in 1916. Since he was the first Jew to receive this honor, the conservative forces in the country were aroused: seven former presidents of the American Bar Association, including William Howard Taft, opposed confirmation; so, too, did A. Lawrence Lowell, President of Harvard University (although Brandeis was a Harvard Law School Overseer at the time). But Charles W. Eliot, Harvard's President Emeritus, favored Brandeis; so did Newton D. Baker, who became Secretary of War in March 1916, and Frances Perkins, who was to become Franklin D. Roosevelt's Secretary of Labor. In the Senate committee named to consider the nomination, ten Democrats voted for and eight Republicans voted against confirmation. After five months of public controversy, the appointment was approved in the Senate by a vote of forty-seven to twenty-two.

Brandeis was sixty years of age when he took his place on the Supreme Court. He retired in 1939 after twenty-three years of distinguished service. His name and his record stand with those of John Marshall, Joseph Story, Roger B. Taney, Stephen J. Field, and Oliver Wendell Holmes.

A major contribution of Justice Brandeis was to deepen public consciousness of the significance of civil liberties. With Justice Holmes, Brandeis worked incessantly to teach his colleagues and the American people that unless basic human freedoms were respected, protected, and strengthened, American society and institutions would hardly be worthy of a notable place in the history of mankind. This conviction was expressed by Holmes and Brandeis consistently and repeatedly, most of the time in dissenting opinions, some of which have become important historic documents.

In a case before the Court in 1919, Justice Holmes first formulated the clear and present danger doctrine; it remained, however, for Justice Brandeis to give the clearest articulation of this doctrine in an opinion he wrote in 1927. The fundamental freedoms enumerated in the First Amendment, he said, may not be denied or abridged; yet the freedoms of speech and assembly that were involved in the case are not absolutes. They may be restricted by necessity, but constitutionally the necessity does not exist "unless speech would produce, or is intended to produce, a clear and imminent danger of some substantive evil which the state constitutionally may seek to prevent." When a state enacts a law to meet an evil, and the law limits the exercise of a fundamental liberty, it is the duty of the Court to determine for itself whether the enactment was in fact necessary; the Court is not bound by the fact that the vast majority of a state's citizens believe that the dissemination of certain doctrines is fraught with evil consequences. At one time, said Brandeis, "man feared witches and burned women. It is the function of speech to free men from the bondage of irrational fears." To justify, constitutionally, restrictions on free speech, said Brandeis, there must be "reasonable ground to fear that serious evil will result if free speech is practiced; reasonable ground to believe that the danger apprehended is imminent; reasonable ground to believe that the evil to be prevented is a serious one."

The clear and present danger doctrine, as stated by Holmes and Brandeis in numerous opinions, has become an accepted constitutional interpretation. Though it has not always been followed, even those who attack or question its force do not disregard it. The doctrine stands as a "fence" to protect the First Amendment freedoms against attempts to whittle them down in the name of alleged national security or state emergencies. To all persons who would play fast and loose with these freedoms, the words of Brandeis stand as a reminder and a warning: "Those who won our independence by revolution were not cowards. They did not fear political change. They did not exalt order at the cost of liberty."

Brandeis' second most notable contribution as a Justice of the Supreme Court was his insistence that Congress and the states have constitutionally the discretion to experiment with economic and social institutions in the light of facts that show a need for action. While a clear and present danger—and only such a danger—may justify an abridgment of a fundamental liberty, much more freedom is vested in the legislative judgment as it is brought to bear on economic and social problems. There is no right to experiment with human rights, but there is a right to experiment with economic and social institutions. It is, said Brandeis, "one of the happy incidents of the federal system that a single courageous state may, if its citizens choose, serve as a laboratory, and try novel social and economic experiments without risk to the rest of the country." As long as the statute setting up the social experiment is not arbitrary, capricious, or unreasonable, the United States Constitution should not be interpreted to stand in the way.

The same open-mindedness for which Brandeis pleaded in his economic brief submitted to the Court in *Muller v. Oregon* appears in his work as a Supreme Court Justice, mainly, however, in his dissenting opinions (with which Justice Holmes generally agreed). The scientific attitude, he argued, must be permitted application to social and economic problems faced by the nation and the states. The advances in science have shown that what seems to be impossible sometimes happens. The progress made in science and technology attests to the value of the trial-and-error method, the method of experimentation. The Due Process Clause of the Fourteenth Amendment, Brandeis contended, must not be used to stand in the way of efforts to improve our social institutions—and improvements can be brought about only through experiments, some of which may fail and some of which may succeed. In 1931, in a dissenting opinion, Brandeis told his colleagues on the Court that to stand in the way of experimentation in social and economic matters was a grave responsibility; the denial of this right may bring about serious consequences; the right should not be denied unless the legislative measure is clearly arbitrary. The Court should not strike down a statute that seeks a solution to a difficult social problem by interjecting prejudices into legal principles. "If we would guide by the light of reason," said Brandeis, "we must let our minds be bold."

The intellectual boldness to which Brandeis challenged the Court often involved the necessity to overcome prior decisions. On this point, too, Brandeis insisted that the Court must follow not precedents, but the light of reason. In constitutional cases the Court should decide either to follow a precedent or to overrule it. In overruling earlier decisions that involve constitutional provisions, said Brandeis in a dissenting opinion in 1932, the Court merely bows to the lessons of experience and to the force of better reasoning and recognizes that the process of trial and error, so fruitful in the physical sciences, is also appropriate in the judicial process. In other words, just as the legislatures may resort to the scientific method in conducting social experiments, so, too, may the courts conduct judicial experiments which entail the rejection of precedents that have not stood the test of time.

The Constitution, if it is to be a living force in the affairs of men, must not be worshipped or venerated but used as an instrument that encourages the exercise of the free intelligence as it struggles with the complex problems of American society. It was not until 1937 that the Supreme Court was won over to the Brandeis logic and method. It was the dissenting opinions of Brandeis—and Holmes—that prepared the ground for the New Deal changes in the Supreme Court—and for the school desegregation decision in *Brown v. Topeka* in 1954.

Brandeis Joins Zionist Movement

It was characteristic of Brandeis, who demonstrated in every aspect of his legal career a passion for social justice, that, once won to the cause of Zionism, he would approach it on the practical, pragmatic level, and give it the fullest measure of his devotion. In 1912, two years after Brandeis' mediation of the ILGWU strike, Jacob de Haas, who had been London secretary to Theodor Herzl, and was now editor of the *Jewish Advocate* in Boston, called on Brandeis for his views on certain aspects of savings bank insurance that might be of special interest to Jewish parents. At one point De Haas spoke of Louis N. Dembitz, Brandeis' uncle, as a "noble Jew" and an early Zionist. De Haas spoke also of Herzl and the Zionist movement. Brandeis was greatly interested. Other discussions followed, which led Brandeis to study published materials on Zionism. When he joined the Federation of American Zionists, this fact was publicly announced at the Zionist convention in Cleveland. In 1913 Brandeis presided at a meeting in Boston to welcome Nahum Sokolow, Zionist intellectual and leader from Europe, and he made other appearances at Zionist meetings in different parts of the country. At the national Zionist convention in Cincinnati in 1913, Brandeis advocated the diversion of Jewish immigration to Palestine, negotiation with the Turkish government (then in control of Palestine) for large concessions, and the industrialization of Palestine through capital investment.

After the outbreak of World War I in 1914, it seemed desirable to move the world center of Zionist activities from Europe to the United States. On August 30 of that year a New York conference of one hundred and fifty Zionists was held, at which a provisional executive Committee for General Zionist Affairs was organized. Brandeis became chairman and thus leader of the Zionist movement in the United States at a time of international crisis.

Chairman of Zionist Provisional Committee

At the close of the New York meeting which elected Brandeis, the administrative committee which he headed worked almost all night and the next day. Characteristically, Brandeis injected into the new task his tremendous drive, capacity for hard work, and an eagerness for facts and practical results.

In accepting the chairmanship Brandeis had told the conferees that he considered it his duty to aid the cause "so far as it is in my power to do so." He was aware of his own "disqualifications" for the important task:

> Throughout long years which represent my life [he was then fifty-eight], I have been to a great extent separated from Jews. I am very ignorant in things Jewish. But recent experiences, public and professional, have taught me this: I find Jews possessed of those very qualities which we of the twentieth century seek to develop in our struggle for justice and democracy: a deep moral feeling which makes them capable of noble acts; a deep sense of the brotherhood of man; and a high intelligence, the fruit of three thousand years of civilization.
>
> These experiences have made me feel that the Jewish people have something which should be saved for the world; that the Jewish people should be preserved; and that it is our duty to pursue that method of saving which most promises success.

In his position as leader of Zionism in the United States, Brandeis subsequently traveled to many cities, where he delivered lectures which were heard by thousands of persons and were read in printed form by many additional thousands. He made a special point of answering the charge of some anti-Zionists that Zionism was disloyalty to America. Zionism "is not a movement to remove all the Jews compulsorily to Palestine," Brandeis pointed out. Zionism was a movement to enlarge —and not to contract—the freedom of the Jew so that, like the Greek, the Irish, or the German, he might exercise an option to live in the land of his fathers or in another country of his choice. By supporting Zionism, an American Jew was not necessarily seeking to change his own home, but rather to win for Jews everywhere the freedom to make their home in Palestine or elsewhere. For Jews who did not wish to leave the United States, a Jewish state in Palestine would serve as a center from which Jewish values radiate and as a spiritual force to preserve Jews from assimilation; it would give Jews everywhere "that inspiration which springs from memories of a great past and the hope of a great future."

Brandeis brought this same message to audiences of young people at Harvard, Columbia, and other universities. In 1915 he wrote that "Zionist affairs are really the important things in life now." Not a day went by that he did not do some work on behalf of the cause. He insisted on frequent and detailed reports from the Zionist organization staff—no detail was too small for his interest. He sought opportunities to address groups hostile to Zionism so that he might win them over. He was deeply moved by the disclosures of wholesale miseries suffered by Jews in Russia and Poland, and in his speeches he appealed for funds, linking relief and Zionism, the immediate needs and the future hopes of the Jewish people.

Anticipating the end of the war and settlement of international political questions, Zionist leaders in Europe and the United States prepared themselves to place before the Allied Powers definite demands with respect to Palestine as well as for equal rights for all European Jews. Since Brandeis thought it essential to unite American Jewry, early in 1916 he joined in a call for a democratically constituted American Jewish congress, to help win Jewish rights in Palestine and the rights of Jews in other countries. Twenty-six organizations agreed to establish this congress. Brandeis was temporary chairman and honorary president. Just at that time he was confirmed as Associate Justice of the Supreme Court, and he felt it necessary to resign from these positions. Though he cut all his other ties with social causes and organizations, his Zionist work, however, did not cease.

Balfour Declaration

As a Justice of the Supreme Court, Brandeis enjoyed even more prestige than he had in the past; and this increased his usefulness for Zionist ends. Zionist leaders everywhere were intent on winning a settlement of the Palestine question as part of the over-all peace settlement that was to follow the end of World War I. In 1914 Brandeis had discussed the Palestine question with President Wilson and later with the British and French ambassadors to the United States, and in the next few years he continued discussions and negotiations with the Department of State and Allied officials. On April 6, 1917, the United States entered the war, which facilitated negotiations with regard to Palestine. In May, 1917, Brandeis met Lord Balfour, Foreign Secretary in Lloyd George's coalition ministry, at the White House, where the latter had come as head of

Britain's war mission. Balfour had expressed his eagerness to see Brandeis, and later Brandeis conferred with both Wilson and Balfour. He was also in close contact with Zionist leaders in Britain, notably Chaim Weizmann and James Rothschild.

On November 2, 1917, the Balfour Declaration was issued, pledging British support to the establishment in Palestine of a national home for the Jewish people. At the 1918 Zionist Convention, held in Pittsburgh, Brandeis offered a five-point social justice code for Palestine, which was adopted and became known as the Pittsburgh program. It called for political and civil equality of all inhabitants without regard to creed, race, or sex; public ownership and control of the land and its natural resources and all public utilities; the leasing of land on conditions that would insure fullest opportunity for development and continuity of possession; the setting up of all economic institutions on the cooperative principle; and a system of free public schools. Since American Zionists supported these principles, but European Zionists resisted making them part of the Zionist policy for and in Palestine, the two groups began to drift apart.

Brandeis and Weizmann

On November 11, 1918, the war came to an end. The following year Brandeis travelled to London, where he met Weizmann for the first time. In his autobiography, *Trial and Error*, Weizmann described his impression of Brandeis as follows:

> Justice Brandeis has often been compared with Abraham Lincoln, and indeed they had much in common besides clean-chiseled features and lofty brows. Brandeis, too, was a Puritan: upright, austere, of a scrupulous honesty and implacable logic. These qualities sometimes made him hard to work with; like Wilson, he was apt to evolve theories, based on the highest principles, from his inner consciousness, and then expect the facts to fit in with them. If the facts failed to oblige, so much the worse for the facts. Indeed, the conflicts which developed between Brandeis and ourselves were not unlike those which disturbed Wilson's relations with his European colleagues when he first had to work closely with them.

* See Chapter 9.

Weizmann thought of Brandeis as a doctrinaire theoretician whose mind worked from premise to fact; this was, however, a complete misconception because actually the mind of Brandeis worked in just the opposite way, from fact to concept. In truth, Brandeis was the least doctrinaire of men: his hunger for facts was insatiable, and he searched them out without fixed preconceptions.

After Brandeis left London, he went to Paris to confer with Wilson, Balfour, and others; he then travelled to Palestine, where he visited all the cities and most of the colonies. This trip confirmed his belief that Palestine must become the Jewish homeland.

The following year (1920), a World Zionist Conference was held in London. Weizmann was elected president; Brandeis, head of the American delegation, was named honorary president. But it was apparent that these two men did not agree on fundamental policies, and that a break between them was inevitable. In Brandeis' view, the future called for practical work in Palestine: acquisition of more land, reforestation, public health, immigration, capital investments. He wanted men with business and executive abilities to take over the main portion of the work, and he was prepared to welcome the cooperation of non-Zionists in the practical work of upbuilding the land. To Weizmann, however, political Zionism still had important functions to perform; the Balfour Declaration and the acceptance by Great Britain of the mandate over Palestine in April 1920 were only the start of a new era of Zionist political work and political action. Weizmann did not want to see Zionist forces compromised in any way by non-Zionists working within the organization. When Weizmann's views prevailed at the London conference, Brandeis resigned as honorary president.

The Cleveland Convention

In time Brandeis also lost the support of most American Zionists. In 1921 the Zionist Organization of America met in Cleveland, and Weizmann came over to attend the convention. Brandeis' administration lost on a vote of confidence; he resigned as leader but refused to lead a secessionist movement or leave the organization. Thereafter he devoted much time and energy to those Palestine agencies that had undertaken practical tasks in the rebuilding of the land.

As later years demonstrated, Weizmann had been right in thinking that the political activities of Zionist organizations had much work to accomplish before Palestine would in fact become the national homeland. But Brandeis had also been correct in stressing the practical work that needed to be done. Perhaps if each had accepted the other's point of view without relinquishing his own, Zionism would have made much faster strides, both practically and politically, during the period from 1921 to 1948.

Even after Brandeis had ceased to be an official leader of the Zionist forces, he continued until the end of his life to give the movement his moral and financial support. At the time of his death, the residue of his large estate, beyond what was willed to his immediate family, was divided as follows: one-fourth to Survey Associates for the maintenance of civil liberty and the promotion of workers' education, one-fourth for the library and law school of the University of Louisville, and the remaining one-half for "the upbuilding of Palestine as a national home for the Jewish people."

Brandeis' Zionist Philosophy

What did Zionism mean to Brandeis? Why did "the upbuilding of Palestine as a national home for the Jewish people" have such a profound hold on his mind and heart?

First, he saw the Jewish homeland as a small country, free of the curse of bigness. Being small, it could conduct daring experiments in social living and social justice, and the citizens would be able quickly and effectively to judge of the success or failure of their new ventures.

Second, Brandeis felt that given the character of the Jewish pioneers in Palestine, the new settlement would be an almost pure democracy, with women and men equal partners in economic and political rights and activities. In the colonies, economic differences, if they existed, were not to serve as a basis for the enjoyment or denial of political and economic democracy or the rights and duties flowing from democracy. Brandeis was certain that the ideals of freedom and equality would flourish in the Jewish homeland, and lead to extraordinary spiritual and social developments.

Third, Brandeis sensed that in the Jewish homeland the settlers would enjoy the fundamental right to be different, to be themselves. A people, no less than a person, he felt, has the right to mold and order its life in its own way, expressing its own genius, ideals, history, and traditions. The Jews collectively should enjoy the rights and freedoms to develop as do other groups of people. In Palestine, Brandeis stated, Jews would enjoy not only the personal rights and freedoms they should have as citizens of any democratic state, but, in addition, they would also enjoy group rights and freedoms, to develop their own language, ways of thought and living.

By achieving these group rights and freedoms in their own homeland, Jews could make an important contribution to their coreligionists living elsewhere. The American Jew would thus benefit from the development of Jewish culture in the homeland. Furthermore, like all other peoples, American Jews should have the option to remain in the United States or go to Palestine. The establishment of a Jewish homeland would thus give Jews everywhere freedoms hitherto denied them by the tragedies of their history—freedom of choice, freedom to be different, and freedom to enjoy spiritual ties with their own people.

The Jewish nation in Palestine would be different, for the Jewish settlers there would bring to a common center qualities of character and moral and social ideals that were the fruit of their history, tradition, and experience. Brandeis put high among those qualities and ideals the reverence for law and the concept of morality. He also included commitments to brotherhood and righteousness, democratic and cooperative living, social justice, and peace. Further characteristics were, in his view, a strong sense of duty and right, high intellectual attainments based on the belief in universal education, and a strong sense of community responsibility.

"Such is our inheritance," said Justice Brandeis; "such the estate which we hold in trust." What obligations are imposed by this trust?

> . . . The short answer is *noblesse oblige;* and its command is twofold. It imposes duties upon us in respect to our own conduct as individuals; it imposes no less important duties upon us as part of the Jewish community or people. Self-respect demands that each of us lead individually a life worthy of our great inheritance and of the glorious traditions of the people. But this is demanded also by respect for the rights of others. The Jews have not only been ever known as a "peculiar people"; they were and remain a distinctive and minority people. Now it is one of the necessary incidents of a distinctive and minority people that the act of any one is in some degree attributed to the whole group. A single though inconspicuous instance of dishonorable conduct on the part of a Jew in any trade or profession has far-reaching evil effects extending to the many innocent members of the race. Large as this country is, no Jew can behave badly without injuring each of us in the end. . . . Since the act of each becomes thus the concern of all, we are perforce our brothers' keepers, exacting even from the lowliest the avoidance of things dishonorable; and we may properly brand the guilty as disloyal to the people. . . .
>
> And yet, though the Jew makes his individual life the loftiest, that alone will not fulfill the obligations of his trust. We are bound not only to use worthily our great inheritance, but to preserve, and if possible, augment it; and then transmit it to coming generations. The fruit of three thousand years of civilization and a hundred generations of suffering may not be sacrificed by us. It will be sacrificed if dissipated. Assimilation is national suicide. And assimilation can be prevented only by preserving national characteristics and life as other peoples, large and small, are preserving and developing their national life. Shall we with our inheritance do less than the Irish? . . . And must we not, like them, have a land where the Jewish life may be naturally led, the Jewish language spoken, and the Jewish spirit prevail? Surely we must, and that land is our fathers' land; it is Palestine.

Adapting a phrase of Mazzini, Justice Brandeis said that no Jew may be a moral mediocrity. And that, he added, was precisely how the Jewish pioneers in Palestine felt because they were conscious of their inheritance. "It is the Jewish tradition," Brandeis said, "and the Jewish law, and the Jewish spirit which prepare us for the lessons of life. In Palestine the younger generation is taught that heritage and as a result they live for the highest and the best of what life is and what it may be."

Finally, Brandeis saw in Zionism the possibility for the American Jew of living and thinking in a pluralistic world. A free man who seeks spiritual riches must have many loyalties. "Multiple loyalties," said Brandeis, "are objectionable only if they are inconsistent. . . . Every American Jew who aids in advancing the Jewish settlement in Palestine, though he feels that neither he nor his descendants will ever live there, will . . . be a better American for doing so."

Zionism and Americanism Compatible

Since "the twentieth-century ideals of America have been the ideals of the Jew for more than twenty centuries," and Zionism is committed to the preservation and strengthening of these ideals in Jewish living in a Jewish homeland, it followed for Brandeis that "to be good Americans, we must become Zionists." The Jewish rebuilding in Palestine, furthermore, would enable American Jews better to perform their duty to the United States, for it would help them to make "toward the attainment of the American ideals of democracy and social justice that large contribution for which religion and life have peculiarly fitted the Jew." The "Zionist ideals, the highest Jewish ideals," Brandeis said, "are essentially the American ideals."

Thus, with a logic that is unanswerable and with a conviction that went to the deep recesses of his heart and soul, Brandeis found in Zionism a home for all his important values and ideals, both Jewish and American—for his faith in freedom and democracy, his love of experimentation, his pluralistic philosophy, his social conscience, his prophetic commitment to righteousness and justice, his strong sense of group loyalty, his belief in equality and in the right of the person and the group to be different.

In an opinion he wrote in 1927, Brandeis said that "the greatest menace to freedom is an inert people." While in saying this he had in mind the American people and American civil liberties, Brandeis could have applied the same thought to the Jewish people. In Zionism, Brandeis saw a way to maximize the living forces in Judaism and in the Jewish people: free acts on behalf of freedom.

FOR FURTHER READING

Abrahams, Israel and Yellin, David, *Maimonides* (Jewish Publication Society, Philadelphia, 1936).
Adler, Morris, *The World of the Talmud* (Schocken Books, New York, 1963).
Bein, Alex, *Theodor Herzl: A Biography*, translated by Maurice Samuel (World Publishing Company, Cleveland, 1962).
Brandeis, Louis Dembitz, *The Words of Justice Brandeis*, edited by Solomon Goldman (H. Schuman, New York, 1953).
Complete Poetic Works of Bialik, translated and edited by Israel Efros (Histadruth Ivrith of America, New York, 1948).
Essays on Maimonides, An Octocentennial Volume, edited by Salo Wittmayer Baron (Columbia University Press, New York, 1941).
Finkelstein, Louis, *Akiba: Scholar, Saint, and Martyr* (World Publishing Company, Cleveland, 1962).
Halkin, Simon, *Modern Hebrew Literature* (Schocken Books, New York, 1950).
Herzl, Theodor, *The Diaries of Theodor Herzl*, abridged, edited and translated by Marvin Lowenthal (Grosset & Dunlap, 1962).
James, Fleming, *Personalities of the Old Testament* (C. Scribner's Sons, New York, 1939).
Liber, Maurice, *Rashi*, translated by Adele Szold (Jewish Publication Society, Philadelphia, 1906).

Mason, Alpheus Thomas, *Brandeis, A Free Man's Life* (The Viking Press, New York, 1946).
Orlinsky, Harry Meyer, *Ancient Israel* (Cornell University Press, Ithaca, New York, 1960).
The Pentateuch and Rashi's Commentary: A Linear Translation into English, translated by A. ben Isaiah and B. Sharfman in collaboration with Harry M. Orlinsky and M. Charner (S.S. & R. Publishing Company, Brooklyn, 1949-1950), Volumes I-V.
Rabinowitz, Shalom (Sholom Aleichem), *The Great Fair: Scenes From My Childhood*, translated by Tamara Kahana (Roundai Press, 1958).
...., *The Old Country*, translated by Julius and Frances Butwein (Crown Publishers, New York, 1965).
Rashi, Anniversary Volume (American Academy for Jewish Research, Jewish Publication Society, Philadelphia, 1941).
Samuel, Maurice, *The World of Sholom Aleichem* (Knopf, New York, 1943; Schocken Books, New York, 1965).
The Social and Economic Views of Mr. Justice Brandeis, edited by Alfred Lief (The Vanguard Press, New York, 1930).
Rashi, *Pentateuch; with Commentary*, translated by M. Rosenbaum and A. M. Silverman (Shapiro, Vallentine & Company, London, 1929-1932), Volumes I-III.
Zeitlin, Solomon, *Maimonides, A Biography* (Bloch Publishing Company, New York, 1955).

About the Contributors

SALO W. BARON is Professor Emeritus of Jewish History, Columbia University, and author of a monumental *Social and Religious History of the Jews* and *The Jewish Community, Its History and Structure.*

SAMUEL M. BLUMENFIELD is Director of the Department of Education and Culture of the Jewish Agency for Israel, and author of *Master of Troyes, Maimonides the Educator,* and *John Dewey and Jewish Education.*

LOUIS FALSTEIN is an Anglo-Jewish writer whose works include *Face of a Hero* and *Sole Survivor.*

LOUIS FINKELSTEIN is Chancellor of the Jewish Theological Seminary of America and author of *Akiba, The Pharisees, The Beliefs and Practices of Judaism,* and editor of *The Jews: Their History, Culture, Religion.*

M. Z. FRANK is the author of *Sound the Great Trumpet,* and a frequent contributor to the Anglo-Jewish press.

ALFRED JOSPE, National Director of Program and Resources for the B'nai B'rith Hillel Foundations, is author of *Religion and Myth in Jewish Philosophy, Handbook for Student Leaders,* and other works.

MILTON R. KONVITZ is Professor of Industrial and Labor Relations and Law at Cornell University, and author of *Fundamental Liberties of a Free People, The Constitution and Civil Rights,* and other works.

MARVIN LOWENTHAL is author of *A World Passed By, The Jews of Germany,* and editor of *Diaries of Theodor Herzl* and *Life and Letters of Henrietta Szold.*

LOUIS I. NEWMAN is rabbi of Congregation Rodeph Sholom, New York, and author of *Jewish Influence on Christian Reform Movements, The Jewish People, Faith and Life, Biting on Granite,* and other works.

HARRY M. ORLINSKY is Professor of Bible at Hebrew Union College–Jewish Institute of Religion in New York, author of *Ancient Israel,* editor-in-chief of the new JPS translation of the Bible, and Chairman of B'nai B'rith's Publications Committee.

Index